Brambles and Bay Leaves: Essays on Things Homely and Beautiful

James Shirley Hibberd

BIBLIOLIFE

BRAMBLES

AND

BAY LEAVES:

ESSAYS ON THINGS HOMELY AND BEAUTIFUL.

BY

SHIRLEY HIBBERD,

AUTHOR OF "RUSTIC ADORNMENTS FOR HOMES OF TASTE,"
"THE TOWN GARDEN," ETC., ETC.

> " The common, the terrestrial, thou may'st see,
> With serviceable cunning knit together,
> The nearest with the nearest, and therein
> I trust thee and believe thee! But whate'er,
> Full of mysterious import, Nature weaves
> And fashions in the depths—the spirit's ladder,
> That from this gross and visible world of dust,
> Even to the starry world, with thousand rounds,
> Builds itself up, on which the unseen powers
> Move up and down on heavenly ministries—
> The circles in the circles, that approach
> The central sun with ever narrowing orbit—
> These see the glance alone, the unsealed eye."
>
> *Schiller's Piccolomini.*—COLERIDGE.

SECOND EDITION, CORRECTED AND REVISED.

LONDON:
GROOMBRIDGE AND SONS, 5, PATERNOSTER ROW.
1862.

PREFACE TO THE FIRST EDITION.

THOUGH somewhat miscellaneous in subject, the reader will perceive a consonance of purpose in the various Essays contained in this volume. The papers were written at various times during the intervals of severe, though not uncongenial duties, and are but several expressions of the same sentiment. That sentiment is the love of Nature, and more especially of that portion of Nature which is represented in the out-door life of " green things," embodying, as they do, a thousand suggestions of their relations to the life of man, closely woven and encircled as he is by a network of beauty, which gives a joy to his calmer hours, and enables him to perceive, both by reason and analogy, his position in the general scheme of creation. If the love of simple things does no more for us than to quicken our perceptions, and enlarge the circle of our pleasures, it is certainly a love which, in that direction, exalts us, and gives us many whisperings of the greatness of the Power under whose control the worlds perform their ceaseless march, and the seasons observe the times appointed them. If we can now and then turn aside from the common-place of daily life—a life fraught with tendencies to deaden the finer sympathies of our nature—if we can now and then turn aside to breathe and enjoy the cool air of mountain groves, and to listen to the music of falling waters, and the murmurs of many voices—we shall thereby enlarge the circle of our emotions, and quicken our sense of appreciation for things which lie around and above us.

This ministration of dew-drops and red sunsets is not appointed in vain; it is a ministration to the heart rather than to the brain of man, and teaches him the lesson of his moral life, of which, under the excitement of worldly avocations, he too often becomes oblivious.

These papers, such as they are, are expressions of thoughts arising out of the observation of natural changes and simple things, all of which, viewed through the imagination with the help of thought, afford us an insight into the poetical uses of natural forms and phenomena, and add to our life solaces and resources, for the augmentation of our earthly joy,

The merits and demerits of " BRAMBLES AND BAY LEAVES " are equally to be attributed to enthusiasm; and should my enthusiasm, as expressed herein, prove welcome to a few congenial spirits, I shall have the satisfaction of having added to the enjoyments of those who see in a wayside pebble, or a green leaf, a subject for meditation not to be exhausted at one effort.

into this professedly simple category.   A story, *certes*,
should be in chapters, have a beginning and an end, and
at the end a moral.   My story shall conform to rule
just as its subject is in the way of fashion, and the first
thought that occurs to me will be the best to lead off
with for Chapter

I. THE COLOUR OF IT.

It is a significant fact, that Nature uses but few colours
in the painting of her many pictures.   The scenery of
the whole world, with all its diversities of hill and dale,
land and sea, mountain and valley, exhibit chiefly the
several shades of blue and green, which are respectively
the emblems of heaven and earth.   It is very simple;
but with what cunning art does Nature trick out an
infinity of wild beauty, dotting each little spot of the
broad earth with a picture of its own, which, in all her
multitudinous representations, will never be repeated.
Philosophers tell us that this blue above and green below
is the combination which, while giving the heart and the
eye an equal satisfaction and solace, is at the same time
the best adapted for the continual exercise of the visual
powers.   The soft azure heaven, which folds us in its
dewy arms, and lifts our souls nearer up to God, is said
to derive its beauty from the refraction of the rays of light
in passing through the air.   The lovely green hue which
overspreads the earth like the laughter of Nature herself,
and which, by its winning tenderness, seems planted here
to make the soul contented with its earthly lot, is caused
by the abundant and universal growth of grass, which is,
indeed, the poetic spirit of the world, for it hides, with

BRAMBLES AND BAY LEAVES.

———◆———

THE

STORY OF A BLADE OF GRASS.

"WHAT a desert-like spot would this life of ours be,
If, amid sands of sin, no glimpse could we see
    Of some green-knotted garland of grass,—
Some oasis bright, a glad hope to impart,
That the sun of the sky, and the sun of the heart,
    Still abide in the road we must pass."

JOHNSON BARKER.

"The golden-belted bees humm'd in the air,
    The tall silk-grasses bent and waved along."

THOMAS MILLER.

"We cannot pass a blade of grass unheeded by the way,
For it whispers to our thoughts, and we its silent voice obey."

J. E. CARPENTER.

IT has become the fashion to study "Common Things," and extort biographies from insects, birds, and flowers. I shall conform to fashion in twining a garland of literary "Brambles and Bay Leaves," and shall escape censure as to the choice of the subject for this paper, at least, because a blade of grass is the commonest of common things, and has as good and copious a biography as the rarest curiosity that has ever been placed

In preparing this edition for the press, a few papers have been omitted, because the lapse of time had destroyed their value. The places of those few papers have been filled up with essays written for the work. The reviewers of the first edition are not responsible for these; and if this edition is anywhere deemed worthy of notice, it is but right I should call attention to the papers on " The Rainbow" and " Fido Fides," as new, and as expounding views in which, possibly, neither my reviewers nor my readers will concur.

S. H.

PREFACE TO SECOND EDITION.

WHEN the first edition of "BRAMBLES AND BAY LEAVES" had been committed to the press, a dark cloud overspread my domestic life, and rendered me altogether careless whether the book should find readers, or make its way silently and secretly to the trunk-maker or cheesemonger. The cloud has not cleared away, but has changed its form, and acquired a few additional touches of blackness; though, thank God, it has a golden fringe, so that there are gleams of light afar off. I name this fact to explain that not the slightest effort was ever made to give publicity to the work, and but one single guinea was expended in advertising it. Yet the edition has been sold, and a new one demanded; making good an observation, which I think Mr. Dickens is the author of, that a good book will find readers, even if privately printed, and utterly denied the assistance of an art known in the book trade as "push-ing." It is no doubt bold of me to take credit to myself that *this* is "a good book;" but I may as well confess that I so regard it, else why should I publish it? In truth, the sale of the edition is to be attributed solely to the kindness of reviewers, who made it known for me, when I simply contented myself to place it on a publisher's shelf; and their generous recommendations of it demand from me this acknowledgment and record of thanks.

a delicious verdure, the grim realities of Nature, and clothes the sordid facts of earth and iron with a garment of life and beauty. From the constant freshness, fragrance, and fruitfulness of grass, it has been held in tender regard in all ages of the world, and has mingled alike with the outpourings of the human heart, under the inspirations of poetry, with the voices and harmonies of Nature in her teachings of love, with the struggles of nations for power or freedom, and with the grim scenes wherein the human heart has paid the tribute of its blood to super-stition, oppression, and despotism. It would seem meet, therefore, that something should be said about Grass, in order that those who tread on it unheedingly, may know something of its history; and that those who have listened to the teachings of the out-door world, and welcomed its verdure into their sanctuary of love, may have its memories and images awakened within them, and so learn to love it more.

> "Then to the enamell'd meads
> Thou go'st; and as thy foot there treads,
> Thou seest a present God-like power
> Imprinted in each herb and flower."
>
> HERRICK.

To mention the greenness of the grass is to awaken at the same time a thousand remembrances of green things generally, for the mind calls them up in numberless pictures, that the heart may feast upon their beauty. "Green things," and we think of Virgil and his brown bees; Longus and his happy children; Keats and his green trees, " sprouting a shady boon for simple sheep;" Chaucer and his imperishable daisies, which he rose early to see "against the sun spread;" Robin Hood and the Lincoln green; Shakspere, Spenser, and Herrick, with their multiplied images, pictures, and allusions; all living and fresh from the green world itself, and redolent of lime-tree perfume, dank moss, woodland echoes, velvet meadows, and all the associations which cling like halos of light around them. With green things the human heart grows larger, and human life more real—for we are fast rooted in the earth, even when imagination makes its boldest flights; and there is a practical suggestion offered us by the blue heaven, which, as a curtain, hides from us the city of God, that the green earth is our best place until His purpose is accomplished.

In No. 387 of the *Spectator* occurs a passage on the colour of grass, which will fit into this place most appropriately:—"There are writers of great distinction who have made it an argument for Providence that the whole earth is covered with green, rather than any other colour, as being such a right mixture of light and shade, that it comforts and strengthens the eye, instead of weakening or grieving it." A word from Sir William Temple may well follow this:—"There are besides the temper of our climate two things particular to us that contribute much to the beauty and elegance of our gardens, which are the gravel of our walks, and the almost perpetual greenness of our turf." This chapter cannot better end than with a terse couplet from Dan Chaucer—

> "Colours ne know I non, withouten drede,
> But swiche colours as growen in the mede."
>
> FRANKELEINE'S TALE, v. 1535.

II. WHERE TO FIND IT.

Everywhere! In all climates, all soils, all positions. It will make a prostrate pillar into a cushioned seat for the meditative traveller among the ruins; it does not disdain a home on a dust heap; I have seen many a brave tuft high up on the shaft of a chimney; and last summer *Poa annua* grew luxuriantly at the foot of the statue of King William, on the city side of London Bridge. Many years ago there used to be some fine tufts of this *poa*, and also *cynosurus cristatus*, on the square blocks of stone above the steps leading to the water, on the City side of London Bridge, and in the midst of them, rooted firmly in the crevices between the stones, was a little cherry tree. Just about that time M. X. B. Saintine published his charming story of "Picciola," which was translated into almost every language of the world; and here, through an abridgement published by the Messrs. Chambers, was read by thousands of persons. I remember once halting in front of the pigmy cherry tree, and revolving in my mind all the points in that enchanting story, in order to make a "Picciola" of it. I think it was a wall-flower which the reflective Charney set his heart upon with a fondness almost fanatic, and it was, therefore, a true prison-flower. But this cherry tree never put forth a blossom, and there was no prison even within sight of it, and by no stretch of the imagination could I make a decent day-dream; while a thousand elbows made a thousand separate thrusts at my ribs and sides, and the business that

brought me there was being sacrificed by loitering.
How rejoiced was I, however, when, in a volume published by Mr. Alfred Smee (I think it was upon
" Instinct "), an account of this tree was given, and its
origin traced to the deposit there of a cherry stone by
some wandering bird. It always seemed to me, however, that it was much more likely a wandering boy,
like myself, after having made a purchase of cherries at
the adjoining fruit-stall, had tossed a cherry stone over
to the stone buttress, and with a million chances to one
against it, the million had failed and the one had
triumphed, and the seed took root and sprang up.
Alas! it was like the seed that fell on stony ground,
that we read of in one of our Lord's parables, which
endured only for a while, and perished. There, too, it
once more resembled " Picciola," but there was no prisoner to appeal for it, and no emperor to command the
lifting of the stone, and the supplying of its roots with a
handful of soil to save it.

The *Graminea* comprise thirteen very distinct tribes,
over three hundred genera, and not less than fifteen
hundred species, of which the British Isles can lay claim
to at least a hundred and fifty. There is no part of the
world but in which some of the members of the family
are to be found. In the tropics they rival oaks in magnitude, and mingle with the arborescent vegetation as
essential elements of the jungle and the forest; and
where life expires in the embraces of perpetual winter,
grasses are the last of flowering plants that linger on the
verge of those silent regions of frost and death. In
South Shetland islands, at an elevation of 7,000 feet,

Aira antarctica blooms alone in a region of "thick-ribbed ice;" and in the far north, in Iceland, Greenland, and the extreme latitude of 70½°, *Trisetum subspicatum*, which has perhaps a greater geographical range than any plant with which we are acquainted, braves the sleet and darkness, and during the short Arctic summer puts forth its pretty blossoms, and ripens abundance of seeds.

In the exercise of that spirit of thankful affection, with which the true naturalist surveys the world around him, the universality of grass is a fact accepted as a distinct teaching of the kindly regard for the happiness of all creatures, which is so prominent a feature in the plan of creation. In herbage and grain the grasses furnish a larger amount of sustenance to animal life than all other tribes of plants together; and so profusely have they been shed abroad in every conceivable variety, as climate, soil, and situation may influence their growth, that the earth has taken their colouring for a garment, and presents a firmament of green almost as unbroken as the upper firmament of blue, which is the only other prevailing tint in Nature. No matter how elevated or how barren the spot, grasses of some kind will make themselves a home in it; and when every variety of soil and climate has been furnished with its appropriate kinds, others find for themselves sites in water, carpeting the bed of the brook, or binding the shingle together on the shore of the sea; others on ruins, house-tops, and subterranean retreats, if but a glimpse of daylight reach them. In that remarkable work, "The Flora of the Colosseum," in which Dr. Deakin has described 420

plants found growing spontaneously on the ruins of the
Colosseum at Rome, there are no fewer than fifty-six
grasses entered as flourishing in various parts of that
venerable ruin; those fifty-six include examples of *Arenaria, Avena, Briza, Bromus, Festuca, Hordeum, Lolium,*
and *Poa,* besides that farmer's friend, *Anthoxanthum
odoratum,* which is said, but erroneously, to be the sole
source of the fragrance of the new-mown hay. This
universality of grass is one of the most poetical of facts
in the economy of the world. There is no place which
it will not beautify. It climbs up the steep mountain
passes which are inaccessible to man, and forms ledges
of green amid the rivings of the crags: it leaps down
between steep shelving precipices, and there fastens its
slender roots in the dry crevices which the earthquakes
had rent long ago, and into which the water trickles
when the sunbeams strike the hoary snows above. There
it shakes its plumes in the morning light, and flings its
sweet, sweet laughing greenness to the sun; there it
creeps and climbs about the mazes of solitude, and
weaves its fairy tassels with the wind. It beautifies even
that spot, and spreads over the sightless visage of death
and darkness the serene beauty of a summer smile, flinging its green lustre on the bold granite, and perfuming
the lips of morning as she stoops from heaven to kiss
the green things of the earth. It makes a moist and
yielding carpet over the whole earth, on which the impetuous may pass with hurried tread, or the feet of beauty
linger. Wherever it is seen it makes a velvet carpet of
emerald beauty—a carpet on which the heavy heart may
sometimes tread, but on which joy mostly wanders; and

from this universality of growth grass derives its name, as will be proved by Chapter

III. ITS NAME.

The word "grass" means simply that which grows. The Greek κράστις, or γράστις (*anglicé* grass), must be rendered *gramen* in the Latin, and gives the idea of something sprouty, verdant, lusty, and herbaceous—*par excellence* "grass." In the Gothic, it is *gras*; in Anglo-Saxon, ʒρaρ; German, *grasz*. In the Anglo-Saxon form the more precise meaning is, to grow, to sprout; applied to grass by the common method of converting generals into particulars. Thus, we get by a slight transition, to the Latin *crescere*, to grow; and hence to cress, simply a sprouting herb—*quod in agris ubique crescit*, "that which grows in every land;" grass, if you will, the universal source of verdure. Junius obtains the *A S græs* from *growan*, and certainly from one of these two we have the word *green*; the designation of the colour of grass, and of the cheerful, everyday serviceable garment of nature.

IV. ITS USES.

All our corn plants are grasses; so a blade of grass is a proper emblem of utility, and of the physical basis of all civilization. Our bread is made of the seed of cereal grasses; our cattle browse the herbage of pasture grasses; the culture of cereals and the preservation of domestic cattle mark the progress of man from barbarism to industrial enterprize, from a degraded subsistence on the precarious crumbs of life, in abject dependence on spon-

taneous growths and the flesh of wild creatures, to the
enjoyment of plenty and comfort, and the establishment
of a home.   Wherever grass grows, beauty and utility
are brought together ; society is possible, and life ceases
to be a strife and a pain.   This chapter might be extended indefinitely, without it being possible to exhaust
the subject of it.   Corn and sugar, rice and paper,
matting, cordage, thatch, the most substantial of our
common necessities, and almost all our ordinary beve-
rages—excepting coffee, tea, and wine—are furnished
directly, or indirectly, from this wide-spread family of
indigenous herbs.   Amongst our native grasses are some
that accomplish uses little thought of by the collector of
specimens for a *hortus siccus*.   Let us take one for an
example :—here is *Psamma arenaria*, a British grass,
considered rare by inland botanists, but plentiful enough
about Hastings, and other parts of the coast.   Thousands
of acres of land washed by the sea owe their preservation
to it, for it forms creeping roots, which extend horizontally in all directions in its sandy bed, and it weavesthat
sand into a matted felt capable of resisting the denuding
action of the tides, and thus prevents the encroachment
of the sea, by binding the drifting material of its margin
together.   Where you find this, you may also look out for
Elymus arenarius, *Carex arenaria*, and *Festuca rubra*,
and you will doubtless find them all combined in preserving our sloping shores intact against the sea, where,
but for such frail defences, the waters would eat away
their boundaries, and swallow up vast tracts of fertile
country.   The protection of this grass was the subject of
an enactment, in 1742, just as, at an earlier date, the Scot-

tish parliament passed an act to protect *Elymus arenarius*. By the act of 1742, the cutting of the grass was prohibited, and the prohibition extended even to the proprietors of the soil. This same grass is the chief defence of the coast of Holland against the encroachments of the ocean; and a closely allied grass, *Psamma Baltica*, performs a similar service on the sandy coasts of the Baltic. This grass has hard elastic foliage, and tough culms, and at Hastings has been long in use for the manufacture of baskets, mats, and fancy goods, of which samples were exhibited by Miss Rock, of Hastings, in Class IV. of the United Kingdom Products, in the Great Exhibition of 1851. Suppose a waste of sand, on which, according to the superficial dicta, "nothing will grow;" place this Hastings' grass on it, and let a thousand delicate fingers find tasteful and useful occupation in the conversion of its stems into articles of household use and ornament, and one despised weed may become the founder of a town, a city, or a colony. *Phragmites communis*, the common reed of our ditches, is another of these basket grasses, as well as one of the best of thatching materials; this makes culms of six to ten feet high, which are used to furnish the strong framework on which the finer grasses are woven, in the making of mats and baskets. What the mat grasses accomplish for the defence of sandy shores this giant grass does for river banks and the sloping sides of pools and ditches; its roots convert the loose boundary lines into firm water walls, and stay the progress of denudation.

We might take each of the known grasses, and specify their uses, without lapsing into commonplace; but the temptation must be resisted, and a sufficiency of illustration found in the few special instances that occur to our memory, as we indite these chapters. Here is the Guinea grass in our collections of growing specimens of *graminea*. It reminds us of Robinson Crusoe, whose supplies of corn and rice were obtained in a way that the reader well remembers. The owner of an estate at Shuttleworth, Jamaica, says Mr. Gosse, in his charming Naturalists' Sojourn, received from Africa a cage of finches; with these birds a bag of seeds was shipped to serve them as food during the voyage. The birds died, and the few seeds left were thrown away. Presto! on the bank where the seed-bag was shaken out, sprang up a splendid mass of grassy herbage; the horses smelt it out, and left their pasture to crop it, and in time that bank became the favourite feeding ground for the horses and cattle of the estate; and *Panicum jumentorum*, the Guinea grass, became famous as the most nourishing of all the grasses used as fodder. All the low land parts of Jamaica are covered with it; and even rocky soils, where few other grasses thrive, produce its dense tussocks of juicy and ever-verdant growth. Here, under the hedge where we have waged a war of extermination against it for years, is the couch-grass, in common parlance the most hateful of all weeds, for it has not the beauty of bear-bine, nor will surface-cleaning remove it, as in the case of our rural weeds. Not long since, the Agricultural Society of Clermont (Oise) recommended that, instead of exterminating this grass, farmers would do well to use it instead of malt in making beer, for, like the rest of the grasses, it is largely productive of saccharine matter. To make one more step in this catalogue of instances, we may call the perfumer into court, to inform us how it happens that oil of verbena, and other perfumes bearing the same name, are produced from a flower which we generally consider to be without scent altogether, for the true scented verbena is not a verbena at all, but an aloysia. The witness will depose that it is a misnomer, for verbena perfume is in reality the produce of the lemongrass, *Andropogon schœnanthus*, a native of India, where it is also used by Europeans as a tea-plant, the infusion of which is tonic, and valuable as a febrifuge.

But its highest use is in its beauty after all, and this prepares the way for the chapter that follows. But we must here, in the list of utilities, class the village green, the smooth, bright, and springy cricket-ground, and the close-shaven lawn, where the children play; for the sunshine of life should be reflected on the verdure of Nature, in a world where there are so many cheap sources of physical health and social happiness. These things follow of necessity, if we write down distinctly that the grass carpets the playground of the children, when they make the sky ring with their laughter, and the elastic turf rebound to the tramp of their tiny, lively feet. The very ground is blessed where children tread—is blessed already by its own greenness, and sprinklings of gold and silver, it is doubly-blessed, when children make their sport upon it, and ignore all laws and all history in wild abandonment to the impulses of nature. God bless them; and if a tear starts while we say so, it shall fall upon the grass that weeps a million better tears than these every-day breaks, for beauty, and simplicity, and truth.

" The sweet songs of the vineyards and the bees,
    Fell lullingly upon the soothed ear ;
And nightingales among the orange trees,
    Piping their gurgling notes so soft and clear,
The old and the young came from the fields to hear
Some gathered flowers by the meadow side—
    Of bright and beautiful there was no dearth—
Or picked up daisies, which they strove to hide,
    Then threw at each other, gay with mirth,
Or planted garlands for the nymphs who loved them from
    their birth."

LONGUS, PASTORAL, *Shepherd's Spring.*

V. THE BEAUTY OF IT.

It seems as if nothing could be said under this head,
because, in truth, there is so much to say. To get a good
idea of the beauty of the grass, endeavour in imagination
to form a picture of a world without it. It is precisely
to the scenery of Nature what the Bible is to literature.
You remember that in the dream, " Eclipse of Faith," that
the Bible had been obliterated, and every other book had
thereat lost its value, and literature was at an end ? Take
away this green ground colour on which Dame Nature
works her embroidery patterns, and where would be the
picturesque scarlet poppies or white daisies, or the
grey of the chalk cliffs, or the golden bloom of a wilderness of buttercups ? Its chief service to beauty is as the
garment of the earth. It watches night and day at all
seasons of the year, " in all places that the eye of heaven
visits," for spots on which to pitch new tents, to make
the desert less hideous, fill up the groundwork of the
grandest pictures, and give the promise of plenty on the
flowery meadows where it lifts its silvery and purple

panicles breast-high, and mocks the sea in its rolling
waves of sparkling greenness. It is beautiful when it
mixes with orpine and *turritis* on the ruined bastion or
grey garden-wall—beautiful when it sprinkles the brown
thatch with tufts that find sufficient nourishment, where
green mosses have been before; beautiful when it clothes
the harsh upland, and gives nourishment to a thousand
snow-white fleeces; still more beautiful when it makes
a little islet in a bright blue mountain lake, "a fortunate
purple isle," with its ruddy spikes of short-lived flowers;
and precious as well as beautiful when it comes close
beside us, in company with the sparrow and the robin, as a
threshold visitant, to soften the footfall of care, and give
a daily welcome to the world of greenness.

> " If a friend my grass-grown threshold find,
> O, how my lonely cot resounds with glee ! "

Is it only for its velvet softness, and the round pillowy
knolls it heaves up in the vistas of the greenwood,
that the weary and the dreamer find it so sweet a place
of rest? or is it because the wild bee flits around its
silvery panicles, and blows his bugle as he goes with a
bounding heart to gather sweets; that the hare and the
rabbit burrow beneath its smooth sward; that the dear
lark cowers amid its sprays, and cherishes the children of
his bosom under its brown matted roots; that the daisy,
the cowslip, the daffodil, the orchises—the fairies of the
flower world—the bird's-foot trefoil—the golden fingered
beauty of the meadows, the little yellow and the large
strawberry trefoil, are all sheltered and cherished by it;
and that when the brown-visaged mower—rustic image

of the Last Enemy—sweeps it down, it scents the air
for miles with the sweetest perfume ever breathed by
man? If only for its fresh green hue, let the dreamer
love it, let him lie thereon—

> " Vnder ye curtaine of ye greenwoode shade,
>   Beside ye brooke vpon ye velvet gras."
>   GODFREY OF BOULOUGNE, B. x., s. 64.

And if thou, O reader, hast any nobler hope imprisoned
in thy heart than that of cooking partridges, or measure-
ing tape; if thou hast not exchanged the Druid's harp
for bell-metal, nor suffered thy heroism to sink into
hypocrisy, go out into the green wilderness, lie down
upon the cushion of the grass, and pillow thy head upon
its virgin beauty. Then shall the songs of the golden
age be warbled in thine ear; then shall the spirit of love
sweep thy heart-strings, to awaken the melodies of the
Empyrean within thee; and a heritage of eternal beauty
shall be thine, in the place of the fleshless fancies which
now allure thee. Stay not here, creating dusty heavens,
from which, like a wild beast, thou shalt be thrust hereafter, but go out free and glad, and commune with the
grass, and listen to its stories of the ages. Look back
at the past, and learn the lesson of its faded peoples and
crumbled empires; learn the ephemeral fleetness of
human things, and the grand supremacy of Nature.
The temples of the Sun, where eastern multitudes knelt
in worship, have sunk down into white and ghastly ruins,
and the grasses wave over their broken sculptures. The
mighty caves of India, where darkness and mystery
aided in the fearful work of bloody superstitions, are now

choked up with weeds and herbage. The stately columns of Athens are woven with ivy, and violets, and grasses. The Roman Forum is a cow-market; the Tarpeian Rock a waste; and the Palace of the Cæsars a rope-walk! Rome herself, where is she? She is—

> "At once the grave, the city, and the wilderness;
> And where her wrecks, like shattered mountains, rise,
> The flowering weeds and fragrant copses dress
> The bones of Desolation's nakedness."
>
> SHELLEY

It is the fate of all: the white stone obliterates the turf, but the stone crumbles, and its ashes nourish the very grass which it had crushed before. London, Paris, Boston, go the same way, and grasses will one day cluster round the monuments of their highest glory!

It is always in rich grassy places that the little springs and water runnels bubble up into the light, and start off on their journey of fertility, down in the dark dell of the old wood, where the huge roots of the trees are matted all over with green and golden mosses, which sometimes hang like green beards, and dip into the pebbly waters; where the little squirrel finds a home, and the lizard and the shrew-mice burrow. There it is that, in rich circles of waving grass, the fresh sparkling waters bubble up with a gurgling sound, and go tinkling along under the shelving banks, kissing the willows, and chiming their soft songs as they jump over the clumps of timber.

The little brooks always make their pathway where the grasses grow; for the little brooks and the grasses love each other, and they creep along together plotting

c

how to bless the world. The harebell and the purple loose-strife, the woodbine, and the meadow-sweet, may each peep up here and there, and get refreshing splashes as the waters leap over the stony ledges in their way, but the grass is the streamlet's favourite, and wherever the one is, there is the other to be found. Oh, what a sweet life hath this grass of ours! his is the true Arcadian transport; the music of the rivulet, the soft bleating of the sheep, the drowsy hum of wild bees, the rich perfume of thymy knolls, and the shadowy beauties of "faërie land." These are his food and pastime, and the bonny brook that wets his feet is his chosen companion.

> " The deep recesses of the grove he gained,
> Where in a plain defended by the wood,
> Crept through the matted grass a crystal flood,
> By which an alabaster fountain stood."
>
> CHAUCER.

Here comes the summer, swift as the succession of night and day; once more the sun will blind us with his golden beams, and the "clear heat upon herbs" will touch us with the sweet lassitude that makes a "shady covert 'gainst the hot season," with a cool mossy lawn to roll upon, the very perfection of listless happiness and abandoned heart-ease. Oh! the bright, smooth bowling green, how its shines in its close shaven neatness of verdure, and what a fragrance is emitted from it on dewy summer evenings, when the foot gently bruises the green sprays, or the bowls make glaucous lines upon it! Oh! the rippling summer meadows, where the moles have made hundreds of soft hillocks, that invite us to bury ourselves in the herbage, and rest our heads on pillows of wild flowers. Oh! breezy evenings, under orchard trees, where the grass makes a cushion on which the juicy pears may tumble unhurt; and oh! bright eyes, laughing cheeks, and lips made for kissing, how will you people the garden with angel faces, when the lawn has been rolled and swept, and every tint of earth and heaven has taken possession of the dazzling beds and borders. A garden without grass is no garden at all, but if there is not a single flower in it all the summer long, a patch of well-kept turf may do its share to make you happy, and entice you to the sunshine and the healthy air. If any one created object is to be selected as a fit subject for the application to it of the immortal lines with which Endymion opens, none so fit as the grass, which is emphatically, "a thing of beauty, and a joy for ever."

VI. IT IS A FAVOURITE WITH THE POETS.

Chaucer, the morning star of English poetry, makes allusions to green things in a way which always evidences a thorough acquaintance with them. His "Gras in the Grene Mead" is not the accidental utterance of a mere maker of verses, but of an observer and lover of Nature. This same remark applies with equal force to Spenser and Shakspere, who may be classed with Chaucer as of the "Pre-Raphaelite" school of poetic-word painting. Milton took more of an artist's and scholar's view of Nature than his great predecessors. His mind was not sufficiently of the Saxon order for a realistic view of Nature; to him the rural had higher claims than the rustic, and we do not get such fresh breezes and vivid breadths of greenness from his natural scenes and images as from the

poets who were less severe in their recognition of
the limits of the art. Falstaff "babbling o' green
fields," is a subjective incident of priceless value, whether
we adopt the view that he was muttering the 23rd Psalm,
or that he was renewing, in the visions of his death-bed,
the sports and pastimes of his youth. Transferring the
incident to the poet himself, who bore some likeness to
his own wondrous creation, how it suggests the scenery
of the Avon, the musings of the boy, the earnest activity
of that marvellous spirit which must find room for action,
now in Sir Thomas Lucy's park, and anon in the wide
empire of Nature and human life. Silently flows the
river through its wall of willows, past its bright bays of
white ranunculus, eddying round its little green islets, all
unconscious of the fame it is to have hereafter in every
language of the world, by association with a name which
stands highest and brightest in all the records of the
human race. The playground of the great poet was also
his school, and by carrying in his marvellous mind the
memories of the Avon, he was enabled to intermingle
with his grand conceptions, pictures of natural scenes
that stand all alone for their truth and beauty.

The "verdant mead" is an expression that acquires
a sickly hue beside Shakspere's "lush and lusty grass:"
the "smooth lawn" is an unattractive object when
he presents his "grassy carpet;" and the speech of
Lysander has the freshness of the scene it paints :—

> " To-morrow night, when Phœbe doth behold
> Her silver visage in the watery glass,
> Decking with liquid pearl the bladed grass."*

---

* Midsummer Night's Dream, Act 1., sc. 1.

Again, in the song of the fairy :—

> " To wander everywhere
> Swifter than the moon's sphere :
> And I do serve the fairy queen,
> To dew her orbs upon the green."[*]

It was on the " green plot,"[†] too, that Quince and his companions held the rehearsals of their revels. It is in the allusion to Grass that the consolation which Gaunt offers to the banished Bolingbroke derives its cheering freshness and its sunny hope ; he tells him :—

> " All places that the eye of Heaven visits
> Are, to a wise man, happy ports and havens.
>
>   •   •   •   •
>
>   Suppose
> Devouring pestilence hangs in our air,
> And thou art flying to a fresher clime.
> Look, what thy soul holds dear, imagine it,
> To lie that way thou go'st, not that thou com'st.
> Suppose the singing birds, musicians ;
> *The grass whereon thou tread'st, the presence strew'd ;*
> The flowers, fair ladies, and thy steps, no more
> Than a delightful measure or a dance."[‡]

The most noble of Shakspere's songs are those which partake most of the rural character, and these embody choicer, fresher, quainter allusions to green things than the songs of any other poet, either ancient or modern, of this or other countries.

Where shall we find anything which bears comparison

---

* Midsummer Night's Dream, Act ii., sc. 1.
+ Midsummer Night's Dream, Act iii., sc. 1.
‡ King Richard II., Act. i., sc. 3

with the magical scenery of the *Midsummer Night's Dream*, and the *Tempest?* Chaucer and Spenser are the only authors who dare be mentioned at such a moment. In his "nodding violets" and "kissing cherries," his "green holly" and "strawberries" which "grow underneath," or in such passages as :—

> " The even mead that erst brought forth
> The peckled cowslip, burnet, and green clover."

Or that finest of wood songs in the English language, which the wild Caliban, in his rugged simplicity, babbles as if it were no better than mere drunken talk :—

> " I pr'ythee let me bring thee where crabs grow ;
> And I with my long nails will dig thee pig-nuts;
> Show thee a jay's nest, and instruct thee how
> To snare the nimble marmozet ; I'll bring thee
> To clustering filberds, and sometimes I'll get thee
> Young sea-mells from the rock."

The dew-spread grass has furnished many charming images to the poets. One sees therein the tears of heaven; another calls it manna; all agree that a dew-drop is more than a watery globule.

> " So sweet a kiss the morning sun gives out
> To those fresh morning drops upon the rose.[*]"

> " ——— Sip from herb the pearly tears
> Of morning dew, and after break their fast
> On greensward ground—a cool and grateful taste."[+]

A more delicious image still is that of Mickle, when he pictures the Spring as glistening with dew :—

---

[*] Love's Labour's Lost, Act iv., sc. 3.
[+] Dryden's Virgil—*Georgics*, B. iii.

" Glistening with dew, the green-haired Spring
  Walks through the woods, and, smiling, in her train,
      Youth glitters gay on cherub wing,
    And life, exulting, lifts the eye to Heaven."*

It comes to this, that if we want to know all that the
poets have said about Grass, or even all that they have
said directly in praise of it, we must read and note down,
and gather together, and compare, and so this chapter
must remain uncompleted; but whoever chooses may
proceed into it as a special department of the study of
"Common Things."   One reason why it is of necessity
a favourite with the poets, gives us the subject for
chapter

VII. IT IS EMBLEMATIC.

It is always of the same colour; it changes its aspect
with the seasons, but neither the frost of January nor the
fire of June ever utterly extinguish its sempiternal verdure, therefore, it is the emblem of constancy; it is
faithful to the brown earth that feeds it, to the blue
sky that hangs above it like a tent, and at the horizon
touches it, as if there the tent-pegs were driven into the
ground.   It is an emblem of life, the stature of its
growth is limited and it clings closely to the earth; the
brightest of its blossoms are demure, as compared with
things of less utility that share the sunshine with it; and
just as man, in the midst of stern utilities and material
thoughts holds firmly to sources of heavenly knowledge,
and cherishes the faith that gives him hope in heaven, so
the grass shelters many a bright-faced daisy, because for-

* Mickle—*Ode* 3.

sooth, the daisy is always looking upward, as becomes an
angel of the herbage.

Dr. Cromwell, in his "Philosophy of a Future Life,"
urges that there are grounds for concluding that plants
are possessed of a principle closely akin to intelligence.
I know not how far knowledge may lead us in this
direction; but I am sure if vegetation ever comes to be
regarded as the depository of sentient powers, it will be
pronounced first of all that grass can think. It is an
emblem, too, of all that is good in life and hopeful in
death. We cannot conceive of human happiness, except
in connection with verdurous scenes; we cannot conjure
up a vision of our heavenly home, without lavishly
clothing it with greenness. The truth is, that the story
of the grass is the story of the world. Ere the creatures
of the flood and field existed, the earth brought forth
grass and herbs, so that when the earth should "bring
forth the living creature after his kind, cattle and creeping thing," they should find sustenance and enjoyment;
and man, waking up from chaos at the will of the
Omnipotent, should find himself in a home of greenness,
with a soft carpet for his feet, a refreshing verdure to
gladden his eye, and a living beauty to imbue his heart
with holiness and peace. Well! upon the green turf he
worshipped his God at sunrise, and upon the grassy
ground he slept at nightfall; and when that greatest
of his benedictions came—a companion to make complete the sweetness of his hours—it was on the green
grass they walked together, singing hymns of joy,
and mingling their affections with the happiness of the
creatures.

" —————— Raised of grassy turf
Their table was, and mossy seats had round."

PARADISE LOST.

The leafy bowers were their mansions of beauty, and the
grass made green the pathway to their temple of love.

All the philosophies and mythologies have had for
their object the same end as that proposed by our own
blessed Christian faith—the restoration of man to the
Eden he has lost—the bringing together of the primal
elements of his life and history. It is certainly humanly
pardonable that men should seek of Nature that which
is alone the gift of God; and the cravings of the human
mind, in striving to solve the problem of destiny, have
about them the signs of a poetry which the world will
not willingly let die.

And what of that ancient metaphor, "a green old
age?" It must have its place here, though it must rest
for its validity on the sanction of prescription, not on its
obviousness, for less lively hues are the more evident
figures of senility, though in truth a hearty old age is
implied by it, an age rich in years and experience, but
with faculties unclouded, and the ardour of youth so
mellowed, that the sympathies are practical, and the impulses governed by wise judgments. How far back the
phrase may be traced I know not; I can only think of
"Dryden's Dedication of the Georgics," where he com-
pares Virgil and Horace, as to the respective excellences
of the works they produced at successive periods of their
lives. He says :—" In the beginning of summer, the days
are almost at a stand, with little variation of length or
shortness, because at that time the diurnal motion of the

sun partakes more of a right line than a spiral. The same is the method of Nature in the frame of man. He seems at forty to be fully in his summer tropic: somewhat before and somewhat after, he finds in his soul but small increases or decays. From fifty to threescore the balance generally holds, even in our colder climates, for he loses not much infancy; and judgment, which is the effect of observation, still increases. His succeeding years afford him little more than the stubble of his own harvest; yet, if his constitution be healthful, his mind may still retain a decent vigour; and the gleanings of that Ephraim, in comparison with others, will surpass the vintage of Abiezer. I have called this somewhere by a bold meta-phor—a green old age; but Virgil has given me his authority for the figure :—

" Jam senior ; sed cruda Deo, viridisque senectus."

It was upon the grassy prairies of the olden time the untamed races chased the deer and boar; within the umbrage of primeval woods they learnt the first lessons of a simple creed, and upon altars of green herbs offered their first sacrifice. Nature was still educating the Man, lifting up his heart to heaven by the splendours of noon and sunset, and filling him with gratitude to the Author of all Good, by the promises of fertile fields, the exube-rance of fruitful jungles, and the enamelled poetry of wood and hill side.

In after times, the grassy herbage was still dear to men, and upon the green floor of the wilderness they made their orisons to the morning star, and chanted their hosannahs to the rising sun, regarding the golden orb as the visible emblem of the Eternal. The green grass was the first altar, and the brown forest with its roof of sky the first temple. The Druids walked in solemn procession over the dewy sward of the forest, when, with shouts of joy and wild songs of gladness, they assembled to commemorate the egress of the ark. Then the caves were festooned with garlands; an altar was built of grasses and vine leaves; the crystal cups of honey were twined with clusters of wild blossoms; the trees were festooned with flowers; and citterns, emblematical of the sun-god, were hung among the garlands. Then in the twilight recesses the priests performed the mystic dance, and as the May smile of morning broke upon the hills and fields, the hymns of the May-women were whispered in wild melodies, and the invocation to May was performed upon the green. The cattle lowed in the meadows, the birds sang in the valleys, and the sun, pillowed on the clouds of heaven, flushed the fountains and the forests with his golden fire. The multitude fell prostrate on the grass. The priests bowed to the pavilion of celestial glory; and with one accord the throngs of worshippers broke forth into hymns of praise, so that solemn music and sweet odours were eminent in the rituals of the grassy temples of the ancient Britons.*

When man, first waking up from rude barbarism, perceived the relations of the world without to the world within himself, he sought to embody the unshapen poetry of his heart in some form of simple beauty, and he took the grass as the first representative of the exuberance of nature. He made manifest his thankful-

* Harrovian.

ness for the fruits of the ground in offerings of the green grass which made beautiful his pathway through the world, and by the seeds of which his fields were sown with plenty. The period is of immense antiquity when the inhabitants of the sacred region of the Nile began first, from the vestal hearth, to sacrifice to the celestial gods, not myrrh, cassia, nor the first fruits of things mingled with the crocus of frankincense—for afterwards, when wanting the necessities of life, those were offered with great labour and many tears, as libations to the god,—"but grass, which as a certain soft wool of a prolific nature, they plucked with their hands." "They gathered the blades and the roots, and all the germs of this herb, and committed them to the flames, as a sacrifice to the gods, to whom they paid immortal honour through fire."* Hence, too, the patriarchs and poets of the olden times painted Damater, the mother of the gods—the same that was Cu-bell, the chief goddess of the Chaldeans, the Cybele of the Ionians, and the Rhoia of the Doric people—as sitting amid green grass, and surrounded with fragrant flowers. On the oldest coins of Syria she sits beside the hive, with ears of corn in her hands, to denote the return of the seasons and their exuberance of fruits ; while at her feet the grasses grow and wave, to typify the seasonal renewals of green beauty on the earth. So, too, the benefactors of humanity were represented as surrounded with emblems of rural beauty, and as such, Saturn, the man of piety and justice, is described with the sickle in hand, going over the earth to teach its people the tillage of the soil. It was in the

* *Porphyria de Abstinentia.*—Book II., sec. 5.

season of spring grass, too, that the band of heroes
under Jason set out under the guidance of the dove,
which was directed by the hand of Minerva, to regain
the Golden Fleece. It was at the time—

> " When first the pleasing Pleiades appear,
>   And *grass-green* meads pronounced the summer near,
>   Of chiefs a valiant band, the flower of Greece,
>   Had planned the emprise of the golden fleece."

But leaving the shadowy records and traditions of
buried years, let us turn to the aspect of the grass itself,
for it is everywhere a thing of beauty, whether gladden-
ing the mountain solitude with its angel smile, greening
the soft slopes of the mossy glades, where the red deer
wanders, and the child loves to play; whether gliding
down into the deep, deep valleys, where the fountains
murmur and the bees sing; whether clothing the sharp
granite on the crown of the world, and making a
cushion for the only flower which there looks up to God,
or clinging, like an eternal friendship, to the roots of the
gnarled trees, where in summer the rabbits burrow and
the linnets sing, and in winter the storm-cloud gathers
and the branches crash; while the hurricanes howl in
chorus, scattering the growths of ages as they sweep the
march of God.

In all its states and stages it is emblematic of human
sentiments and human fate; especially is it emblematic
both of life and death. All imagery fades into common
place beside the imagery of the inspired volume; and
there the grass is again and again the subject of similes
and comparisons that reach deeper into the heart than it

is possible for the highest secular poetry to do. How
sweet is the opening of the song of Moses in the 32nd
of Deuteronomy—"My doctrine shall drop as the
rain, my speech shall distil as the dew, as the small
rain upon the tender herb, and as the showers upon the
grass : because I will publish the name of the Lord."
See the mournfulness of the climax in that reply to
Hezekiah's prayer against the mocker Sennacherib, who
had ravaged Israel—"Their inhabitants were of small
power, they were dismayed and confounded ; they were
as the grass of the field, and as the green herb, as the
grass on the housetops, and as corn blasted before it be
grown up," 2 Kings xix. 26. There are more than forty
such comparisons of the fate of man to the grass of the
field, and each has its own peculiar power, adaptation,
and use, in the precious words of divine wisdom, and
serve to bind closer the relationship of man and Nature,
which are so distinctly set forth in the grand revelation,
that all that is of earth shall perish, even as the grass of
the field, "which to day is, and to-morrow is cast into
the oven." If we dare not say that the grass is a
symbol of God, we may say that in some measure its
perennial verdure and plentifulness, and as the source
of sustenance to myriads of creatures, represents the
exhaustless affluence, the limitless energy, the boundless
supervision and incessant exodus of benefits that combine in Him, "by whom, and through whom, and to
whom are all things." It is most true, says Isaac Taylor,
that the pious contemplatist finds in the sere herbage of
the wilderness, and on the rugged and scorched surface of
granite rocks, symbols enough of God ; and he thinks

himself richly furnished with book, and lesson, and
teacher, when he descries on his solitary way only a blade
of grass.

VIII. PERORATUS.

It is worth noting here that, according to the teachings of Geology, the tribe of grasses was ushered into
being only a short time previous to the appearance of
man upon the earth.   There are no grasses in the old
red sandstone, none in the carboniferous rocks, rich as
they are in other vegetable forms which gave their bulk
to the formation of the coal measures.   Myriads of ages
went by, and myriads of plants succeeded race upon race,
but not a grass was fashioned until of the entombed generations, as we find them, "God had made the pile complete."   *Then*, and not till then, when the earth was to
be the abode of man and the creatures that especially
minister to his wants, God said, "let the earth bring
forth grass;" and the black vallies became savannahs—
the dreary plains prairies of grasses and wild flowers.
The grasses were made especially for man, and that is
man's title to draw from them sustenance for both body
and mind.   Hence the moral beauty of green things
generally, best perceived through the aid of a healthy
sentiment, and a mind ordered after the will of God.
Dear to man are they as things which .solace him and
beguile life of its harshness ; which surround his home
with poetry, and fill his heart with peace.   How dreary
would be the lot of man in a world where green things
were not ; with no green valleys dotted with homely
sheep, no broad savannahs rustling a million golden

tassels in the wind; no flowery meadows folding us in
their grassy arms; and no magic chain of love-like
songs and bleatings, and tender associations, and soft
stirrings of the heart, filling the soul with joy upon joy,
till life itself becomes but as an hour of sunshine.
There is a moral beauty and a teaching for the spirit in
all the budding things of the green out-door world,
which to the wise man afford inward satisfaction, and
never fail to renew his hope.   Their very frailness and
evanescence hint of our short stay here, as their renewed
growth with each return of spring symbolizes the spring
season to which we shall awake in another world.   The
story of the fig-tree but emblems the condition of man:
if he be without fruit he shall be accursed; if he do
naught for the service of men, he shall fall under the
doom of the fig-tree which the Lord condemned.

> "He gafe ensample in His parsone,
> And we the wordes have alone,
> Like to the tre with leves greene
> Upon the which no fruit is seene."
>
>   GOWER.

Let him, while his outward deeds are fair and goodly to
behold, cherish also the inward sympathies and high
thoughts which tend to fruitfulness in the future; and
he shall then become as a tree whose harvests are equal
to its spring promises; and the fruition of his heart
shall endear him to his age and generation.   "The
greene leaves outward sheweth that the tree is not drie
inwarde; and the good workes oftenlie notifieth the inwarde heart secretlie."*

* Golden Boke, Letter 7.

Over the field where human blood has flowed, and
thousands have fallen in the fight for freedom, the grass
waves as greenly as before; and where the martyrs
sleep, it grows in rich luxuriance, to hide their blanched
bones from the gazing of the world. They who sleep—

> " Deep beneath the grass-grown soil,
> Far in the common field,"

will awake no more to the sunshine of this world, but
meet the reward of the justice or the injustice of their
fight beyond the grassy shores of this. And so the
world revolves; and on the spot whereon armies have
assembled, where emperors have achieved territory and
martial glory, where crowns have been lost and won, and
thousands have sunk down unknelled to rise no more,
the grass comes again with its refreshing verdure, glad-
dening the husbandman with its assurances of plenty,
cheering the heart by its spring light and whisperings of
love, and surrounding the life of man with perfumed
benedictions. These are the teachings of the grass,
these the lessons of its verdurous beauty. It is alike
the symbol of exuberance and the teacher of fate. In
the wilderness it welcomes man to pitch his tent and
become a peaceful sojourner; and, amid the ruins, it
mocks him for his work : the city which he rears sinks
into the dust, and—

> " Desolation o'er the grass-grown street
> Expands her raven wings, and from the gate
> Where senates once the weal of nations plann'd
> Hisseth the slimy snake, through hoary weeds,
> That clasp the mouldering column."*

---

* Akenside—" Pleasures of Imagination, B. ii."

D

But from that ruin shall other cities arise, and a nobler race of frank-browed men shall pass in the streets, and maidens fair walk on the green lawns to welcome in the morns of spring. There shall be flowery islands in the future, and the summer's-shine shall fall on meadows green, on which the children of the future men shall play. The young birds shall carol from their leafy homes, as if the trees sang forth themselves, and the new generation shall have the dreams of the present all fulfilled.

Heart! be thou like the grass; welcome man and woman with thy smile: be thou green in winter as in summer; assort thyself with brown bees, and homely things that bless the world, keeping thy blossom by thee to gild the pathway of the future. Thy days are as few as the grass; as the grass that groweth to-day, and to-morrow is cast into the oven. "For euen as the flower of the grasse shall he vanishe awaye. The sunne ryseh wyth heete, and the grasse widereth, and his flower falleth away, and the beautie of the fashion of it perisheth."* Heart! be thou like the grass—fragrant, fair, gentle, and fertile in good works; for which God be thanked, for its beauties are beyond description, and its uses beyond enumeration.

* Bible, 1551.

THE SEASON OF BUTTERCUPS.

> " ALL is silence—silence deep;
> Hark! what chanting faint and low!
> Leaves and flowers awake from sleep,
> Murmurs from the blossoms flow."
>
> HERR FREILIGRATH.

NOT alone is the spring-time the genesis of life; it is also the genesis of joy,—the soul's season of promise. Nature and Man come back again to childhood; childhood itself has lighter laughter; infancy a fresher heart. Spring! oh dear spring, with thy tender voice and holy tears, how do men bless thee for thy gifts of love! greener moss, greener grass, blinking sunshine, softer air, daffodils, buttercups,—

> " As if the rainbows of the fresh mild spring
> Had blossomed where they fell."

Buttercups, the freshest and the welcomest of all. Buttercups! splashes from the wheels of the chariot of the sun, that haunt every meadow, and roadside, and sunny bank, and with the white daisies, make the gold and silver of the fields,—a gold and silver more precious than the dirt men dig from mines, because appealing to their highest faculties, mingling in the play of their senti-

ments, and while glittering before the eye, filling the
heart with the noblest emotions.

Hail, beautiful Season of Buttercups! thrice beautiful
in thy timid gentleness, thy confiding innocence, and thy
fulness of rich promise! Welcome, fragrant season of
slanting sunbeams, fresh birth-time of yellow flowers!
When the dear children go with hearts full of spring-
time, and hopes yet in the unfolded bud,—searching for
the snow-flakes and the spangles, the daisies and the
buttercups, which they think heaven has let fall as
manna; then, wearied with prattle, to loiter home, in
twos and threes, laden with their flowery spoils, to lie
and dream all night of worlds made of flowers, and
people with yellow faces and white daisy eyes, and yellow
hair, walking upon yellow ground, on which there is not
room to tread without crushing the buttercups. Welcome, bright birthday of flowers and song; soft season
of verdurous freshness, bringing back the growth and
glory of the world, and filling manhood's heart with
dreams of boyhood, and the fairy pictures of the past!
Welcome, Season of Buttercups, and soft gales that kiss
the cheek with coolness! When the honeysuckle peeps
in for the first time at the open window; when we venture out once more with heads uncovered, and watch the
sparrows as they flutter round the ivy; and, forgetting
hawks and cats, imagine their life a more joyous one
than our own; when the hills come nearer to us with
their fresh green flanks, and the wild wood warbles with
a full heart's song; when the bare branches wake from
the night of winter to the morning of spring, to peep at
the buttercups and blades of light green grass that

cluster round their knees; and then watching the amber bars of the east; as the old sun climbs the slopes of Heaven, so wink and blink in the glare of the sunlight, that tears start from their eyes, and form thousands of yellow drops which take root on every spray and twig, and form their summer coat of leaves. Beautiful, fresh season! sanctified at thy shrine of flowers by all the little birds that woo and wed in the brown branches; by all the new buds which break into emerald greenness; by all the dreamy bees which sail singing after luscious honey; by all the milch kine that breathe a "smell of dairy," and wallow, knee-deep in the new grass; and by every milkmaid whose cheek blushes with the rose of health, whose breath is ever like the meadowy breeze of June, and who "makes her hand hard with labour, and her cheek soft with pity."

Spring is the Season of Buttercups; it is the season also of bursting buds and germinating seeds. First, we have troops of snow-drops and flame-like crocusses, varied here and there with the bright yellow of the winter aconite, and crowned with the iron leaves of the butcher's broom. Then come the pale primroses "that die unmarried," sprinkling the hedges with sulphur; violets with breath as sweet as from an angel's mouth :—

> "As if Nature's incense-pans had spilt,
> And shed the dews i' the air."

Coltsfoot, the emblem of maternal care; the rare whitlow grass, both white and yellow, so small that they seem like legacies from the fairies, who perished when Faith fled

from the people : white wood anemone, the spirit of the
spring breezes ; the pilewort, and the celandine that
Wordsworth loved. On the edges blue speedwells peep
up in cloudy clusters ; the chickweed and the cuckoo
flower show their silver petals ; the daisies sprinkle the
sward with millions of white starry eyes ; and the buttercups wreathe and twine over the green mounds, the
forest dimples, the grey stones, and the graves of a
former summer's beauty.   And amid them all—

> " The silver streams go singing in fine lines—"

splashing, trickling, washing banks of moss where harebells, yet unfolded, cluster ; creeping through reedy
banks, where the water fowl learn maternal joys ; past
grassy meadows that swell with fatness, and beneath
broad, arching boughs, where a thousand wild birds con-
gregate amid the leafy darkness :—

> " The Winter with his grisly storms no longer durst abide,
> The pleasant grass with lusty green the earth hath newly dyed ;
> The trees have leaves, the boughs do spread, new changed is the
>   year,
> The water-brooks are clean sunk down, the pleasant boughs ap-
>   pear ;
> The Spring is come, the goodly nymphs now dance in every place ;—
> Thus hath the year most pleasantly of late changed her face."
>   EARL SURREY.

More glorious still when the gardens heap up their crimson foam, and apple orchards brim over with blossoms ;
when the green corn waves high above the furrows,
playing with every wind that skips over the field, and
clustering in thick patches round the skylark's nest,

where the brooding mother crouches, listening to her gallant as he dashes upwards to the sun, singing in the blue his roundelay.

In the hedges nestle all manner of wild herbs and creatures, while, along the banks, the hawthorns stretch, like boundary walls, for miles and miles, making the air so full of fragrance that we seem wafted to some old region of enchantment, amid the scenery of the " Fairy Queen," or within reach of the " sleep soothing groves " of the " Castle of Indolence."   Good old friend! flinging its perfume over the sheep-fields, waving its boughs over the thatched roof, and suggesting to the wayfarer the merry days of Robin Hood, when the good folks went before daybreak to the woods—

> " To gather May-buskets and smelling brere,
> •   •   •   •   •
> With hawthorn buds and sweet eglantine,
> And gurlonds of roses, and soppes in wine."

The Season of Buttercups is also the season of the sweet birds'·song. It is the heyday of Nature, in which the blood trips more freshly through the veins of every creature, and love stoops down once more to possess all things with his warmth and vigour.   How could the little birds woo and wed at any other time? How, except at the season of Buttercups? when the world is surfeited with beauty, when—

> " Each leaf upon the tree doth shake with joy,
> With joy the white clouds navigate the blue,
> And on his painted wings the butterfly,
> Most splendid masker in this carnival,
> Floats through the air in joy."
>
> ALEXANDER SMITH.

How, but at that awakening season, when

> " The clodded earth goes up in sweet breathed flowers;
>   In music dies poor human speech,
> And into beauty blow these hearts of ours,
>   When love is born in each."
>
> ALEXANDER SMITH..

It is this passion, dawning in the Season of Buttercups, which gives new life to the heart of the most timid creature; works a change in the attitude and habit of the most courageous and the most retiring; gives the quadruped his noblest bearing, and the bird his brightest plumage; makes the creature, which before was startled at the falling of a leaf, or the dancing of its own shadow, energetic, affectionate, and fearless; brings out the highest capabilities of the meanest and most despised, and makes even a sparrow musical. There is the bonny lark,—dweller on the brown earth, companion of the daisy, a little tawny bird, shy, and crouching in the dust —Love lifts him up into the blue heavens to beat his wings against the morning star, and drown the voices of angels with his torrent of song :—

> " Seeming to rain down music from his wings,
>   And bathe his plumage in a fount of light."

It carries him on the wings of a wild passion away into

> " ———— the abysses dim
> Of lornest space, in whose deeps regally
> Suns and their bright broods swim;"

and makes him the companion of the sunshine and the amber cloud, all the while warbling to his bride as she sits brooding and listening under the shelter of the bents.

How fares it with a hundred others? Mute all the year till now, Love seizes them, and they become spirits of gay song, so full, free, and concordant, that the forest is no longer a mere fleet of brown stems, but "an orchestra of mighty sound."

In the very dawn of spring comes the wryneck, with its cry of "pee,", softer and fuller now, because uttered from the heart, telling of the hours, when—

> "The balm, the beauty, and the bloom
> Recall the good Creator to his creature."

Then, simultaneously, the chaffinch, who had begun to sing long before, attains the fulness and fluency of his cheerful song; the thrush, who whistled when the snow lay thick, is hurried with the rest, and has so much to express that he is constrained to sing by night as well as by day; the blackcap, with uncontrollable delight, mocks all the songs it hears, as if employing all the languages of the bird-world to express what language never can express at all; and, from the midst of this "full-throated chorus," rise the soft modulations of the nightingale, first, "jug jug," then in a liquid strain of flute-like music which melts us into tears, as if it were the voice of a happy spirit, singing songs of gladness in the gardens of Paradise. "It breathes," says old Isaak Walton, "such sweet, loud music out of its little instrumental throat, that it might make mankind think that miracles had not ceased. He that at midnight, when the very labourer sleeps securely, should hear, as I have often, the clear airs, the sweet descant, the natural rising and falling, the doubling and redoubling of that sweet voice, might

well be lifted above the earth, and say, 'Lord what music
hast thou provided for the saints in heaven, when thou
affordest bad men such music upon earth?'" No wonder
the old poets wove it into their wild fables, and made it
the emblem of tenderness, affection, and slighted worth.
No wonder that Hesiod sang of the "dappled Philomel,"
Homer of the "tawny Nightingale," Æschylus, Sopho-
cles, and Euripides—himself the nightingale of Grecian
poetry, drawing his inspirations from the beautiful in
Nature—Theocritus, dreamy and musical as a summer
sleep—Longus, spiritual and tender, like the flowers in
the gardens of Philetas;—all that have known how to
love and sing, from the mountain bard, charming the
shepherds with impromptu songs, to Milton singing
of—

> ———— "the pleasant time,
> The cool, the silent, save where silence yields
> To the night-warbling bird, that now awake,
> Tunes sweetest his love-laboured song."

And not those only that sing deserve honourable mention,
but many others, whose throats have no ravishing harmonies, are yet susceptible of the rose-hues and summer
breath of that blind god who tips his arrow with an
amra bloom to make its point pierce keener. There is
the little wagtail—dear to the Season of Buttercups—a
consequential, striding wiseacre, for ever foraging by the
unfrozen spring for delicate morsels of insect life; a
thorough Briton, nevertheless, who sticks to the land
that gave him birth, and disdains to turn his back on
our northern climate, because a few fogs and frosts give
the British winter. There are the rooks, too, a

clamorous, croaking, sable-plumed race of petty swindlers, spending half the spring in stealing each other's sticks, and fighting no end of battles in the thick of the branches, until that universal conqueror—the god of the Season of Buttercups—has them in his grasp, and then they build nests, and prattle of love, and hatch large broods of baby rooks—destined, like their parents, to be alternately devils and doves—the very models of parental care and social union. Besides these, there are the wood-pigeons, which now gather back to their old mossy haunts, cowering together in the leafiest of coverts, besides the loveliest of grey old nooks, where little runnels flow unseen, and little seeds burst into yellow sprays, under the matting of the last year's leaves, to spring up into waving heads of greenness, and sit in the shadow of the oaks, beguiled by the soft, heart-touching "coo, coo," which tells of love amid the branches. April bringing up the rear of spring visitants, gives us quails, turtle-doves, swifts, puffins, swallows, martins, and lapwings; and life in innumerable forms assumes its noblest aspect, warmed into new vigour with the expansion of the season, enhanced in its beauty by the development of increased provision for its support, and lifted half-way into the region of the unreal by that divine impulse which is the soul of living Nature, and which, while it adds heroic attributes alike to man and brute, conserves that succession of creatures to which all the provisions of Nature are attached as to one continuous thread.

Poets, painters, and gossipers, have all dealt with spring as a season of beauty only, as a time of renewal and regeneration; forgetting that it is the season also of

strife and terror, alternating between sunshine and storm,
and, in some climates, the most to be dreaded for its
ravages of wind and wave. The vernal equinox is not
more strikingly marked here in its bright hues, its bursting of leaf-bud and flower-bud, its softness of sunshine,
and its gush of song, than it is in other climes by its
sweeping hurricanes, its sand-storms, and ice-storms, its
crash of forests, and fall of avalanches—for it is everywhere the season of rapid change, and the summer of
fruitage which follows it is but the ripening of the influence, which, in its birth, had so many startling features.
The spring of the world has its analogies in the spring
of time; for in the ages the seasons are repeated, and
from the beginning to the end of creation, times, and
seasons, and things, are counterparts of each other.
Geology, astronomy, history,—each have their spring-
time,—their Season of Buttercups. Far back into the
twilight of tradition, spring shows its mask of beauty,
and its phase of many-coloured strife. The mountain-
heights that crown the world were the growths of former
springs of forces, as buttercups are now the growths of
fair springs of sunshine. Entombed within the rocky
ramparts are the ferns and flowers of that old season of
renewal, and beside those very plants are the indelible
traces of up-heaving forces, writhings, fusings, and con-
tortions, by which the giant masses were blasted and
flung about the world,—played with, as the March hurricane now plays with the stray feather of a bird, or as
the ocean, whirled in the equinox, plays with the froth
that forms the crest of its waves. Spring in the world
and spring in man are only different sides of the same

fact. Infancy opens into youth, like the unfolding of a
flower. All is promise; the blossom of life breaks upon
the ruddy cheek; the freshness of spring-life is there;
the laughing lip and the daisy light of boyhood's eye
proclaim how lovely is the stormless spring. But the
equinox of life comes on, and fierce passions rage; March
hurricanes ride upon the breath; March madness usurps
the will; the heart becomes a region of storm and tempest; and sometimes the spring folly withers the blossom
which should light up manhood's summer.

It has its use, this spring of beauty in Nature, this
spring of passion in Man. As the winds try the branches,
and the frosts try the buds, sweeping away those that
are not worthy to bear fruit, so the passions of Man serve
as tests of the good that is in him. When they lead not
to licentiousness, they impart a virtuous fire, which
impels him to noble deeds, and upon the shoulders of
impetuous youth, Love is borne in triumph to a home of
virtue. Bless thee, bright season of greenness, birth-
time of out-door joys, harbinger of plenty, genesis of
love; fresh, fragrant, and fertile season of Buttercups!

A HAPPY FAMILY.

WE are a cosy quiet couple, not frequently haunted by cares, or excited by varieties. We live just far enough from town to be free from temptations of pleasure, yet near enough to avoid lapsing into vapid dullness; in fact, we manage to combine town and country life together in our little household, and to adorn our rustic pursuits with a few of the graces of literature, and some touches of homely art. I might perhaps amuse you by a relation of our every-day life, its whims and oddities and the utter abandonment to impulse to which, since our first wedding-day, we have been addicted; but it is the family we have reared that I think I may most profitably talk about, and, at the risk of being thought egotistical, I shall give you a brief account of it.

I venture to say that few strictly private families are so truly happy as ours; for though it comprises *thousands* of children of all ages,—some older than ourselves, many of them differing in temper and taste as widely as the pole differs from the equator,—yet the most perfect harmony at all times prevails amongst us, and the only anxiety that possesses us is to render each other happy. To be sure, the elements of " a row " are never wanting; and were the heads of the family for one single day to forget their responsibilities, bloodshed and cannibalism would make a total ruin of our model Agapemone.

Ten or twelve may be considered a fair number for any ordinary family, and on such a limited scale, some little generalship is essential for the preservation of domestic peace: but, as I first remarked, our family consists of thousands—in fact, *we* ourselves have never attempted a numbering of the people, and frankly confess we do not know how many within a thousand or two are dependent upon us. If I tell you they are all children of adoption,—for as yet we are unblessed with children of our own,—you will conjecture that we are keepers of an orphan asylum, a workhouse, or a prison; but such ideas will vanish when I assure you that we are strictly private folk, renting a humble country cottage, with a moderate amount of garden attached, and with a very pretty variety of rural scenery adjoining. The fact is, we are victims of a hobby. How many have gone mad, been ruined, traduced, ay, transported or hanged, for hobbies! Yet we live in no fear that *our* hobby will entail future penalties, for it is simply a love for animals: and the passion is fed and strengthened by a strong curiosity to learn more and more of their histories and instincts, their relations to each other and to the general scheme of nature, and, above all, their capabilities for human companionship. Our little house is a sort of menagerie; not in imitation of the Zoological Gardens, or the Jardin des Plantes, nor yet on the plan of the Hospital for Animals at Surat,—for we have nothing about us that is obnoxious, and not a single cripple.

We are just now ready for breakfast, and we sit at the fire surrounded with cockatoos, macaws, and parrots. All the voices of the animal world salute and deafen us. *Old* Poll, the pet of the parlour, can bark, growl, bleat, purr, or whistle, and in addition, ask for every thing she wants, and for many things she does not want. She can be insolent or polite; and, as a result of our teaching, she is a very expert thief. I could tell a hundred anecdotes about that one patriarchal parrot: how she takes tea from a spoon and beer from a tumbler; how she cracks nuts and crows like a cock; how she leaves her cage to steal sugar or fruit; how she can recite two complete stanzas of *Johnny Gilpin*, and bandy small talk with any body. When her noise and impudence cease, we turn to the cockatoos, of which we have three elegant, docile, loving creatures: one pure white, with a crest that looks like flakes of turbot; another with pale sulphur crest; and a third with white and crimson plumage—strictly a cockatoo-parrot, the most loquacious of the whole family, but so gentle in her demeanour that she never was guilty of a single mischief yet. To visitors, the gray and green parrots, of which we have two each, are a perfect bore; they scream and yell and bark, and, if a chance were afforded them, would dig their pickaxe beaks into innocent faces and hands; but these gentle crested favourites are determined to be loved, and at the first sound of a strange voice, up go their crests, down go their heads with a soft ejaculation of "Cock-a-too;" and if they do not get their accustomed

scratching on the poll, they seem dejected for the day.
As for Betty, the cockatoo parrot, she says plainly,
"Scratch poor Betty's poll; Betty wants her poll
scratched;" and scratched it must be over and over
again before Betty will turn to her bread and milk, and
allow an interval for conversation. Then we have a pair
of Australian ground parroquets; two splendid macaws
that dazzle the eye with their oriental plumes of azure
and vermillion; a pair of slender and brilliantly-coloured
lories, that have never yet, and never will, acquire more
speech than the utterance of their names; and a pair of
Brazilian toucans, with enormous bills, and plumage
more dazzling than the dress of a harlequin.

You would just think yourself in Babel, were you to
be spiritually present when we sit down to breakfast
surrounded by these, the noisiest members of our happy
family. But if you were present in the body also, I
would insure complete silence by one clap of the hand
and you should hear a pin drop if you wished it. Then
one by one each should go through its performances of
imitating a farm-yard, a fiddle, a pair of bagpipes, or a
series of incoherent but very comical speeches. Old
Poll is the only one that would occasion trouble; and
she is so self-willed, that you would have to take your
chance whether she would take breakfast with us and
talk like a Christian, or cough, bark, and growl you into
a state of stupid deafness. But if all went well, Polly
would be a polyglot; for she can gabble French,
German, and Latin with very tolerable accent, and mix
with her classical quotations the more familiar sounds of
"Beer, ho," "Ba-ker," and the words and air of "Pretty,

E

pretty Polly Hopkins." When Betty's turn came, she
would, in a nasal singing tone, ask you some impertinent
questions, such as "Can you spell Istactepetzacuxochitl
Icohueyo?" and before you could give her an answer,
such is her want of politeness, she would hurry through
a whole string of small talk; ask for tea, beer, cakes,
nuts, grapes, and finish off with Quin's "incoherent
story," which, with a slight blush, I confess to have
spent the occasional leisure of a whole year in teaching
her. While this went on, the other birds would get
jealous; and to keep peace, we should have to scratch
no end of proffered polls, and make a compromise with
master Tommy, the elder of the green parrots, by the
present of a chicken bone for him to pick and chuckle
over. The exhibition always finishes by feeding the
toucans, which are the "lions" of the collection; we
hand them each a choice morsel—a task which you
might think dangerous, seeing that their beaks are large
enough for the seizure of a fat baby, and you would
think it no trifling matter to appease appetites having
such formidable representatives. Yet, immense as are
the horny appendages with which the toucan takes his
daily bread, his mode of eating is decidedly pretty and
amusing. The food is taken on the point of the bill,
it is then tossed high in the air, the immense jaws open
like a pair of park-gates, and the descending morsel falls
straight into the gullet with "a cluck" that makes one
roar with laughter. The conjuror who catches knives
and rings might take a lesson from these comical
creatures.

It is not every body who cares to be shut in with such

a gabbling noisy crew as our parrots; and fortunately we
can give our visitors a choice between fountains and
water-gardens, tropical and British ferns, and homely
songsters; or accommodate them with the scientific
seclusion of a cabinet stocked with living and dead
insects, aquatic larvæ that glide about like ghosts,
beetles that kick and plunge in their vessels of water
like imps on the verge of despair, together with tame
spiders, toads, frogs, and snakes, and a very attractive
display of stuffed quadrupeds and birds, and some prepared and mounted skeletons of various animals. This
cabinet-room is my own especial pleasure; *cara sposa* only
finds her way there occasionally; and, indeed, none but
choice scientific friends, who have sufficient enthusiasm
to stare themselves tired with a compound microscope,
or feed their imaginations into a "fierce frenzy" by
discussing the technologies of entomological nomencla-
ture, ever get permission, much less invitations, to enter
it. The most attractive things there are the Aquaria
and water-cabinets, which together fill up the window-
spaces, and shut out a large portion of the daylight.
In the right-hand window stands the river-tank, pellucid
as crystal, and luxuriant with many forms of bright-
green vegetation. Within it five-and-thirty fishes glide
and gambol, and exhibit their several habits and instincts. I should not mention this as a part of our
happy family were it not so in reality. In that vessel
more than three-fourths of the finny innocents are as
tame as cats; they know me, love me, and not only feed
from my hand, but assemble when I call them, and obey
my every look and motion as readily as if they were

terrestrial kith and kin.   There are three splendid tench
—naturally the shyest of British fishes—now so familiar
with the prison which has housed them for more than
two years, and the keeper who has tended them during
that time, that they not only flounder out of the dark
weeds and rise when I call them to receive a few worms,
but, without the offer of food, they will assemble at the
surface and remain still while I play with them, and seem
to enjoy familiarities as much as parrots do to have their
polls scratched.

I have a whole school of Crucian, British, and Prussian carp, all docile and loving as is their nature; but
one huge Prussian carp is the captain of the tank—the
special pet, the ancient and trusty friend whom I ever
delight to honour.   He is a magnificent fellow, plump,
iridescent, seven inches in length, and as playful as a
spaniel.   He commands universal admiration.   His easy,
gliding, and dignified motions,—for he is never in a
hurry,—and his constant association with seven other of
his kindred, who to him are as babes to a giant, and
above all, his confiding fondness, make him a piscatory
marvel.   Whenever I enter the room, " the boomer," or
" master carpenter,"—for those are the names he seve-
rally bears,—at once recognizes my voice or step, and
straightway he comes " booming " to the side, with his
dolphin-like head and splendid eyes, and there poises in
mid-water to watch me.   If I sit down to write, he
remains there, slowly rising and sinking, never leaving
the side next me even for an instant; he seems to watch
and listen; and I could sometimes bitterly reproach
Nature that she does not allow him to speak.   As to

eating from my hand, or rising to the top when called, or rolling on his side to be played with, these are common-place matters; he will nibble my finger gently for ten minutes at a time, play with a stick, dart about at a game of touch, or assemble his little band of juvenile carpenters, and get up a frolic with them for my amusement. But he is a gentleman in every thing—easy, dignified, never put out; and if a shoal of saucy bleak or daring minnows steal the choicest morsel even from his lips, he yields the point at once, takes no revenge, but looks with expectant eye to his protector for more.

As to chub and bream and dace, I have as many as the tank will support, all of them thoroughly tame. The minnows and bleak are "the fun of the fair," and the loach, the untameable savages that hold aloof from the general society, and, spite of every kindness, persist in leading a life of their own.

Above the river-tank are the shelves containing my aquatic curiosities. There the ravenous water-beetles and their larvæ, with other creatures of similar habits, plunge and kick in their crystal jars. Give them a minnow, how they plunge their fangs into the palpitating flesh, consume their prey piecemeal without first killing it, dragging the viscera from the trembling creature, or boring into the gills while it yet struggles for life! If now and then a death occurs in the tank, these carnivorous gluttons have the carcase tossed to them to riddle and consume; but as this very seldom happens, they have to remain content with earth worms from the garden, which I find answer very well for every one of the flesh-eating aquatics.

In other jars I have specimens of the magnificent *Hydrous piceous*, the largest aquatic beetle found in Britain, and the most docile and harmless of the whole family; boat-flies; lovely specimens of Colymbetes, with jet-black backs and silver bellies; eccentric whirligigs, that emulate the dervishes in defying giddiness; quaint species of water-scorpion; and that most curious of all the smaller inhabitants of the streams, the diving spider, with its silken cocoons suspended beneath the surface. These occupy a whole shelf; and a curious sight it is to watch their various motions and proceedings as they dive, spin, kick, quarrel, or engage in comical courtships.

But these are not the most prized among the minor members of my family. The shelf above them contains the rare treasures, though to the casual eye it exhibits nothing more than a row of crystalline jars filled with clear water and very emerald-green tufts of starry vegetation. But here are my Nitella, my Vallisneria, my sorted species of Chara, Riccia, and Lemna; and if I want to observe the circulation of the sap in plants or the blood in animals, these jars supply suitable specimens, that under the penetrating eye of the microscope enable me to pierce at once to the most secret chambers of nature—to the fountain-head (materially speaking) of life itself, wherein I may observe the development of a cell, or the production of the primal germ of organization. Some honoured members of my family are here, too. I have thousands of the living ghosts of gnats, dragon-flies, and beetles, that glide up and down in the clear lymph, like souls just taking shape, and with but one film of earth about them. Here, too, are small larvæ of all kinds,—some ravenous as wolves, some that do nothing but jerk themselves into spasms, others that wriggle and twist into all manner of inconceivable forms. Here is a cluster of perhaps a thousand of the larvæ of the common gnat,—a lot of lively jerking imps, that seem as if their bodies were made of spiral springs, and that conduct themselves as if life had but two pleasures to sweeten it one skipping like Spring-heeled Jack, the other hanging from the ceiling by the tail, as the American adventurer lately astonished us by his antipodean perambulations. Indeed, all the aquatic larvæ that I have here—numbering some sixty different kinds —are given to this same feat of suspending themselves by the tail from the surface of the water; for in that way only do they breathe, by means of the plumes, and rays, and prongs with which their tails are furnished.

In other jars I have some pretty water-mites that are incessantly on the trot, not swimming or diving, but literally running hither and thither, as if at any depth and any where the water presented to their feet a solid surface. I have thousands of Cyclops, Monads, Vorticellas, wheel-animalcules, a few Hydras, and no end of common and rare infusoria, that nightly occupy me under the glare of the microscope-lamp, in exploring their inner and outer constructions, their actions and instincts, and the many marvellous indications they afford of the perfection of the economies in things ordinarily invisible—the work of the same Hand from which the worlds themselves were launched, and which sustains, without ceasing, the balance of huge incomprehensible forces.

My other window is adorned with a marine collection
similar.y arranged. The tank contains the choicest of
the gorgeous sea-flowers—

> " Blossoms that ope in the oozy deep,
>   And ne'er lure the bee to thoir green retreat."

I have all the well-known anemones, and a goodly
number of new and rare species. Some are like daisies,
others like the bundles of hissing snakes the ancients
wove around the heads of furies ; one kind is an exact
imitation of a rosette of blue ribbons, another of a coral-
coloured chrysanthemum ; but the most prized of all for
glorious form and colour is the huge carnation or plumed
anemone, which expands its thousands of living fringes
into the form of a very fabulous carnation of mammoth
dimensions.   These are ever changing in form and
aspect ;—now they are lifeless lumps of jelly, now
alabaster columns, now transparent balloons puffed to
bursting with absorbed water, and again the flowery form
predominates, thousands of petal-like fingers expand ;
and the sea-bottom, transferred to my room, shows me
its floral gems, that rival those of the garden in splendour, but which move and change mysteriously, and show
themselves to be endowed with a mute but wonderful
life.   Lifeless as they may appear for hours, their will at
last determines them to prove that they can glide and
climb, and float and cling ; aye, and grasp in an embrace
of death whatever livelier creature may unwarily come
within reach of their barbed threads and flower-like
fingers.

Besides these, I have the pretty Serpulas, that make

for themselves stony tubes; Madrepores, that build up
ocean reefs, and that here in the glass vessel are positively manufacturing coral before my eyes; some crabs,
that walk sideways on tiptoe, and that carry their eyes
on stalks; and hundreds of other things, of which it
would require huge volumes to recount the history or do
justice to their beauty, and the intense interest they
excite in those who delight in preserving them as objects
of study.

After all, I think you would perhaps find more to
amuse you in a little singing-party, to which we have
assigned a room upstairs. This is the special care of my
better half, who, indeed, shuts me out from any partici-
pation in its anxieties, though I am very freely admitted
to the performances of the pupils.

In a snug attic, well lighted, adorned with a fountain
and mirrors, the windows and skylights embellished with
gay plants, a collection of about forty song-birds pass
their time in as jolly a way as one would wish. You will
think of happy couples and nest-building, and the maternal incubation of baby-broods of dickey-birds; but we
long ago found out, as did Mr. Kidd, the prince of bird-
masters, that a bird-room is not the place for breeding.
If love sanctifies life, and gives it its noblest development, it also is the parent of strife and jealousy; it ruined
Troy, its dark side blots with some vengeance or madness or
villany every page of the world's history; and how should a
community of such warm-hearted creatures as birds
escape the desolating effects of a fire that warms when
kept in check by wisdom, but which scorches and blights
when passion only fans the flame? Not to philosophize,

suffice it that none of the fair sex are ever permitted to co-
lonise here; we have in other parts of the house a goodly
number of happy feathered couples that enjoy connubial
bliss and connubial cares; but in a general assemblage
hen-birds are but a source of contention and bickering.

But what a merry and familiar lot are these bachelor
vocalists! how they—

> " Ring roof and rafter,
>   With bagpipes and reeling,"

from the first dawn of day to evening dusk, and even
after that for hours, if indulged with a lighted lamp!
They are all familiar, too; they cluster round their mistress when they have their daily supply of buns and
insects and seeds and paste; they swarm on her head
and shoulders, and actually chaff at her in impudent
tones and gestures, and make such a flutter, and confusion and row as would drive a nervous person utterly
mad.   There are siskins, canaries, white-throats, tits,
woodlarks, wagtails, buntings, linnets, goldfinches, red-
poles, a young thrush, a pair of Java sparrows; a common
sparrow, that has learned a few notes of respectable
music, and that delights in quarrelling with everybody
about nothing; a couple of black-caps, a nightingale,
and a most musical brambling, that imitates the note of
every other bird, and almost equals the nightingale in
some of his finest passages.

The garden is as much a menagerie as the house.   I
have my triangular Cochins and my squatty Bramapoo-
tras, my noble crested Polands and my neat little
Sebrights, that look like poultry for a doll's house;

besides a herd of tame jays and jackdaws, that drive me
crazy by their destructive tricks. These would not interest you, for you see such things everywhere; but here
is a flock of mountain goats that make a daily bleating
on the adjoining common; they are pure Angoras, with
silky fringes of milk-white hair hanging from their flanks
to their fetlocks, and beards that would not disgrace the
most hirsute Crimean hero that ever voted razors to be
ridiculous. The father of the flock is a' noble fellow—
such horns, such a curly head and massive forehead, such
a delicate splash of fawn on his withers, and, O, the
purity of his snow-white back and silky flanks! He
hears my voice or footstep; and away flies Billy, clearing
the five-feet fence at a bound, and trotting towards me
with a playful air of defiance, and with an evident consciousness of his capability to represent a traditional
dilemma. As soon as he comes within a few paces, he
draws himself up on the very tips of his toes, then leaps
up and curvets sideways, and finally springs forward at
me, and butts full at my chest in a manner that would
alarm a stranger unprepared for defence. But that is
only Billy's mode of romping with me—it is always a
rough kind of play; but the noble-hearted fellow always
takes care that his frontal *sinus*, not his crescented *cornua*,
shall make the bold contact that, were I not prepared for
it, would make me measure my length at his feet *hors-
de-combat*. His pranks are all of them characteristic;
he will leap up and plant his hoofs on my chest, and
explore with his nose every one of my pockets to find a
hidden bunch of acorns or a few bean-pods, all the while
winking his splendid large eyes close to my face in a look

of intelligence that is as eloquent to me as the richest flow of human speech. If I move aside, he will mount my back, plant his paws on my shoulders, and continue prancing up and down, and throwing his enormous weight upon me till I yield the point he seeks, and give him a choice morsel. What he will eat in this way is prodigious; yet the fare he seeks when turned out on the common is the dry and sapless leaf, the thorny sprouts of the whin or the hawthorn, half-withered elm-leaves, and, indeed, anything that appears dry, tasteless, woody, and indigestible. It is a fact but little known, that goats *never drink*; this, coupled with their love of dry, scrubby forage, enables them to crop fatness from bald granite, and completes their adaptableness to barren mountain. heights.

If I am bitten with any of that enthusiasm which is popularly called "a fancy," it is certainly a fancy for goats. I have kept goats of every known variety, from the sleepy and fertile Spaniard, to the bold and sprightly Welshman, or the real chamois of the Alps. After all, I prefer these picturesque Angoras; *they* are the goats for the artist—every attitude is graceful, every line, from the beautifully shaped head to the clean fetlocks and polished hoofs, is suggestive of sylvan solitudes and rocky heights. Of all the domestic creatures that associate with man in the conquest of the earth, the goat is certainly the most ancient and classical. The earliest records of civilisation mention goats and sheep as representatives of pastoral wealth, and the most cherished property of the simple nomad patriarch; whose flocks were his household gods, his daily and nightly care, and

his whole support during his bold migrations over path-
less wilds. His great anxiety was to find a succession of
"fresh fields and pastures new;" and the sheep and
goats were the real founders of the earliest states and
dynasties. In the records of later ages the shepherd has
ever a high place. And though in the old chivalric narratives the horse is the subject of many a splendid apostrophe, the domestic life of antiquity finds its truest
utterance in the associations that attach to flocks and
herds; for the shepherd was always the predecessor of
the husbandman, or the builder of cities. The earliest
and the latest pastoral equally derive freshness from the
presence of the mountain goat. Longus, the first and
most tender writer of pastorals, reaches his highest excellence where he paints the foundlings, Daphnis and
Chloe, feeding their flocks together, and at the same time
learning to love. Theocritus, the true cottage-poet of
antiquity, gives us the most homely and rustic pictures
ever sketched in pastoral verse; and in every group he
places the goat in the foreground to suggest the flowery
hills and knolls of wild thyme, amongst which his shepherds breathe fragrant air in the tendance of their
flocks. Horace, thoroughly proud of his garden, was
too much of a parlour-poet, and too much addicted to
the shadow of Mecænas, to cultivate the truly rustic.
But see what Virgil did in his highly polished pastorals
and the graphic "Georgics" in honour of the jaunty,
self-willed, strong-limbed, but tameable and affectionate
Capricornus; and when John Keats shook the dust of the
grave from the inner life of Greece, and rekindled the flame
on the altar of Pagan .worship, the shadowy pomp of

Hellenic mythology received its finest finishing touches in his hands through the help of the sheep, and goats, and bees, that bleated and buzzed in the brightest of his sublime pictures. Then the goat was intimately mixed up with the origin of the drama: for tragedy, which was at first called *trugœdia*, or " the song of the cask," came to be known as *tragœdia*, or " the song of the goat,"—the cask of wine giving place to the higher prize of a goat in the public festivals.

Are you fond of bees? Here I have them in a house to themselves, aspect south-east, a causeway cut for them through the belt of shrubs that screens them from the July sun, along which they pass in buzzing streams to the bramble-hedges and clover-fields, that divide and splash the landscape round. I am passionately fond of my bees. Many a dreamy hour of joy do I find in sitting beside them on a summer afternoon, to watch them go and come, to note the several labours on which they are engaged, every one of which I can determine as well as a master who keeps a rigid register of the labours of his workmen. Some of my hives are made of glass, some of wood, or straw, with glass windows; and in times of commotion, when the bees insist on non-interference, I can retire to the rear of my hive-board, and watch all that takes place within the several abodes of concord and industry. You will not doubt the difficulty I have in determining the exact number of the members of my family, if I tell you that my hive-board now contains ten strong stocks, every stock numbering not less than fifteen thousand bees—some, indeed, containing as many as five-and-twenty or thirty thousand, as I could

prove by experiment. Reaumur first hit upon a mode
of counting bees: he *weighed* a swarm; the result was
four pounds. Now a pound of bees contains five thousand individuals, and as many as half-a-dozen pounds of
bees is the common weight of a strong and prosperous
stock. Hence, if I tell you that nearly half a million
hard-working folks recognise and love me as a father,
you will at least allow I am a true *pater familias,* and in
that sense, more worthy than even old Priam of Troy,
who, I think, was the father of *only fifty* children.

Of course I read the " Georgics " of Virgil, and make
many a brown study over Columella, and Schirach, and
Reaumur, and Huber, and Cotton ; nor do I forget old
Tupper, who has a grand place in my library—no, nor
Wildman, nor Nutt, nor Taylor, nor any other true
student of this wonderful insect. Here, indeed, I can
verify with my own hands and eyes many of the most
startling discoveries that have been made as to the habits
and instincts of the bee, and become daily familiar with
facts that the majority of those who *only read* about
them *must* regard as extravagant fictions. I see the
queen, surrounded by her state attendants, every one of
which right loyally faces the supreme female magistrate
and mother of the state : never one of that dutiful train
turning its back even for an instant to the royal mistress,
who represents all, and more than can be imagined, of
dignity and command concentrated into the compass of
less than an inch. I see the progress and development
of new broods, the deadly hate of rival queens, when it
happens that two come into contact. As two claimants
to a throne cause civil war in human states, so with the

bees, that in every thing represent the *serious* side of
human life in all its minutiæ with wonderful accuracy.
But the bees are the wisest; they never suffer the community to waste valuable energies in deciding a personal
quarrel. They urge the rivals to single combat, and
recognise the victor as their future mistress; the dead
body of the vanquished being cast out from the city.
There is no end to the marvellous in the history of the
bee; and the studious possessor of them may have daily
proof that neither classic lore nor modern scientific
research has yet exhausted the catalogue of sober facts
which in bee-history are every one too marvellous for
credence, except to those who claim the bee as a member
of the family. That they know and love their keeper,
and submit cheerfully to his decrees, repelling the invad-
ing stranger from their causeway and neighbourhood, is
the crowning mark of their sagacity, humble as they are
in the scale of nature, and the trait that endears them to
me more than any other; for I can safely say, "My
bees know me," and give proof of it to any who shall
choose to challenge their capability for distinguishing
one man from another.

My catalogue does not end here. Oh no! but it is
time to stop, waiting till, on a future occasion, some further particulars may be given from the Family Register.
Suffice it for the present that ours is a happy family, the
members of it, though various in tastes and appetites, are
knit in strong household bonds, and are very dear to us
for their confidence and affection, and the many lessons
they daily teach us of the ways and means of nature.
Indeed, we lead a very merry life in the midst of so in-

congruous an assemblage. We wake to the bleating of goats and the song of birds; we breakfast with our parrots about us like a family-party; we dine, like royalty, to music; for then the parrots give place to some little golden-plumaged pets that glory in the clatter of knives and forks and dishes. Tea and supper are also musical meals; for we train many of our birds to sing by lamplight. And we sleep very pleasantly with the odour of ash-tree fires pervading the house in winter; and all the rest of the year fragrances of all kinds are wafted through the open windows from our little flowery garden, or from the miles and miles of haw-thorns and haycocks that stretch on all sides around us.

F

THE JOY OF A GARDEN.

"A wilderness of flowers around us lying,
   Tangling our steps the hidden pathway throng;
Myrtles and vines bloom there above thee, sighing,
   As the wind wakes their fibres into song.
      *   *   *   *

Life here is Eros, that hath ever been,
The sigh of Death forgot, the shadow Time unseen."
                    JOHN E. READE.

O BLINDING sunshine and green coolness! O fresh
morning air and dew-powdered gossamers! O wakeful
colours and sleepy odours! O shivering leaves and
rustling bird's-wing! O joyful dawn, with hum of
voices! and O sultry noon, with dead stillness, silent,
and oppressive! O mossy turf! O sparkling fountain!
O dark mould, that, out of thy dead heart, sendest up
the joy of summer in flowers that rise like souls
released from the sepulchre! O emerald spring, crouching in shyness! O lusty summer, confronting the sun
in thy bold strength and ardour! O fiery autumn,
gathering the glories of all seasons to thyself, to swell
the grandeur of thy flaming sacrifice! and O hoary
winter, magician and destroyer, by whose touch the
world is hushed to rest, and the grave of beauty gar-

nished with a robe of whiteness! Where, but in a garden, shall we see and hear, and press to our heart of hearts the precious wealth of a whole creation? Where, but in a garden, shall we meet with genuine heart-ease? Where, but in a garden, learn the sweet idleness that seems like a dream of Eden? Where, but in a garden, acquire the quick action and the anxious thought that prove us to be fallen creatures? Where, but in a garden, realize our dependence upon God, and understand the links that bind us to Him? Where else see the lilies "how they grow," and the sparrows that fall not but at His bidding? Where, but in a garden, feel the full remembrance that man fell from God in the very morning of his creation, and thenceforth read reproaches in the thorns and thistles that choke the pathway of His life? Where, but in the world of greenness, and life, and everlasting change, and the growth on growth of things indissolubly linked together, read the true lesson of God's love for us, and see the upward yearning of all things that teach us we may be saved? O heaven and O earth! in the garden is your meeting-place, for there God talked with Adam, and there the Saviour wept in agony for all. O polar frost, and O torrid sunshine! O bright orient, and O mysterious occident, your delicatest darlings here blossom side by side, and shake their honey-bells together; for a garden is a microcosm of the world, a living map of climes and seasons, a gathering of all things curious, and useful, and beautiful, from "the cedar that is in Lebanon to the hyssop that groweth on the wall;" and if it may be looked on as an open scroll of pictured emblems by

Almighty fingers, it also illustrates the parti-coloured structure of the human brain, which draws its knowledge from far sources, and spreads abroad ten thousand busy hands to grope and gather from darkness many sources of light and power. O moist palate! longing for luscious fruits. O dainty eye! seeking festivals of colour. O heart! panting for a lovely ministration, and expanding in the bliss of this hushed beauty, seek your joy in the garden, where the voice of God may still be heard among the trees, and a deep sense of peace shall possess thee.

A garden is a Divine institution, a Biblical reminiscence, a present solace, a refuge, a retreat. It is a joy all the year round, it keeps the mind active in invention, the hands diligent in labour, and the heart warm in its capabilities for love. It is the first hope of childhood, and age clings to it as an anchorage to earth, for in its presence it seems as if we could not die; for we talk of " next summer," when Death is already clasping our hands in his; and, as the chill of mortality freezes up the sources of life, the sight of a flower seems to dispel the darkness, and bring light and warmth from the very dust unto which we shall soon return. If I were to recount all that is comprised in the joy of a garden, I should have to sketch out a complete catalogue of human pleasures, from that highest and first of all, the contemplations of the Deity as He is revealed in His word and His works, to the hopeful labour of an infant planting a garden for a doll.

But, apart from things too high and reverend to be treated lightly, or things too trivial for a grown man to try his pen upon, I think the first and chief pleasure of a garden is, that it compels one to be a gardener, which, of all wordly occupations, is the noblest, the most useful, and the one which promises the richest mental and material rewards. Compare the life and habits of a man who loves a garden to one who never in his life felt one touch of enthusiasm on the subject. Your gardener is a healthy, jovial fellow, with a hearty word for everybody; when he laughs, you hear him, for he cannot simper; when he greets you, it is with a grip of the hand that makes you feel, for he is incapable of a touch of finger-tips, or a slow squeeze of cold palms; and it will be a rare thing if he does not live a "righteous, godly, and sober life," at peace with the world, and happy in the bosom of his family. A garden compels a man to be patient, diligent, and temperate—there is no compromise possible. The day-break is no signal for a "second sleep," but a call to fresh air and exercise, for one day's neglect may cause the ruin of things that represent many months, perhaps years of anxious care and watchful attention.

This out-door life not only keeps the blood in a healthy glow, and the brain active in its search for knowledge, but the meanest tasks are elevated even to dignity by the fact of their necessity. Hence, a man who is a thorough gardener feels no shame in handling the spade, or in wheeling rubbish to the pit; for though his means may enable him to enjoy all the refinements of life, it is his pride that there is not one manipulation but he can perform himself, and so a brown skin and hard hands give him no fear that he shall lose his claim to the title of

gentleman. And the world is very forgiving on this
matter—its sympathies are *with* a gardener.

Here it is that a striking social and political feature
arises out of gardening—that is, the levelling nature
of it as a pursuit. In the presence of things for which
men's sympathies are mutual, they forget distinctions
of birth, and rank, and condition, and measure each
other's worth only by their several degrees of skill;
so that if Hodge adorns his fence with a new rose of
his own raising, my Lord will drop all superfluous dig-
nities, and discuss its merits with him as a neighbour and
a friend. This genuine feeling of manly regard, measured by worth only, ought to rob rivalry of every
bitterness, and make even professional competitors glad
of each other's successes; that it does not do so is to be
charged against the fickleness of human sympathies, and
the natural sordidness of man's heart; for gardening in
itself suggests the purest ethics.

It would, indeed, be a folly to say that bitterness never
did creep into the minds of rival florists, but it is the
exception, not the rule, for every grower knows that what
one does, another can do, and to acknowledge merit is
to pay homage to intellect, and patience, and vigilance,
and instead of hating the man for his success, we learn
to emulate his virtues; so that rivalry in gardening is a
school of practical morals, in which the pupils increase
in excellence as they make progress in the successful
prosecution of their favourite art.

This truly fraternal feeling, to which every petty pride
yields up the ghost, manifests itself in a thousand pleasing ways, which prove that gardening, whether followed

as a livelihood or as a pleasure only, is an art that ennobles all who share in its exercise. Make note of a man who has attained to high excellence in any one department, and measuring him by the world's rule, you will not expect him to impart to you one jot of information which may help you to similar success. But, put the thing to experiment, and once let him see that the spirit of a true gardener moves you in questioning him, and he will lay before you his whole routine, will show you his compost, and tell you how it is prepared; will tell you when and how to make your cuttings, let you into the secrets of stopping and training out, and put you in the way to beat him, if you can, with his own weapons. Look at our leading nurserymen, one and all, they do their best to help the amateur in his pleasing occupation; the results of years of observation and experience are placed at the disposal of all to whom they may be useful, and they would be as incapable of any paltry exclusiveness as they would be of paltry dealings and low chicanery.

A spirit of generosity is a most distinctive feature in the character of a gardener; he is perfectly miserable if he can find no one to accept a pinch of seed or a few cuttings of some choice thing; to keep it to himself is as much agony as a boy endures when he sees no opening for the investment of his pocket money.

Go through the whole catalogue of gifts, and what can equal flowers and fruits? It is not only a diffusion of God's bounty, but a sacrifice to friendship of the most valued labour of our hands; so that if we have toiled a whole season to produce a noble crop, we find our highest pleasure in giving it away. You will find that the genuine gardener, who enters heart and soul into his work, has no selfish manner of enjoying the results of it; he grows many a row of beans and peas, many a score bunches of grapes, many a dozen melons and cucumbers, expressly to give away; and, if you were to watch him when he packs up the hamper for a friend, you would see that he chooses the best, and reserves those that are ill-shaped, badly-ripened, or in any way defective to the eye or palate, for himself. I believe I have given away a good third of all I have grown for many years past, and I do hope my heart will not so shrivel up that I shall ever cease to dig, sow, train, and reap expressly for those whom I esteem as dear to me, who have either no opportunity or no skill to produce garden products for themselves.

A thousand anecdotes of the active nature of the generosity that grows up in a garden might be told here, and no end of historical events might be shown to have their chief interest in connection with such things. I shall never forget how Margaret Fuller describes her "first friend," as heightening the ideal beauty in which she floated before the child's imagination by her precious gifts of flowers. Here is one passage from her diary to the point:—

"She has just brought me a little bouquet. Her flowers have suffered greatly by my neglect, when I would be so engrossed by other things in her absence. But not to be disgusted or deterred, whenever she can glean one pretty enough, she brings it to me. Here is the bouquet—a very delicate rose, with its half-blown bud, heliotrope, geranium, lady-pea, heart's-ease—all sweet-scented flowers! Moved by their beauty, I wrote a short note, to which this is the reply. Just like herself!—

" 'I should not love my flowers if they did not put forth all the strength they have, in gratitude for your preserving care last winter, and your wasted feelings over the unavoidable effects of the frost that came so unexpectedly to nip their blooming beauties.' "

If the toils of a garden were not to be ranked among the highest pleasures of life, their reward would be found in the joy of giving away the fruits of our labours, for in this, above all things, the words of Holy Writ are lovingly verified, that " it is more blessed to give than to receive."

Then look at the knowledge one gains in all this. The gardener must learn the exact limits of adaptability in the vegetable kingdom, so as to make plants of opposite habit and different constitution, natives of diverse climes, and naturally accustomed to soils of the most heterogeneous nature, prosper side by side in one common soil and climate. He must learn how to subdue luxuriance in one, and promote it in another; how to hasten this plant into a state of rest, and how to prolong the growth of another beyond its natural season; for it is by such coaxing, forcing, checking, and persuading, that we are enabled to adapt to our own peculiar seasons and temperature, so many interesting productions of the world; and whether they come from the regions of everlasting snow, or from the burning jungles of the tropics; whether from the cool clefts of alpine solitudes,

where nature waters them with the tricklings of glaciers;
or from the dry lava of volcanic sites, where, perhaps, rain
never falls, to compel them to shake hands as friends,
and cease all disputes about the superiority of their
native lands and seasons, in full content with the circumstances with which the vigilant gardener has surrounded
them.

It is at this point that gardening rises to the dignity of
an art. Let any one take a survey of one of the best modern
gardens, in the height of the season, and say whether
gardening should not be classed as one of the highest
of the fine arts, for it paints not *from* life, but with life; it
models not after a form, but into endless forms of grace,
and symmetry, and power, and it performs its best works
by the aid of subjects that are foreign to our soil, our
seasons, and even, in some cases, to the very sunshine
under which they grow ; yet the gardener has so moulded
their habit and altered their constitution, that they take
to their conditions as if they were " to the manner born."
Then, if we go a step higher, and consider how a few
poor pelargoniums, dahlias, chrysanthemums, tulips,
hyacinths, and other such things, which at their first
introduction were not much more attractive than the
commonest weeds, have, under the manipulations of the
hybridizer, become the parents of thousands of varieties,
to which every season makes additions of still better
ones, we shall see that, in a secondary sense, the gardener
is a creator as well as a modeller of beauty.   Give him a
thin, ragged, and almost colourless weed, and as soon as
' ˙ sharp eye detects its capability for improvement, he
    ˙ it to some kindred flower, or to one of its own

family which may present desirable qualities; the progeny will be one step in advance, and by steady repetition of the process, the plant will at last rise to the dignity of a florist's flower, its varieties will be counted by thousands, and glad eyes will gaze upon myriads of gorgeous blooms set out on the exhibition stage, little dreaming that the parent of all these variously coloured and diverse varieties was but a poor, slender, unnoticeable thing, which a passer-by would have spurned with his foot as "a weed" worthless of attention. What would the first dahlia, or the first half-dozen pelargoniums, or the first chrysanthemum now appear, if placed beside a few of the best of their progeny raised of late years? And who, except for the proveable and admitted nature of the fact, would believe that the thousands of different varieties, glowing in all the hues of the rainbow, and conforming to severe rules as to forms and properties, are the descendants of such unattractive things as were, for the most part, the parents of what are known as florists' flowers? Nor can one fail to feel astonishment at the patience which has been shown in attaining such results. It may take twenty years to convert a "self," or one-coloured tulip, into a "feathered" flower, and it is seldom that they "break" in less than seven; yet look at the collection of such a man as the late John Lawrence, or go over the ranunculuses of Tyso, or the chrysanthemums of Salter, or the pelargoniums of Turner and Henderson, and, remembering the original materials, it will be almost hard to believe that human agency alone has brought such results about.

It might seem absurd to drop down from the consideration of these high departments of the art to the

humblest example, as seen in a cottage plot; but the
best joy of a garden is, that it levels all distinctions, and
makes every sincere labourer, however mean under ordinary comparisons, alike meritorious. Look at the old
Granny in her mobcap and gray gown: she is a picture
of the past, worthy to live for ever on Frith's canvas,
and call tears to the eyes of many in the future; but see
how, in spite of age, wrinkles, and indigence, a little of
the poetry of youth clings about her dear old heart, in
the love she bears her half-dozen flowers. She has known
keen want, for her home is an almshouse; she has lost
all that were dear to her of kindred, and in her night-
watches counts over the last words of her dear Betty,
who died in childbed many, many years ago; over her
mantel-piece is the old-fashioned black paper profile of
him who was her stay on earth, her friend, and companion, and to whom she gave herself with all her heart,
in the freshness and fulness of life's first love. She looks
on it as she sits smoothing her apron at her daily meals,
and wonders whether God will call her to him "this
winter," for her cough grows worse, and she thinks she
cannot live through another; and with all her weight of
painful remembrances; with all her bodily afflictions,
age has not so chilled her feelings but that she loves her
window pets as much as ever. Her geraniums are no
one knows how many years old, their stems knotty and
dark, and you would think, if you were to see them in
January, that all life had departed out of them. But
Granny knows to a day when they will begin to break
again, and she goes out into the road on the first sunny
ing-day, and gathers a little fresh soil in a fire-shovel,

and dresses up their roots, and brings them into the light again, and gives them but little water at first, and this year they will grow as bravely as ever, filling the whole of her window with a leafy screen, and blooming to a certainty on Midsummer-day. Her heliotrope is just as old, and is grown like a shrub, and she says it always comes into bloom about Lammas-day, and she half believes that the boys make their oyster-shell grottoes on that day, in celebration of the opening of her sweet-scented flowers. God has not left her utterly desolate; she can still read her large-print Bible, and, as long as she can keep on her feet, those precious flowers will sweeten her little room with their fragrance, and shed a soft light on her pathway to the grave. Look at her prying into the buds to see if any thing has come to hurt her darlings. Her white cap, and twinkling eye, and grey hair, make her beautiful as the sunlight glances on her, and one might believe her to be an angel tarrying for but an hour on this side of heaven, beguiled by the love of something so suggestive of her proper home— and she *is* one. You can almost see the glory of a better world shining on her brow as it did on the brow of Stephen. Her stay beside those flowers will not be long; and others like them will beautify her grave.

But who can tell the joy of a garden? Who but those who know, through sweet experience, can realize, either by remembrance or anticipation, the hearty fulness of life in which a gardener's happiness consists? Take the year round, with all its lights and shadows, and what pursuit can offer so many joyous hopes, so many glad realizations, so many exquisite pleasures! Look at the

dark, crumbly, fertile mould, how it rolls over from the
spade, smelling rich and earthy, and showing a promise
of plenty as it falls into friable powder in the ridges!
Look at the well-dressed border, when hoed over for the
last time, ready for the seed that is to be committed to
it; it is nothing to a passer-by, but its neat, swelling
outline gives a pleasure to the gardener's eye that is not
of the moment, but one of future promise! Then, with
what faith is the seed committed to the earth; a few
grains as fine as dust thrown by the skilful hand, and
left to the care of the elements, in the full assurance that
Nature will do her best to reward the husbandman!
Then there is the daily observation of the growth of
things, whether they be the commonest kitchen crops,
or the choicest flowering exotics, how we rejoice to see a
bud break here, or a shoot start there, or, on a sudden,
and as it were in a single night, a potted plant sends up
from every joint its bold trusses that are to cover it with
glory, and prove before the world that patience and skill
spent on worthy objects, are sure to bring their good
rewards.

However refined may be the pleasures attendant on the
culture of flowers, and the production of scenic effects in
ornamental gardening, a few rows of well-grown edibles
have special charms for most people. What can be more
jolly in appearance than a well-stocked kitchen garden
in autumn, when the potato ground has been cleared
and planted, when many of the summer crops still linger
to say "good bye," the bowery "runners" still holding
their blooms, and weighing their sticks down with thousands of tender pods; the kale, and broccoli, and winter

cabbages dressed up in their hearty green, like files of
riflemen, full of strength, and suggestive of knife-and-fork
battles before good fires, when the beef will have its right
flavour, because honourably accompanied ? Peep into
the shed or store-loft of the good gardener, and see the
rosy-cheeked and russet apples stored away all shining
with ripeness, and beating the sweetest flower-bed in
their perfume; the onions drying ready for the very
goose that is waddling yonder; the potatoes swelling
their sacks tight, every tuber of them ready to transform
itself into a snow-ball; all reminding you of baked and
roasted delicacies, that butter and pepper are to make
additionally savoury on winter nights, or that at Christmas
—the grand feast of the year—are to proclaim gardening
to be the homeliest, the prettiest, and the most profitable
of arts. Then, in early summer, what among gardening
scenes more attractive than the rows of peas laden with
snowy blossoms, like clouds of butterflies, or trying to
topple their stakes over with their weight of plump pods,
that make your mouth water as you involuntarily conjure
up the smell of the mint that goes before them to the
table, and the mingling of the green marrowy smoking
things, with the brown gravy, that compels you to
chuckle "delicious!" as the palate revels in their flavour !
See there, the pretty lettuces in their clean drills, so
delicately green and vigorous; see the tender spring
onions, silvery at the root, and ready for pulling; the
coral radishes; the cheerful small salads that seem to
grow as you look at them, all of them hurrying towards
the salad-bowl, crisp, and cool, and relishing, and ready
to enchant the appetite on the very first warm day that

shall make a radish, or lettuce, or cucumber the very completion of table enjoyments.

Then think of the beautiful gourds that always astonish you and everybody else, at their size and rapidity of growth, and that admit of half-a-dozen modes of cooking yet always delicious; the fresh summer cabbages that take one leap from the morning dew to the bubbling pot; and, above all things, who can know the real flavour of peas but those who grow them within sight from the kitchen door, and who eat them an hour after the gathering? You have only to tell a friend you will dine on such a day on peas "out of your own garden," and he'll go any number of miles to taste your marrowy, bright green beauties, that have never been fermented in bushel baskets, or shaken out of flavour by the jolting of the market cart. Talk of high art and classic gardening, the sight of a row of well-grown kale, or a broad patch of kidney beans just coming into flower, or well-trained fruits on a south wall, swelling with luscious juices, and almost crying, "Eat me, eat me!" is one that cheers the heart of man, and appeals as strongly to the sympathies of a noble duke as to a ploughman in want of a dinner. The matrons say, "The way to a boy's heart is through his belly;" but the adage applies to human kind of any age. These are very material considerations. We *do* like to see something eatable in a garden; and the man who makes a hobby of raising the best kinds of edibles, whether of the class of necessities or luxuries, adds to the productive power of his native land, increases the national resources, and in his day and generation does some good for the world. Who *can* sneer at a cucumber with the bloom on, a fragrant mushroom hot from the gridiron, a basket of strawberries to dip in the breakfast cream, or even a dish of marrowy green kale with a savoury joint on a frosty day?

And there are higher pleasures, too, in this department of gardening. If our wits are not exercised in the arrangement of figures and colours to please the eye, or our ingenuity taxed to acclimatize and bloom choice varieties, there is much to employ thought, and not a few pretty spectacles, as the seasons work their changes, now smothering the fruit trees with snowy bloom, and now loading their branches with the lovely fruit; the very beet is pretty as its richly bronzed foliage meets from row to row; and as to most crops in full luxuriance of growth, there is much real beauty in a well-disposed, and well-kept profitable garden, the charms of which are much enhanced by the idea of utility that accompanies the enjoyment of them. One would not be in haste to condemn a poor cottager for striving to excel in the growth of flowers; but there would be greater interest in his success if we saw that his cabbage and potato plots were not neglected, and that, in the aching of his heart for something beautiful, he did not forget the kale pot and the appetites of his little ones. Nor would the thriving citizen, who takes a pride in his beds of asparagus, his trellises of tomatoes, and his creamy cauliflowers, ever need to fear the criticism of his friends and neighbours, for that which is really useful has a dignity peculiar to itself, and makes its own assertion of its right to encouragement. Whoever turns his skill and patience to account in the creation of the material neces-

sities and luxuries of life, finds a source of special enjoyment in the work, as well as a welcome addition to the
family means, and, to some extent, adds to the resources
of his country; so that in profitable gardening a national
end is served when personal and private benefits are
aimed at only. To be sure, there are people who say
that a kitchen garden is an expensive affair, for " the
cabbages cost five shillings each ;" but whether it shall
be a gain or a loss depends entirely on how it is
managed. By right management, on either a small or
large scale, the culture of edibles is immensely profitable,
as everybody knows who is practically used to it ; but it
is quite an easy matter for folks, who take no real interest in a garden, or who have foggy notions of econo-
mical tillage, to pay very dear indeed for their luxuries,
and at last to get tired of the attempt to fill a basket at
its market value.

Depend upon it, it is no mean art that enables a man
to take off potatoes at the rate of five tons to the rood,
to gather a thousand cucumbers from one vine, and then
strike cuttings, and go on again without the help of
seed ; or to manage a succession of crops, so that there
shall always be plenty and variety, and not a single
waste leaf to cumber the ground. It is not a sordid
feeling that stimulates a man to cultivate such things as
shall increase the enjoyments of his family, and prove
welcome as gifts to friends ; and the task of rearing
handsome crops of eatables, each in perfection at its
season, and some thrust out of their season, to gratify
an honourable caprice, is one that has its rewards in
many ways besides the profit ; or, rather, the profit

should be understood to include the pleasure attendant on the exercise of skill and industry, and the source of health that a garden always proves to a man who loves it. And this is equally true, whether a man be called to the hurry of commercial life in town, or be blest with country air and singing birds in the midst of farms and gardens. The subject invites one's heart as much as one's head, and the world is never more ready to pardon enthusiasm than when it is the sign and token of a love of out-of-door pleasures, and has for its end and aim the improvement of the social ties that bind the human family together.

To enjoy a garden, a man must be a student of Nature, a good weather prophet, something of a botanist, very quick-sighted in matters of vegetable physiology, accustomed to observation, and that "forecasting of the whole," which Cowper notes as so essential to success. Those who dabble with little town plots, and never soar beyond paternal laurels and sweet-williams, have an idea that the gardener's season begins in May and ends in September; but your genuine gardener finds as much to do, and as many pleasures in his work in the depth of winter as in the height of summer. I do not know but what the winter pleasures are the best, as they certainly are the most intellectual. Philosophers say that "anticipating" is a greater joy than "realizing;" and when a man sits down to sketch out his scheme of culture for the next season, to plan his beds and arrange his planting, he has to exercise some very high faculties of mind. Perhaps he has done verbenas and geraniums, and lobelias, till he is sick of the repetitions, and now he

means to work out a new style of bedding altogether.
He looks over his stock, and by a strong effort of imagination pictures out a plan, and sees it planted in its proper colours.   Here, however, "is the rub," and the man
of experience must be the man of invention; for when
his plans are all conceived, the colours marked, and the
scheme completed, the thing *has yet to be done* in actual
plants; and, strange to say, no gardener, however talented
and rich in experience, can predict to a certainty how
any scheme of bedding not before tried will answer. It
must be done first, and judged on the ground; and
hence the risking of a whole season, and perhaps thousands of plants, on an idea, is a bold adventure, and
success proves a far-sighted sagacity.

But consider the anxiety of the winter work where
new patterns and styles are tried every year. Think of
giving a man a bit of golden-leaved stonecrop, or a new
variegated balm, or ground ivy, the gift being perhaps a
mere scrap of an inch long, and what would you say if
you were to see a hundred yards of it forming the most
delicate edging to geometric beds next summer? Yet
this is just the sort of achievement in which an earnest
gardener delights. Your scrap of something new or
curious is made to root in heat; then the tender top
nipped off and struck, and then the shoots, as fast as they
appear, taken off and rooted again, till, in the course of a
few months, your valued gift has been multiplied a thousand fold, and a simple sport of Nature, which an unob-
servant eye would have passed unheeded, is, once secured
in its entirety, converted into garden-stock, and the
splendour of a grand show made perfect by it.

The vigilant gardener is always on the look-out for novelties and improvements. He observes an early pea come into blossom before any one in the row shows any signs of bloom. He does not look at it in idle wonderment, but at once secures it as a prize. He tears down the whole row, clears a space about it, gives it extra light, air, and nourishment, and ripens its pods a fortnight before any of the rest; and thus secures seed of an earlier sort, and lays the foundation of a fortune.

But, apart from the daily work, apart from the season-changes and the calls for various operations consequent on the growth and decay of things, what a joy is a garden as a place of retreat from worldly cares, from anxieties and worry of all kinds! There is our school of Nature, where we watch the first greening of the leaf, the growth of the full summer's verdure, and the slow but sure passage of autumn's " fiery hand " among the branches. There are the glittering constellations, and the soothing odours, that beguile one into the belief that God lets some fragments of heaven fall upon man's lot, that when he feels "of the earth, earthy," and the pressure of sordid musings, or the fever of worldly ambitions eats up the heart, and threatens to crush every tender emotion out of it, he may, in the freshness of the innocent world of flowers, feel that life has its lovely compensations, and its rewards *here ;* and that the words of the Saviour appropriately answer his complaints—" If God so clothe the grass of the field, how much more shall He clothe you, O ye of little faith !"

Think of the morning walk, all coolness and fragrance ; think of the mid-day lounge under embracing branches, where the mind sinks into sweetest dreams, and all our past readings of old lore, poetry, and Holy Writ take shapes, and float before us like realities!   Think of the mid-day summer glow of all things when the parterres burn with colour, and the cool green grass defies the sun to brown one ravel of its mossy carpet; think of the "quiet cigar," all alone in seraphic contemplation; think of the in-door readings of the works of men who have loved gardens, from Bacon to Wordsworth, whose avenues of hollyhocks were the pride of Rydal; think of the summer visits to the gardens of friends to make notes of comparison; the trips to botanic gardens, not forgetting *fêtes* and exhibitions, where the genuine gardener has pleasures that the mere sight-seer knows nothing of; think of the pride with which you show your friends over your ground, and display your stock to those that have sympathies kindred with your own; and think of the fame you acquire in your circle as a clever gardener, a man of worth, a gentleman, and a Christian, for you must be all these to love a garden rightly, and then say if there is any pursuit besides this that can match it in its fullness of joy, that can take its place for even one hour; for it comprehends the love of Nature in its most extended meaning; it comprehends the love of man in the reality of affectionate kindness, good-will, and sober behaviour; and it comprehends the love of God, in the daily witnessing of His works in their loveliest of aspects!   Who would not be a jolly gardener? Who would not have at least some living flowery thing to set an earthly love upon; who would not ever keep at least one flower near the heart, to cheer it in a gloomy hour, and read it an easily-learnt lesson of love and duty to man and God? Surely, without a garden, life is hardly possible; with it all the foes of man may rise up against him, and he may turn aside for a moment and catch a glimpse of his roses through the open window, and say, "My peace is there, there will I seek God, my refuge."

THE SOUL IN NATURE.

THERE are certain philosophers who maintain that all existence is essentially material; while there are others who hold, with equal stubbornness, that there are no entities but those of a spiritual kind. Not to-day only, but from the birthday of the world, have these two opposite doctrines been repeatedly brought into collision; and the question, as far as philosophers are concerned, is as much unsolved as ever. But it is not always the philosopher who deals most acutely with philosophy; and it sometimes happens that the idea of a poet, or the tradition of an uncultivated antiquity, throws more light on a topic under dispute than the most elaborate reasonings of men schooled in disputation. So it is in regard to this question of matter and spirit. The ancient poets, in their strange fables, asserted the prevalence of soul in Nature, and continually carried back the mind from material to spiritual things. The ancient creeds of the world embodied the same thought; and, whether we refer to the Indian, Egyptian, or Grecian mythologies, we find that a spiritual existence is everywhere granted, and that body and soul in man, body and soul in nature, are unities universally adopted as respectively essential to each

other. The Hindoos say—when Brahme sleeps, all
existence passes away; but when Brahme wakes, his
thoughts take shape under the agency of Brahma, and
creation follows. What is Brahme but Deity, whose
will controls Brahma or Nature, and through thought
gives impulse to a perennial birth of beauty, each separate
birth being the expression of that thought or will which
called it into action? The Greeks had Proteus, who
took many shapes, yet never lost his identity; and Proteus was an impersonation of the creative power working
underneath and continually revealing itself, never in two
forms alike, yet ever the same in purport and essence.
Proteus is Brahma at three removes, degraded somewhat
by his passage through the Egyptian mythology, into
which he passes with other gods from India, and so into
the fanciful, but scarcely sublime category of Hellenic
deities.

Literatures, mythologies, traditions, all attest the
union of matter and spirit; and instinct, turning a deaf
ear to the propoundings of the spiritualist and the dogmas
of the materialist, declares for the two elements, and holds
them essential to each other. Science completes this
work, and marries the two worlds together by the
wedding-ring of universal law, which it is the task of
science to comprehend and apply in accordance with the
strictest generalities. Let it not be thought, however,
that this work is yet complete—for in the infancy of
science we can only expect approximations; and such of
these as physics are capable of affording, the labour of
Oersted has thrown together in one of the most enchanting volumes ever published, which has attained a cos-

mopolitan celebrity, under the title of the "Soul in Nature."

In this work, the great Danish philosopher employs the reasoning which scientific facts supply in the defence of that part of the popular faith which asserts the universal existence of spirit, or rather the universal prevalence of thought in Nature. As far as it is possible to reduce his views to the compass of a short essay, let us endeavour to do so, and with a hope that such a reduction of ample particulars into brief generalities will not, in any way, mar the profound reasonings of so genuine a philosopher.

First, then, how do we gain a knowledge of the outer world? Not surely by the senses only; for in our quick views of things we apprehend their meaning readily by merely viewing portions of them, *inferring* the remainder of the conditions which are requisite to a complete appreciation of the object. We have a perfect idea of a tree, with branches, leaves, bark, buds, and fruit, from a mere glimpse of a portion of the trunk through a window or crevice; and we recognize a book, *as a book,* by merely laying our hands on a portion of it in the dark. What then? why;—inasmuch as we do not grasp the things themselves, but infer their existence by mere glimpses of them, so we are indebted for the knowledge of the world to the impressions which things are capable of producing upon us, such impressions being converted into thoughts by union with the collective experience with which former impressions have furnished us. Now, to make an impression on a being capable of thought, requires in the object an active existence; but a stone, lying still by the roadside, appears the deadest thing, the most immobile and passive existence it is possible to conceive; and to assign it an active existence seems absurd. Yet that stone is dragged downwards by the force of gravitation; it presses towards the centre of the earth, and meets with the resistance offered it by the stone on which it rests. That second stone is pressed upon by the first, and is also impelled downward by the force of gravitation, but is prevented from descending by other stones on which it is super-imposed; while all of these again are in the same condition—driven down by gravitation, yet prevented from descending further by the objects which support them. Again, the second stone, which bears the weight of the first, and the third stone bearing the weight of the second, are each subjected to the pressure of the body above them, and that pressure—comparatively immeasurable though it is—tends to compress the particles of the body pressed upon; while the elasticity inherent in the particles of the body pressed upon, causes them to rebound, and so prevents them being crushed or altered permanently in shape. It is just such an assemblage of forces—pressure in one direction, resistance in another, general tendency towards a centre and repulsion from the centre by virtue of the accumulation already there—of which the globe consists, and to which it owes its shape, rotation on its axis, and motion round the sun. If, then, each separate stone by the wayside plays a part in a system so extensive and so complete, how can its existence —lifeless, motionless, as it seems—be anything than the most active that can be imagined?

Again, if we look round on Nature, we discover certain forms of existence which we may term permanent; yet,

these very permanent forms only exist by virtue of the
incessant change which they are undergoing. The oak-
tree, which gave Adam its shadow in the happy garden,
and the nightingale which hallowed Eve's connubial
sleep, are seen again to-day; the oak-tree has the same
shaped leaves, the nightingale the same warbling song,
though the *identical* oak and nightingale which we are
supposing to have inhabited Eden have both long since
perished. We view a waterfall, and make drawings of
its shape and measurements of its altitude, and we consider it the same waterfall ten years afterwards, when we
find it occupying the same place and exhibiting the same
form as the one represented in our drawing of ten years'
old. Yet no one will suppose that, after an interval of
ten years, we see the same water, the same plants, or even
the same rocks; for, while it will be readily admitted that
fresh floods have been continually flowing over the pre-
cipice, and fresh plants springing up in the surrounding
soil, it must be remembered also that the rocks have been
also wearing away above, while a deposit of fresh particles
is being continually made by the water below. Yet, in all
these mutable things—and Nature is equally mutable all
through—the Invariable in type is to be easily traced,
for that does exist even more definitely than the very
mutation which we see. The *idea* of a waterfall is the
invariable result which the fall of an *ever-renewing* flood
—the dispersion of an endless *succession* of drops—the
roaring and foaming of particles which *never remain an
instant in the same position,* convey to the mind; so that
out of *a series of effects* we gain *one thought,* which may
be called the thought of Nature inherent to this parti-

cular phenomenon. There is no animal, plant, mineral, or gas, but is passing through a succession of changes, growth, decay, dissolution, re-combination; yet each one has a permanent existence by virtue of the thought which it represents, because the laws of Nature are constant; and however fleeting and fading the forms of the world, the idea of creation is continually reproduced, and through the medium of the ever-changing material, the unchanging and eternal spirit is to be seen.

The moment we arrive at this stage of thought, we perceive how hollow are those assertions of the superiority of matter—how vain those endeavours to disprove the existence of mind, over which so many have wasted their lives, hopelessly forswearing the very intellect which by its partial views led them into a complexity of errors. Before this fact, the very earth passes into the condition of a shadow; and beyond the almost intangible forms of material existence lies a thought more solid than the adamant—a thought which operates silently, and finds representation in that world of change which lives only to embody the idea of permanence. The flower, the tree, the cloud, the sunbeam, the granite rock, have no existence but as letters of the alphabet of Nature. As letters in an alphabet, they are woven and interwoven into syllables and words, and as letters of an alphabet again displaced to enter into new combinations. As letters of an alphabet they exist also, not for themselves, but as elements through which Intelligence is spelt into expression, and thought fashioned into visible form. What is the flower but an assemblage of tissues, which is again but an assemblage of gases? What is the cloud but an assemblage of water-drops, atmospheric air, electricity, and ammonia? That same water, air, electricity, and ammonia, fall in a shower, and are each absorbed by the plant; and, to-morrow, the very same elements, which appeared in the heavens like a golden car for the sun, or a group of cherubim winging upward through the ether, are seen in the form of a lowly violet, the elements that formed the cloud lend softness to its purple tint, freshness to its grateful odour, and healthy-greenness to its heart-shaped leaves; how, then, could the cloud which yesterday floated in the blue heaven, and to-day forms the tissues of a plant, be said to have any existence but as a letter in an alphabet which Nature is everlastingly weaving into prose syllables or poetic rhymes?

But there is a higher fact revealed in this philosophy, namely, that the laws which we perceive working as instruments of power are the laws of reason, and are as truly in harmony with the human mind as with that higher mind from which all things spring. So true is it, that naturalists have frequently deduced natural laws from reason alone, and have afterwards discovered them really existing in Nature. From the fact that bodies mutually attract each other, Newton deduced, that as the distances of bodies increase, their mutual attraction decreases; and that an effect proceeding from one point becomes weaker in proportion as the square of distances increases. Both these conclusions have been verified by appeals to Nature, and the true laws of planetary motions have thus been traced out as fruits of human reason resting on its own strength alone, and asserting that such and such *must be*, because such and such already

exist. Kepler's great laws of the motions of the
heavenly bodies were discovered in this way; and it is
well known that Leverrier measured the weight, velocity,
distance, and constitution of the planet Neptune without
having seen it, and so determined its existence by the
aid of reason alone.

By the very fact that man is part of Nature, so his
reason is also natural, or in harmony with the reason
manifested in natural law. Were the laws of nature
antagonistic to the infinite reason, they could not exist;
were they inconsistent with human reason, man could
not comprehend them;—hence we know that, in the
great unity of the spiritual and material, man is also
concerned, and inseparably united in the living idea of
the Almighty power by whom all things are created.
From the moment that we perceive this truth, the walls
of space and time fall down, and the soul finds an
inheritance of immortality in its merely spiritual existence, needing none of the aids of external reasoning to
endow it with everlasting life.

The philosophy of the beautiful is wrapped up in this
fact. Metaphors and poetical images derive their origin
and significance from it. The analogies which the
imaginative mind readily perceives between objects
which to ordinary apprehension seem so dissimilar, are
traceable to the same source. Indeed, strictly speaking,
the whole creation is only a bundle of analogies.

We are accustomed to the recognition of beauty, and
seldom pause in our admiration to inquire the source of
the beautiful. Yet the beautiful is to be found by the
man of science, and is merely the last expression of a

series of minute facts. Take the instance of the fountain:—in this, the rising jet of water consists of a
number of particles, all spherical in form, which, as they
ascend, gradually increase in breadth, and at last bend
over in the form of a parabola and descend to the basin.
The velocity continually decreases from the point where
the jet first rushes forth to the point where it bends
over in a graceful curve, and it is this decrease of velocity
in ascending which gives the column of water its tapering form,—for it always tapers downwards from a broad
convex sheet to a thin compressed jet. This downward
tapering of the column and parabolic outline of the
falling summit are what most readily strike us as beautiful in a fountain, and these phenomena are simply the
result of the opposing forces of the rising jet and attraction of the earth. The prismatic colours and the rich
musical tones also combine to complete the harmony,—
and thus the idea of the fountain is the result of an
assemblage of details, each of which contributes an
essential part of the whole.

Man, too, is a part of this; his soul is a part of the
great soul which pervades Nature; and to every beat of
his heart the great heart of the universe answers with a
kindred throb. By his relationship to outward things,
he is enabled to comprehend them, and, in so doing, he
finds that the laws of the external world are consistent
with the thoughts within himself. Does such a conclusion make him dread mortality? if so, let him trust the
history of his soul to faith, which is as much above
reason as reason is above the brute matter on which it
impresses its speaking image. If the " clodded earth,"

sending up its breath in flowers, has a soul by which it is united to all the links of diversified being; if man, too, has a soul not merely obedient to reason as in the brutes, but awakened to self-consciousness and so far free in agency, then, by all these links of causation, he shall trace up his relation to God, the first link in this trembling chain of spiritual impulses. Into his nostril did Deity breathe the breath of life, and this soul, which beats its wings eternally within his brain and bosom, is the incarnation of that holy breath which brought him into being. For this reason, while he fears not to admit that the material forms of the world are the least tangible, so, for his own soul, he can afford to rest on faith.

H

THE SPARROW.

WE confess to a great partiality for the sparrow. There is something hearty in his impudence (London boys call him "cheeky,")—something funny in his domestic habit, and in his love very much of the heroic. Our partiality, though, has a deeper source than the superficial traits of sparrow-life, and springs from the constancy of the sparrow as an associate of man everywhere. He is the last representative of bird-life left to the smoke-dried citizen, just as the grass is the last relic of vegetable life which still clings to him. The sparrow will make itself a home in the most sooty covert under grim tiles, and between the blackened chinks in chimneys and waterspouts; and the grass will spring up between the flags in the closest court or alley, or on the most barren heap of rubbish in a dirty corner. This proximity to us, however, is fatal to the sparrow as an object of study, and when an amateur ornithologist commences the formation of a museum, the sparrow is the last specimen that finds a home there. We watch our human neighbours too closely, and very often allow slander to supply what ignorance suffers to escape; but our out-door neighbours, the sparrows, are, from their very neighbour-like qualities, overlooked, and substituted in the attention by things more rare. We shall, therefore, recount the history of the sparrow, and say a few words on his character as a social being, hoping thereby "to point a moral and adorn a tale."

The house-sparrow (*Fringilla Domestica*) belongs to the most interesting of the bird families, being a member of the *Fringillidæ*, or the Finches, which includes most of the birds of song, and those immediately interesting in their association with man. Spread pretty equally over Europe and the north of Africa, on the plains of India, and in the passes of the Himalaya, he is everywhere the companion of man, and is the only bird whose habit it is to be at every season in close attendance on human dwellings. Considered as an individual, the sparrow exhibits a remarkable mixture of opposite qualities. When made to pass through the sanitary processes which a city sparrow requires for the exhibition of his aboriginal clothing, he appears in a true quaker garb, of chesnut, ash, and black, trim in clothing, pert in manner, positively pretty, yet still quakerish. But he belies his looks; for he is a thief, a pugilist, and an everlasting gossip. He is everything by turns, and adapts himself to every new condition and circumstance, without the least regard to that motto of Emerson's which requires us to "walk upright and vital," and to maintain our integrity under all trials. He will eat the daintiest food, and, if that is not at hand, will forage on any dustheap, and eat the veriest garbage. Even in feeding he is a paradox; for if the supply be scant, he searches keenly, and is content with what he finds himself; but the moment he lights in a land of plenty—as, for instance, a stone-pavement covered with crumbs, or a granary with a hole in the roof—he immediately abandons the good habit of foraging on his own account, and filches from his neighbour. He has great faith in the sweet flavour of forbidden food, and eats that which he has stolen with indescribable relish.

But it is as a member of a community that the sparrow appears in his true light. He is a sociable fellow and loves company. Nothing more delights him than to meet a score of his companions on the top of a pear-tree within view of a kitchen "whence smells arise" along with pieces, and there to beguile the afternoon with small conversation, and the first lines of songs which none of them can sing through, with occasional sallies after food, and then a fight or two, and a gossip, as before. At roosting-time he has compunctions; and, for fear he should die in the night—cut off by a black cat even in the act of digesting the stolen provender—he turns religious, and mumbles a few disjointed prayers, with his head leaning on an ivy leaf, and, after another incoherent gossip, dozes off in a state of plethoric sobriety.

The sparrow is precocious. He enters the world "on his own hands" or claws, at six weeks old; he quarrels with his parents, and attempts to kick them out of the nest a day or two afterwards, and goes on all sorts of voyages and travels, and gets steeped in crime within two months of being fledged. When nine months old, he marries and sets up a domestic establishment, and during courtship, and the first of the honeymoon, keeps the neighbourhood in constant alarm with his repeated quarrels and sanguinary fights. He is great in war, particularly that ignoble warfare which may be best likened to an Irish row, wherein ten or fifteen rush pell-mell together in the branches of a pear-tree, each with a war-whoop of his own, while fighting all the rest, and the whole body rushing together in a confused heap of birds and voices, as if they would sacrifice their blood to the last drop. Just as they have converted the highest fork of the tree into a Thermopylæ, and Xerxes and the Greeks are heaped together, beak and claw, the fight suddenly ceases, and a few scattered chirps are all that remain of the fierce din of battle. These rows chiefly take place in spring; towards the middle of June they have entirely ceased; and the summer and autumn pass tranquilly, without a single breach of the peace.

· When on the point of marriage the sparrow's life is indeed one of excitement. He has his home to build, his bride to protect, and what with the search for food and building materials, and the frequent challenges to combat to which his love prompts him, beak, claw, and wing are kept in great activity. He is by no means fastidious in regard to the material of his nest; and, like an Arab in the desert, he makes freehold property of any spot that suits him, and there determines to build his home, and die if necessary in defending it. Every . variety of size, fabric, and locality enters into the details of sparrow nests. If moss and feathers are to be had, none know better how to appropriate them, and if these comforts are scarce, he weaves together bits of rag, straws, wisps of hay, dry grass, and every variety of tex-tile refuse which finds its way out of doors; sometimes

labouring with much pride of heart in the construction
of a neat circular nest, and at others, crowding together
enough "marine stores" to fill a hat, content with the
dirtiest hole at the top of a waterspout for its reception.
When he builds in a tree—which is very seldom, though
Professor Rennie says to the contrary—he usually con-
structs a domed nest; that is, a large globular framework
of straw and feathers, with a hole in the side for ingress
and egress; so that a good shelter is afforded by the
circular roof and walls. In the country he houses under
ricks, and in holes in barns, and very often turns the
martin out of doors, and takes possession of its mud-
cabin; but in town he mostly creeps into the holes and
recesses amongst chimneys, eaves, and broken brickwork;
and always covers the floor of his castle with a thick
matting to protect his mate and her brood from the cold.

Owing to the partiality of the sparrow for bits of
thread and woollen rag, he sometimes gets entangled in
the fastenings of his own tent; and it is not uncommon
for fierce struggles to take place under the tiles, where
some unlucky cock or hen has got entrapped. He partly
deserves this for the careless way in which he builds his
walls, but he scarcely deserves to be hanged in his own
noose when pursuing his calling industriously. Such
fatal catastrophes happen, however, and not a few sparrows fall victims to their propensity for woollen goods.
Rennie relates an instance of a pair of sparrows which
had carried off a long piece of bass, but when this had
been successfully stowed in the nest, it appeared they
had not sufficient skill to work it into the fabric, and
both birds got their feet inextricably entangled in the

folds, and were held close prisoners. Around them assembled their cackling neighbours, who appeared to be occupied in scolding them for their folly, instead of imitating the mouse that released the lion—in assisting them to get rid of their entanglements. They were taken down and freed from their fetters, but were too exhausted to survive their struggles, and a pair of their scolding neighbours took possession of their premises a few days after. A note in the first volume of the *Zoological Journal* states that a pair of sparrows, which had built at a house at Poole, were observed to continue their regular visit to the nest long after the time when the young birds take flight. This unusual circumstance continued throughout the year, and in the winter, a gentleman who had all along observed them, determined on investigating its cause. He mounted a ladder, and found one detained a prisoner by means of a piece of string or worsted, which formed part of the nest, having become accidentally twisted round the leg. Being thus incapacitated from procuring its own sustenance, it had been fed by the willing and watchful parents. A still more tragical occurrence is related in the *London News* of January 20, 1844. A sparrow had built its nest in the eye-socket of the carved head of an ox, which formed part of a frieze of one of the buildings in Sackville Street, Dublin. By some means he had got his neck into a noose, and in struggling to get free had fallen out of the nest, suspended by the neck, like a wretched criminal, from the eye-socket of a skull.

But the sparrow's cares do not end with nest-building. Some fine spring morning he wakes up as usual, and finds

his mate in an ecstasy of chirping, and looking round
him, discovers an oval egg, with a very white ground,
variegated with ash and brown spots and streaks. Before
he goes to roost, the cackling begins again, and as he
comes in with a caterpillar for supper, she shows him
another, and so on, till there are five or six. Then is he
a husband in earnest. No intruding sparrow dare take
shelter near his nest; no cat even warm it with her feline
breath. He is all wings and claws, and his beak is a
dagger to transfix every enemy to his domestic peace.
He is an example of perpetual motion, too, and hurries
here and there for dainty bits of meat which the cook
has thrown out, fat snails, hirsute caterpillars, pickings
from the pig-trough, and bread-crumbs, carrying them
into the nest for his faithful partner, who receives each
with a low chuckle of satisfaction. Not food alone, but
every stray feather, wisp of wool, or bunch of cotton-
thread is carried up also to increase the warmth of the
nest, and preserve the eggs from chill, while both the
parents are away in the morning and evening. He not
only knows no fatigue in his unceasing search for food,
but he takes his turn at sitting while she airs herself at
daybreak, and the moment she returns he darts off again
in search of feathers, grubs, and bread-crumbs. He is
the model husband now, and has given up fighting and
quarrelling. By-and-by there are weak voices crying for
food, and a number of naked children stare him in the
face, all crying in one dismal tone, as they squat in a
confused heap with their wide yellow gaping mouths, for
continued supplies. He is astonished at the voracity of
his own children; they would eat up mother and father

if they had but the strength to do it. He flies here, there, and everywhere; and however much he brings, there is always the same cry, and the same cluster of gaping jaws to greet him. It is enough for both parents now to keep their six juvenile gizzards grinding, while the six juvenile mouths, like separate and determined Olivers, keep crying out for " more ! "

With this attention and good feeding, the babes in the nest soon become babes in the wood, and the fond parents, inflated with pride, take out their chelping children on short excursions over tiles and parapets, and then down into gardens, where they both feed them alternately from their own mouths. While the father is offering them what he has brought in his bill, the mother is foraging elsewhere, and when she returns, he darts off again, and thus protection and food are both administered. A week's exercise in this way completes the education of the fledglings, and then the sparrow colony breaks up; the old citizen birds leave the town to sun themselves in corn-fields, and make acquaintance with the rustics that dwell in the thatch. An ivied wall, which has sheltered fifteen or twenty pairs in spring, is almost deserted before July, and the cheerful chelping that woke the townsman in the morning, and cheered him as he took tea at the open window in the evening, is now scarcely heard, a few young birds of the new brood being all that are left to people the once populous city in the ivy. The sparrow is never silent long, and so these few keep up the sparrow music through the summer; and, to an ordinary observer, who sees wings in motion in every garden, and hears the unmistakable

sparrow chirp all day long, the houses seem by no means
deserted. But he would only need to watch them as
they come to roost, to note the comparison between the
few that remain, and the crowds that haunted the same
roosting-grounds in spring.

Towards September the numbers thicken, and when
the last gleaning is carried from the harvest-field, those
that remained with the gleaners turn their faces to the
town, and in a short time the gardens and the eaves are
crowded. The morning matins and the evening vespers
are as loud as ever, and there is something really cheering in the confused chaos of voices, and the whirring of
wings, and rustling of feathers, which blend so harmo-
niously with the growth of the morning daylight and
the increase of the evening darkness. "Just as the
leaves begin to fall," says Rusticus, "the sparrows begin
to hold their 'evenings at home;' and strange evenings
they are; such chattering and chirping; such hopping
up and down; such changing of places; such bickering and squabbling; such fidgetting and wriggling; the
row often lasting more than an hour, and only ceasing
when they have chattered themselves to sleep." Towards winter, the sparrow grows impudent, bold, and
thievish. He will feed at your feet if you give him encouragement, and may be tempted to the window-ledge
for crumbs, or into the room, even, with a little patience,
and the absence of everything likely to threaten his
safety. As soon as Christmas is past, he looks out for
the green sprigs of bulbous plants, and nibbles down
the snow-drops and crocuses, and enlivens the dull days
of February and March with his incessant chatter and

repeated quarrels. It is not fair, however, to charge him with indiscriminate destruction; there are few garden plants for which he has any regard, and the vast havoc he makes in the insect broods amply compensates for the stealing of a little green meat for his young ones.

But the sparrow has his enemies. He lives no life of uninterrupted enjoyment. His acts of petty larceny bring upon him the vengeance of the farmer, who sets a price upon his head, and thereby encourages vagrancy and destructiveness in all the ragged urchins of a village. Arsenic, *nux vomica*, and baited traps, are offered him, and he takes his choice and dies forthwith, to haunt the fields afterwards in a ghostly shape, and revenge himself by watching the growth and multiplication of cater-pillars—caterpillars which he, if living, would have destroyed, but which, left to fatten on the farmer's crops, entail upon him ten times the cost of a sparrow. Then there is the screech owl, who now and then finds her way to the nest when both parents are out, and gobbles up the callow brood, and, if she could, would do a similar office for the parents. But the windhover hawk is his most deadly enemy. He dreads the high-flying mouser, and has no appetite for growing corn when she is within sight. It is seldom that he suffers in a positive way, for the windhover is mostly content with a few mice and cockchafers, but the dread is instinctive; he knows the hawk-like swoop, and he cowers under cover without making the necessary distinctions. As to scare-crows, he snaps his bill at such in perfect contempt. He views them as demonstrations of eccentricity,—

matters for amusement rather than fear,—and after a
careful survey of a straw-stuffed man, with boots turned
behind, and face without expression, he deems it the
relic of some gunpowder-plot freak, and so far from
being frightened, chooses it immediately as a suitable
spot for his nest.   Old hats stuffed with red rags, dead
dogs and cats crucified on broom sticks, and rows of
gay ribbons threaded on sticks, he holds in equal dis-
regard, and if puzzled by them for a day or two, pays no
more attention to them after he has seen their empti-
ness; and as to boys with horns and clappers, he takes
no alarm from their hideous noises, but keeps at a safe
distance in case of stones.   Thus, in every sense, the
sparrow is very individual; his ways and means are
interesting, though neither song nor plumage claim any
particular regard.   He has character, and that redeems
him from indifference.   Song and plumage are both
poor things compared with character: it is character we
seek in men; and strong individualities make even
rogues tolerable; for, after all, Will, which is the foundation of individuality, compels reverence, no less in
feathered than in coated bipeds.

THE INNER LIFE.

EMERSON remarks in his beautiful essay on "Gifts," that "Flowers and fruits are always fit presents,— flowers, because they are a proud assertion that a ray of beauty outvalues all the utilities of the world. These gay natures contrast with the somewhat stern countenance of ordinary nature; they are like music heard out of a workhouse;" and it is in the sympathy which all natural objects have for the best sentiments of our nature which makes them always acceptable. Man is something more than a bundle of petty cares and jealousies: he has within him a world of living beauty, and an existence ever seeking for closer sympathy with moral worth, and anxiously striving after higher states of perfection. But in the intercourse of men with each other the tendencies, and desires, and passions, which have been implanted within them for purposes of beauty —and beauty is the highest form of utility—get pushed beyond the legitimate sphere of their action, and become characterized in their development as vices. Hence, in all cities and large aggregations of men, the true nobility and intrinsic stamp of human character is sunk below the duplicities which float upon the surface of customs

and usages. Thus civilization, viewed in a narrow and
partial light, has all the appearance of soul-murder; but,
seen through the "optic glass" of a transcendental
philosophy, simply indicates a necessary phase of the
human mind in its progress upward; and is a manifestation, not of the destruction and annihilation of virtue,
but of the perversion and distortion of our legitimate
aims and actions. To look at modern society in its
existing state of complexity and petty warfare, it has all
the semblance of a huge mad-house; but, seen as a necessary condition of the human mind in its transition from
a rugged barbarity to a high and exalted morality and
beauty, it appears as a plain fact, but significant of the
multiform changes and modifications of the same identical purpose, still striving to evolve itself through all
the ages of the world.

But when we leave this inclosed world of antipodean
and twisted interests, where we are eternally compelled
to hedge and dodge, and dance a shapeless game of
evasion, and go into the pine woods or mountain solitudes, where Nature still wears the freshness of a
primeval morning, and awaits with complacent brow,
and meekly folded hands, the appeals of her repentant
children; we come into the sheen and lustre of a new-
made life, and grow young again in the beauty and simplicity of a rugged and heroic virtue. The soul, tattered and despoiled, and weather-beaten in the strife
and storm of petty contentions and mean and degrading
tendencies, awakens again to the vigour and freshness of
its true life, and seems to have been made anew. With
men, the true soul seems ever in the presence of a blight

or pestilence, and droops and fades as in the hot and parching air of a sirocco : but with Nature, the true old love of innumerable ages comes dawning upon it, and it grows and expands in the opening of a new future, a future teeming with truth and beauty; and finds in this new realm of thought and perception an insight into its highest tendencies. In the buzz and distracting whirl of the world, the only hope of satisfaction seems to be in sorrow, for there we expect to meet with "sharp peaks and edges of truth;" but in Nature all is perpetual jubilee and song, and every feature wears the aspect of festive hilarity,—pure, ennobling, and true. The sunshine of Paphian skies seems ever dawning upon the horizon of a holier hope; the warmth and fruition of a new summer seems ever alighting upon the petals of unfading flowers; and in the dark brows of Dodonian oaks we see the type of ceaseless renewal and unspared exuberance. The soul grows and grows, and feels in its inmost recesses the awakening light and divinity of its highest spiritual truths.

Life is a constant flux of moods or conditions, evanescent and transmutable, yet, together, forming a great circle in which the true character is encentred. Be the mood what it may, it is but a reflex of the combined conditions of the true character which lies beneath, and the outward and visible influences which surround us. Every man wishes for good, wishes to attain to the practice of virtue, and to gather to himself the noblest thoughts; but while we glide hither and thither under masks and pretensions, we mutually deceive ourselves and others, and the world comes at last to wear the

garb and colouring of a fantastic dream. But with
Nature all is pure, all is true, constant and abiding, and
from every thread of her endless fabric of loveliness
comes a voice of sympathy and love.

Thus it is, that in our earlier life, before the soul is
enveloped in cobwebs and dust, that the love of nature
is warmest in the heart; and that ever afterward, when
that same love awakens in us, we feel the replenished
vigour of an ascending life, and the untold joy of primal
beauty. We seem to be brought back again to the
flowery brink of our budding youth, and to stand once
more upon the threshold which then separated the sweet
years of childhood from the mysterious, yet promising
future which then lay before us; and in which our
ambition and our hopes were coined into realities, by
the energies of our hands and the firmness of our
hearts.

There is ever hope for that man who feels the freshness of his youth like a soft fragrance fanning his hot
brow, when he wanders into the wild solitude, where
Nature still beams in the radiance of untroubled tran-
quillity, and the hand of man has not yet begun the
work of demolition, but where all is vigour, and freshness, and reality. Beside the mountain torrent, gleaming as with the light of a perpetual morning, and in
the pine woods, where night hovers all day long, he feels
the purple flush of youth once more upon his cheek, and
the generous sympathies of his earlier life burning in his
heart. Then emotions are kindled in the breast, of
which even an angel might be proud, and *to live* is a
joy unutterable. Memory is then a sweet picture;

Love is an odour breathing of Heaven; Hope sits beside us and points upwards lovingly, and the inheritance of life is a boon more sacred than the possession of a world, for it gives us more than a world—an Universe of beauty within ourselves.

This is why, in the first efforts of the anxious heart, that all books which set forth the harmonies of Nature are eagerly devoured. Every genuine student will remember when the most simple and unassuming books possessed inexpressible charms, if they but spoke in harmony with the poetry and moral sympathies which dwelt within his own breast; if they breathed of green fields and flowers, and sought to embody and embalm all that was beautiful in sentiment, and simple in thought. When we look back to our earliest readings in the great book of Nature, and our first communings with Nature's worshippers, we seem carried to some sweet oasis in the dreary wilderness of life, where nothing but beauty, and the aspirations for a higher life could find a place. Then every book which had the least smell of green fields or water brooks, or was in any way imbued with the poetry of Nature, was devoured page by page, as if it were manna but just fallen from heaven.

The high philosophy of beauty, in which the ancients delighted, is a better symbol of the manifestation of the sentiment than any which modern poets can afford. They said "that the soul of man, embodied here on earth, went roaming up and down in quest of that other world of its own, out of which it came into this, but was soon stupefied by the light of the natural sun, and unable to see any other objects but those of this world, which

I

are but shadows of real things.   Therefore, the Deity
sends the glory of youth before the soul, that it may
avail itself of the beautiful bodies, as aids to its recollec-
tion of the good and fair." *   And, although the first
utterances of the Inner Life are seen in the youth in the
love of Nature, and a growing fondness, and a kindling
sympathy for that higher beauty, which is in itself im
personal, and beyond the stretch of thought, and which
may flash upon him from the sunset, the gleam of water-
falls which leap amid wild islands green, the silence or
the sleep of nature, or the dove-like eyes of the loved
one of his heart; yet, this is but the first spark of a sentiment, which shall hereafter enlarge into a warm and
generous flame, to light up all the world with the radiance of a new hope, and to bring the bosom in which it
burns nearer to God.   The awakening of the soul to the
perception of beauty, encircling and multiplied, is its
first step to the appreciation of beauty special.   Then
it expands in a sentiment more lofty and pure, and love
becomes the ruling passion of the heart, and is a wreath
of flowers upon manhood's brow.   This new delight is
but a sympathy made forceful and predominating, and
for us it re-makes the world, and forges all nature into
spangles and stars, and summer sheen, and song, and
makes every leaf and cloud articulate.

> " It gives the brow of age
> A smack of youth, and makes the lip of youth
> Shed perfumes exquisite."

---

* Emerson.

This sentiment is ennobling, because it springs from
that deep well of inexhaustible beauty which lies within
us, unsullied and serene.   It is the bond which shall
unite all men and women together, and form them into
one great circle of good and generous souls.   Love is
our highest assurance of this inward self, for beneath it
Nature hides the greatest purpose which she has to accomplish, namely, the perpetuity of the species.   And if,
when it shall knock at the door of our hearts, we give
joy to its divine presence, and greet it as a ray of ethereal
loveliness flashed out of the abyss of God, it will find us
young, and keep us so for ever.

The province of the soul is not the province of the
intellect.   The spring of all feeling is from within, the
source of all idea from without.   The one is the office of
the mind, the other the possession of the heart.   Sentiment, an innate moral perception, is self-existent ; intellect is the result of experience, and is acquired during
time.   Even Locke admits that "though it be not sense,
as having nothing to do with external objects, yet it is
very like it, and might properly enough be called an
internal sense."   The perceptions of moral beauty, of
conscience, of virtue, of infinity, of God, are the faculties of the soul, and that takes cognizance of the outer
world only to read therein the symbols of its own egres-
sive law, and the constant exodus of its highest intelligence.   It is only through the channel of the memory
that the mind can take cognizance of a state of feeling or
a sentiment ; for the emotions of the heart—love, friendship, paternal care, pity or remorse, are not processes of
logical sequence—are independent and foreign to all

analysis, and are states or conditions self-induced to accord with the symbols which exist outwardly; as positive electricity always generates in the body with which it comes in contact a negative fluid, in order to restore the harmony between them.

To the soul, virtue is aboriginal; self-existent, not induced. It perceives and appreciates there and then, without weighing and estimating what pertains to itself; and plucks its own fruit where it stands, if there the fruit be. It is independent of experience, and does not perceive its objects in any relation as to time. In what bosom soever it abides, it sheds fragrance and music, as though flowers were blooming there, and angelic fingers were sweeping the tough fibres of the heart, to make them overflow with melody. Every scene and home of life is made sacred by it; and Nature, conscious of its high relations to the Most High God, always heralds the great phases of its doom.

The tendency of the age is to sensualism on the one hand, and to extreme intellectualism on the other. But however grand and imposing the achievements of the intellect, in the wonders of the laboratory or the engine-house, that alone is insufficient. We care too much for algebra, and chemistry, and the affairs of the household, and too little for that of the church; nay, every household should become a church, where the pervading spirit of all loveliness may sit enshrined, and where her votaries may kneel with fervent hearts to worship and offer sacrifice. It is our consuming folly to view all things in the cold light of the intellect, and to judge by the acquisition of facts, rather than by the enlargement of the highest sentiments. Are facts so necessary then? Have you exhausted all your previous stock? Or do you sit brooding there for some expected truth which shall show you the hollowness of your ways, but which, while you sit there, and shut your ears to the beseechings of the soul, shall never come, and you shall die at last a beggar. The sovereignty of the intellect has dwindled into cant, as much soul as you can muster avails; maugre that, all is barrenness and ashes. Events strengthen not the hope, for no length of time will ever ripen the contents of an empty barrel. If the intellect is our highest faculty, how comes it that so many of those who have been so highly endowed with this inheritance, have only died at last covered with shame at the perverted nature of their lives?—who, while stalking like petty gods among men, and transcending by the giant powers of their minds, have yet left a blight and pestilence in their path, as venemous reptiles leave their slimy tracks behind them. The names of Alexander, Pericles, Aspasia, Cataline, Alcibiades, Mirabeau, and Napoleon, only suggest a thousand more which might be quoted. And much to be deplored are the effects of our systems of trade, commerce, and education, in checking the growth of the best sentiments of our nature. The slow and steady calculations of gain and loss are appended, like badges of charity, to every effort which the pure soul would make to rescue some relic of itself from the wreck and destruction in which it finds itself immersed, and which threaten almost to strike God from the world. The influence of the senses is to circumscribe all things, and make the walls of space and time look solid and real, and to surround us with a world of insanity and corruption; but the moment we suffer the soul to speak, we become advertized of the great possibilities of our being, and a heaven of truth opens before us, in which we may bathe as in an ocean which has neither let nor bound, and even to us, the attributes of God become possible. "The moment we indulge our affections, the earth is metamorphosed; there is no winter and no night; all tragedies, all *ennui* vanish—all duties even; nothing fills the proceeding eternity but the forms all radiant of beloved persons." The moment the soul is assured of its acceptance to this universal realm, it acquires a new life, and a beaming satisfaction. Plato says, "lookest thou at the stars? If I were heaven, with all the eyes of heaven would I look down on thee?" and to the soul which is conscious of its high regard for the plain and solid beauty of its presentiments, the whole universe becomes but the speaking semblance of itself, and the bond of union between it and those it holds most dear.

All that the poet can teach us is his own impotency to express adequately the sentiments and feelings which surround us with each pulsing of the soft air, and with each echo of the wheeling sky. This power which abides within us is higher than intellect, more potent than will, and works through every fibre of our living hearts for good and beautiful purposes. It is the living soul of the world, the Alpha and Omega of this passing life, the *primum mobile* of all the virtues, and the vital force of all heroic actions. It is a power above the bolts and bars of thought, and fills up the space between the earth and heaven. It endows us with the rose of immortality, and gathers round us all the moments of the past and future: it can crowd a whole eternity into one hour, one single hour of immeasurable bliss.

THE LAND OF BLACKBERRIES.

"What tho' no charms my person grace,
Nor beauty moulds my form, nor paints my face?
The sweetest fruit may often pall the taste,
While sloes and brambles yield a safe repast."

BLACKLOCK'S *Plaintive Shepherd.*

TALK not of the luscious land of vines; sing not the
praises of blue heavens and rivers which flow through
vintage banks; of Rhines, and Moselles, and Rhones,
and Danubes; forget that there are regions of towering
palms, and fruitful bananas, and golden prairies reaching
to the sea,—lands all fragrant with magnolia blossoms,
and jungles where the richest fruits rot, untouched, upon
the mould; sigh not for Grecian vales and isles of
Paphos; nor pine for the rose-gardens of Cashmere, nor
for the scented bowers where the bulbul sings. Know
that here, in this island of green meadows and luxuriant
hedgerows, we speak the tongue of Lydegate; that we
are compatriots with Spencer, Chaucer, Shakspere, and
Keats; and that it is the land of beechen woods and
Druidical memorials; and above all, let us be grateful
to the Providence which has placed us in the Land of
Blackberries.

Blackberries! rich, juicy, cool, and gushing, which, in the days of boyhood, lured us with their jetty lusciousness, and made us forget old Horace and the *Pons Asinorum*, and in exchange for the Eton Grammar and the pickled birch, gave us a larger life in the green woods, made our young hearts beat with hopeful enthusiasm, and filled us with the first taste of life's poetry. Who then but would love blackberries, even though less delicious and refreshing to the palate than they really are? Who but would love the simple fruits which recalled the memories of orchard-robbing, school-mischief, April fools, holiday rambles, and frantic dogs with kettles or crackers at their tails? Blackberries,—ah! away we go, the sunshine is still blinking among the trees, and although the air grows chill, autumn is still ruddy, and the hedges are yet fruitful. There is Epping Forest, whither we went from Stepney at eight years of age " Blackberrying." We knew almost every dell, and cover, and tangled copse, and from any path could lead you direct to the richest garden of Blackberries. We knew the haunts of Hornsey, and Finchley, and Old Ford—now, alas! little towns, or appendages to London —long before we were twelve years of age; and many a dream of Robin Hood and Will Scarlet have we dreamt there among the fern, after having sated ourselves, after the fashion of Justice Greedy,—with the blackest of ripe Blackberries. There was always a charm about it, which neither tattered clothes, nor lacerated hands, nor angry looks at home, nor harsh words at school, could ever dispel; and to compensate for all the sorrows and trials of school drudgery and book education, we had the

nobler education to be gained in the land of Blackberries. And now, after having sunned our hearts in
the green ways of Saxon poetry, after having held companionship with the forests, and bugles, and green hills
of Scott, and luxuriated among the lush and leafy coverts
of Endymion Keats, besides many fair-spent hours over
Ritson and Robert Herrick, how can we refrain from
loving Blackberries? Blackberries, which speak so
winningly of "yellow-girted bees," and "golden honey-
combs," and "jagged trunks," and "unseen flowers in
heavy peacefulness." Love them? aye! and away we
go into the thick woods, far from the roar of cities and
the tramp of men, far from the soul's prison house, into
the free air of bosky dells, where ragworts and harebells
tremble, and the brambles hang their clouds of fruits.

This time to Cheshunt, fifteen miles from town, in the
prettiest part of Hertfordshire. Through the ancient
churchyard, glancing at the monuments of the Crom-
wells and the grassy mounds of many a sturdy Puritan,
superseding Hervey's sickly *Meditations*, by thoughts
which are always better suggested on the spot. Gathering as we go any precious little gem which may add to
the herbarium, we reach Cheshunt House, and refresh
our memories with the stories of Wolsey's pride and fall;
thence to the shadow of a great beech in Cheshunt Park,
to dine upon the grass, and discover a new and most
"come again" flavour in the beef and ham, which,
despite our worship of the Blackberries, makes us feel
keenly for the Vegetarians. Dinner over, through the
green lanes to Goffe's Oak, gathering berries as we go,
the first handful being offered as a libation to the earth,

after the manner of school-boys and the ancients. At Goffe's Oak we rest for the night, and enjoy that delicious slumber in a snowy bed which can only be enjoyed at a country inn in the land of Blackberries.*

The mornings are grey and misty at Blackberry time, so before venturing on the great expedition we have in view, let us be internally fortified with a good breakfast. The fragrant coffee tickles the sense until the nose seems to laugh at the conceit, and the palate, beguiled by the bland richness of the fresh butter and new-laid eggs, threatens to forget the anticipations of more Blackberries.

We are away at last, upon the roadside, gathering as we go from the brambles that skirt the pathways. Away with conventionalities; fling away the books; and let us for the present live for Blackberries. The berries are as black as death, and as delicious as the first kiss of a fond lover. There they hang like sugary showers of healing and delectable manna; hatless, on tiptoe, forgetting drawing-room and parlour courtesy, scorning etiquette and the doctrine of appearances, and like children in our aboriginal wildness, we gather and eat, we eat and gather. Satisfied, we walk on, and take the path to the left. which leads to "Newgate Street" and "Little Berk-

* Goffe's Oak stands on Cheshunt Common, overlooking the ancient lands of Guffley, and commanding a splendid panorama of hill country beyond. The tree from which the inn takes its name, is an ancient oak planted in the reign of William the Conqueror, and which is now a hollow ruin, though still bearing a head of foliage. The inn is one of the best samples which remain of the "Good Old Time," and still preserves the English characteristics of female beauty, domestic comfort, and hearty good cheer.

hampstead." The country, with its woody hills and miles and miles of wheatlands, turnip-fields, and meadows, swells grandly around us. There are copses and forests of pine stems; broad fields of cruciferous blossoms glowing like golden seas with ripples and billows of amber. Up above lie the woods; and the partridges and pheasants whirr away in heavy flight to shelter. The toil up-hill has cooled our energies, so we step in here to a small roadside inn, and seated in the only public room, which serves as a kitchen, pantry, and public parlour, regale ourselves with a sweet draught of " Prior's Entire." Here are eight houses and a mud cabin, backed on one side by the splendid park of Squire Ellis, flanked to the left with the richly wooded hills, through which the road rises and falls like an undulating line of foam upon a dark green sea of rolling billows; behind lies the valley we have just left, with its banks of harebells, wild thyme, and yellow ragworts; and on all hands the country lies basking in sunshine, full of fertile promise, beauty, and vegetable exuberance, and dotted and fringed all over with bushy lines of Blackberries. Down the steep hill towards the wood, up again, as the road passes over the upland, and a new scene breaks upon us. Down again into the thick of the wood, and feast our eyes on the interminable silvery birch masts, which gleam away into the dark background, like the spars of an anchored fleet all wedged together in a green sea of fern, while a solemn rustling in the green twinkling foliage above sounds like a chorus of dryads, or the song of liberated fays, which have been imprisoned in the glens since the days of Oberon and Titania. Blackberries again, richer, larger, and more pregnant with the cool mulberry flavour of any yet. Appetite grows keen, and we feel that we could eat all the woods contain, they are so grateful and delicious.

Alternating with Blackberries are crab-trees, loaded with fairy fruit; then clumps of willow-herbs, here covered with rich purple blossoms, there powdered with downy seeds; then again, St. John's-wort, then blue scabious, and then broad flushing sheets of crimson *lythrum*. Blackberries again and again, and stomachs and baskets are filled to repletion. The robins, and chaffinches, and willow wrens, flutter and sing, and chirp about us; and now and then the rabbit limps along through the brown brake, and the partridges run to cover. Between the singing and chirping of the birds, and the flutter of the wood-pigeon's wing, there is an occasional pause—a dead stillness—which is so solemn, so palpable to the sense, which has been all but stunned by the fret and din of cities, that it begets fear, and we tremble lest the rest-harrow which blooms on the bank should convert its spines into spears, and threaten us; or that the earth should gape and let forth some monster of malignity, such as the knights encountered in the olden time. Silence is new to man, and as strange as it is new; it is the searching and listening of the suspended sense which begets the mysterious feeling which accompanies it, and when it comes upon us in the world of green moss, and crushed leaves, and tangled branches, and Blackberries, we feel that we are alone with God, and come nearer to Him in the solitudes, and the silence becomes a new voice, whispering of trust, and faith, and

renewing love, and steadfast hope in the promised hereafter.

And here, sitting on the green bank, which is as soft
and elastic with the mossy growths of many years as any
bed of down; with the smiling face of one whom we love
beside us, let us indulge in a soliloquy on the all-a-b
sorbing topic of Blackberries. Not that the silence of
the woods needs to be broken by the voice of man, for
he, too often, carries strife and tumult into regions which
had else known peace, and blights the fresh face of
Nature with his iniquities and feverish impulses. Nevertheless, it seems meet, and the shadows nod a welcome.

Well, this said luscious, jet-black berry, or fruit of
the bramble, is a thing of no mean degree, either in its
botanical or literary history. Its botanical characteristics
ally it closely to the brilliant roses of our gardens, and to
the velvet peach, and the apple and the cherry. It is, in
truth, a rose, and its blossom, in shape and arrangement,
is a miniature of the rose of the hedges. Its sprays are
long and flexible, its juices are wholesome, and its fruit
salutary and refreshing. The leaves and stems afford a
valuable dye; and its young tops were anciently eaten
by the Greeks as a salad. It grows in every country of
Europe; and over the broad moorlands of the north it
produces abundance of its welcome fruits. Its homely
name of bramble, from the Anglo-Saxon *bræamble,* or
bremel *(anguis crucians),* signifies something furious, or
that which lacerates the skin; * and suggests the hirsute
nature of its stems. Hence, —"Doth the Bramble

---

* *Vide* Skelton by Dyce, I. pp. 187, 216, 278; and Chaucer's
Romaunt of the Rose.

cumber a garden? It makes the better hedge; where, if it chance to prick the owner, it will tear the thief;"[*] though in this sense the term is not confined among the Saxon writers to the Blackberry plant, but applied to others which are ragged and thorny. For instance:—

> " Swete as is the bramble floure
> That beareth the *red hepe.* "[+]

in which the wilding rose is "the bramble floure," and not our own true Blackberry: though in another use of the word there is no doubt but the *Black*-berry is referred to:—

> " One of hem was a tre
> That beareth a fruit of sauour wicke,
> Full croked was that foule sticke,
> And knottie here and their also,
> And blacke as berry or any alo." [‡]

The Bramble was as much esteemed as an important article in the materia medica of antiquity as it is with us for the juicy coolness of its fruit. "The berries," says Pliny, "are the food of man, and have a dessicative and astringent virtue, and serve as a most appropriate remedy for the gums and inflammation of the tonsils." I think it is in Hippocrates cited as a grand specific against the bite of serpents, and both berries and blossoms were used in such cases. Pliny also says the young shoots, pressed and reduced to the consistence of honey by standing in the sun, is a singular medicine,

---

* Grew, *Cosmologia*, III. c. 2.
+ Chaucer, *Rime of Sir Thopas*, v. 13.
‡ Chaucer, *Rom. Rose.*

taken inwardly, for all the diseases of the mouth and
eyes, as well as for the quinsy.   The roots, boiled in
wine, were used by the Romans for all infirmities of the
mouth, for which astringents were necessary; and the
young shoots were eaten as a salad to fasten loose teeth.
This was not a mere fancy of the old doctors, for all the
rubus tribe are eminently astringent; and Withering
assigns the same use to the raspberry as the ancients
did to the bramble.   He says, "the fruit is extremely
grateful as nature presents it; but made into a sweet-
meat, with sugar, or fermented with wine, the flavour is
improved.   It is fragrant, sub-acid, and cooling.   It
dissolves the tartarous concretions of the teeth, and for
this purpose it is superior to the strawberry."*   I
imagine it is the astringency of the leaves of the bramble
that renders it such a favourite food of goats.   On a
bank where there is a thorough good mixture of brush-
wood and wild stuff, goats will invariably crop first the
brambles, and next the shoots that crowd about the roots
of elms.   Withering says of the raspberry, "the fresh
leaves are the favourite food of kids;" and Virgil—keen
rustic as he was—had observed the same thing, for he
says—

> "On shrubs they browse, and on the bleaky top
> Of rugged hills the thorny brambles crop."†

Another note from classic sources is worth making
here.   Pliny says the propagation of trees by layers,
was taught the ancients by the bramble bush, which fre-

* British Plants, Ed. 1801, Vol. iii., p. 459.
† Dryden's Virgil, Georgics iii. p. 489.

quently forms roots from joints along the stem, when these trail on the ground, or arch over, so as to have their tops entangled with moist herbage.

Now a right good plant is this our wayside bramble, and one deserving a nobler vindicator than we. It grows bravely and endures all weathers; it sits beside the old oaks, and sees age come down and whiten their brows, keeping ever youthful and jovial itself. Renowned in story, from the time when it caught the garments of Demosthenes, as he fled, coward-like, from the field;* or when it alleviated, with its rich mellowness, the asperity of the Baptist's "locusts and wild honey;" or was strewed over the graves of Spartan heroes; or wove tassels of leaves and rose-shaped blossoms over the skeletons of Alexander's frozen army; or over the ghastly remains of humanity in Odin's Wood. Fair and welcome art thou, O humble and unambitious bramble, as when thou wert mingled with the earliest offerings of herbs, or scattered on the green altars of the ancient Gauls! Beautiful still, as when mingled with Æsop's happy gift,† when covered with elegies in deification of Rosalind, or when nodding a response to Wordsworth, when he so sweetly sang,—

> " I heard a thousand blended notes,
>   While in a grove I sat reclined,
> In that sweet mood when pleasant thoughts
>   Bring sad thoughts to the mind.

---

* Holland's " Plutarch," p. 765.

† Æsop made an offering of flowers to the god Mercury, and was rewarded with the gift of inventing fables.

> To her fair work did Nature link
> 　The human soul that through me ran;
> And much it grieved my heart to think
> 　What man has made of man.
>
> Through primrose tufts in that sweet bower
> 　The periwinkle trailed its wreaths;
> And 'tis my faith that every flower
> 　Enjoys the air it breathes."

But, alas! the learned in the lore of flowers attach to thy blossoms the idea of remorse. There is no cup so pure but dregs may be found at the bottom; and thou, with thy "gauzy satin frill," and tempting harvest of juicy blackness, art armed from head to foot with thorns,—thorns which lacerate and pierce the flesh, and, like the bitter draughts along the path of pleasure, too often bid us taste of one before we reach the other. Why art thou girded round with thorns? is it that man may not pluck all the fruit, and thus some be left for the little birds who fear not brambles? or is there some lurking medicine in thy many lancets, such as the Indians seek while rubbing their bodies with the prickly sela, or the old Romans pined for, when they sowed nettles to rub themselves?* Heaven knows! perhaps we may get a blessing when we smart the most, and if God wills it, so let it be.

If all this availed not to make the bramble precious, and teach the true glory of the Land of Blackberries, what shall avail against the fact (which we have intentionally deferred till now), that they were the only food of the poor "Children in the Wood," and that

---

* Camden's "Britannia."

from day to day as they wandered through the dreary wilderness—unwatched by men, but cared for by God— he, with his arm round her little neck, she looking up in his face with a tear in her eye, and amid the occasional fears and alarms which beset them, feeling still safe while guarded by her boy. Who could pluck a Blackberry and think of this without letting fall a tear, and again thanking God that he dwells in a land where the lives and liberties of babes are so sacred, that that old story never yet failed to move a heart, unless it were a heart of stone; thanking God that it is the land of baby love, of boyish glee, and of Blackberries. Ah! the robin comes now, year by year, and strews leaves upon the graves of innocence, and the bramble of the hedgerows is historically consecrated to the precious dust of the departed. See the old grave-digger busy in the country churchyard making a new grave "comfortable," with sods of grass bound in their places with hoops of bramblerods. Some of those will take root hereafter in the rich earth of "God's acre," and as Tennyson foresaw that the ashes of his friend would nourish the "violet of his native land," so we may see the far off likeness of the lost in the delicate blossom of the brambles—unless we rest there too before the summer comes. Jeremy Taylor uses this fact finely in a passage on the uncertainty of the life of man:—"The autumn, with its fruits, prepares disorders for us, and the winter's cold turns them into sharp diseases; and the spring brings flowers to strew upon our hearse; and the summer gives green turf and brambles to bind upon our graves." This reminds me that the blossom of our

plant is a most beautiful production, and there are few
of the rich colours of autumn that surpass the fiery
hues with which the foliage of the bramble is occasionally dashed. It is a moot point whether the white or
blush-coloured blossoms are the most numerous; the
authors of "Rubi Germanica" say white prevails, and
I think them correct; but Smith* says, "Flowers erect,
handsome, of a delicate pink, rarely, if ever, white."
The prevailing hue is doubtless dependent on soil and
climate, but in the same hedge, and on the same plant,
nay, on the same stem, pink, blush, and white flowers
may be seen side by side, and the white must be
awarded the palm for highest beauty. As poetical
references for this subject are not plentiful as blackberries, I must take refuge in a lyrical scrap from
Hone's Table Book,† which I note down because written
in the scene of my own boyish acquaintance with blackberries.

THE BLACKBERRY BLOSSOM.

WRITTEN IN EPPING FOREST.

"The maiden's blush
   Sweet blackberry blossom, thou
Wearest, in prickly leaves that rove
   O'er friend-like turning bough.

Companionship
   Thine attributes, thou givest
Likeness of virtue shielded safe
   From foes with whom thou livest.   .

---

* "English Flora."   Ed. 1824, vol. ii., p. 400.
† No. xxxii., p. 270.

What is mankind,
  But like thy wandering?—Time
Leads mortals through the maze of life,
  And thousands hopeful climb.

A sudden blast—
  Then what of hope remains?
Beauty full soon by sickness falls,
  And pleasures die in pains.

But fruit succeeds—
  Thou ripenest by the sky;
May human hearts bear fruits of peace
  Before in earth *they* lie."

August 19, 1827.

Well, with childhood's rosy memories, with antique legends and histories, ranging from that earliest age when men fed upon the simplest productions of the ground, when—

  " Content with food which Nature freely bred,
    On wildings and on strawberries they fed ;
  Cornels and bramble-berries gave the rest,
    And falling acorns furnished out a feast,"*

down to Rosalind and the Children in the Wood, together with no end of uses in medicine and the arts, and that grandest of all uses, the making of conserves, preserves, tarts, pies, and puddings, and mingled with damsons, the richest syrup in the catalogue of modern confectionary, we say again,—Heaven bless the brambles, and all cheer to the Land of Blackberries !

From the silent wood, by a road to the left, we passed into a picturesque region of farm-houses and ancient

* Dryden's " Virgil."

homesteads; down a steep hill which gave us another view of the splendid country we had crossed before, and "up hill and down dale," about three miles, brought us back to the Goffe's Oak again. Tea,—Oh, how delicious! Arranged botanical specimens, and "between whiles," peeped in at the basketful of jet blackberries, and thought of pie crust, sable jam, scalding syrup, and the children in the wood.

Six days pass, and each seems more beautiful than its predecessor, till warned of anxieties and cares, and knowing that commercial interests permit us not without stint to pluck Blackberries for ourselves, we take train, and are once more in a region not of Blackberries, but black bricks, and cold stones, and colder hearts, amid—

> " The weariness, the fever, and the fret,
>   Here, where men sit and hear each other groan,
>   Where palsy shakes a few, sad, last grey hairs,
>   Where youth grows pale, and spectre-thin, and dies;
>   Where but to think is to be full of sorrow
>   And leaden-eyed despairs;
>   Where beauty cannot keep her lustrous eyes,
>   Or new Love pine at them beyond to morrow."

There's the bell for dinner. Avaunt! I smell the Blackberries—the atmosphere is changed to nectar, and the sunshine stained with sanguine streaks, as I toss a libation of the ruby juice to heaven, and shout, " The Land of Blackberries for ever !"

THE SOUL OF SONG.

"From harmony, from heavenly harmony,
This universal frame began:
From harmony to harmony
Through all the compass of the notes it ran,
The diapason closing full in man."

DRYDEN.

PHILOSOPHERS tell us that light, heat, and sound, are but the various effects of an agitated or vibrating medium. That a certain number of one kind of vibrations in a given time produce some definite ray of colour; while a definite number of some other kind originate a peculiar sound. Sounds thus produced by vibrating currents of air may be either noises or musical tones; the distinction being dependent entirely on the nature and number of the vibrations. A mere noise is produced by vibrations which have no mathematical proportion one to the other: musical tones result from vibrations which bear mathematical analysis; each separate tone having its specific number of vibrations, and bearing musical and numerical relation to all other musical tones. Inasmuch as red, blue, or yellow light are the productions of waves in the thin ether, so are all sounds, whether of the dear human voice or the dread "rattling thunder"

but effects referable to ripplings or waving of the air.
So far, sound is but a simple result of natural causes—a
plain prose fact. But as the grey and brown tints of the
earth are lifted out of the region of prose into that of
poetry by the gay hues of flowers, so is human speech,
and all other sounds, lifted out of the dead level of mere
utility into a region of life by a poetry which asserts
itself in song. God has so willed it that while the world
brings forth bread for the body, it shall bring forth
beauty for the soul. We prize the corn because it
nourisheth; we love the fresh green of the waving
wheat because it is a thing of beauty. Words are instruments of power, and among the highest in the list of
mere utilities; but when the jangle of commerce ceases,
and the tender utterance of sympathy begins, how poor
the words of the mind, how rich the music of the heart!
Nature ever climbs up towards the spiritual; she never
ceases with use, she must have beauty; and so she gives
man a capacity for the appreciation of harmonious vibrations; and speech dies out—as if in shame at its own
weakness—where the expression of the soul begins.
Simple in its source—simple in its history, is this fact;
yet how deep it lies in the unity of this circle of the
affections—how closely bound up with the hopes and
joys of living men—how suggestive of spiritual life and
high aspiration—how strong a link in the chain of our
destinies. The most ethereal and at the same time the
most vague musical expressions, stand as high above
verse, as verse—the connecting link between conversation
and melody—does above mere prosy talking. We remember the air of an old song long after we have for-

gotten the words. We may sit unmoved during the recital of the finest verses; but the moment the harper's fingers sweep the strings, the melody rouses us to a fine fanaticism. The song was body before,—it is soul now; its harmonies are complete; and to every march of the melody the heart-strings throb responsive. Nature is double all through;—body and soul, matter and spirit, as if the universe were a repeated marriage of the two elements. To the fertility of the fields is added beauty of tint, and form, and colour: the brown soil has a soul, and that soul is the flower, which would exist in vain were there no other souls to make common cause with its life and history. To man—the prose of the world— is added woman, its poetry.

These many spirits of the world seem made for man. The rainbow may span the heavens; but unless seen by man, its arches have been built in vain. When it bridges over the unpopulated desert, it is but a thousand drops of rain, which the green leaves drink in without knowing of their prismatic beauty; but when it embraces the corn ridge and the village, a thousand loving eyes look up, and angels are seen treading it as a pathway between the heaven and the earth. Hence, knowing its mission, the rainbow only visits spots where human souls abide. It is for the soul of man that all these many souls are born, and the soul of song as truly so as any. Where is the music of nature so rich as on the skirts of cultivated districts, where flowery gardens feed innumerable humming bees, and thick bosses of thatch shelter the trusting robin! It is a fact, that in the deep forest the birds that sing are few; and the more lonely

the spot, the more hoarse and dissonant the voices of the
creatures.   Everywhere the dear birds hover and flit on
hasty wing; but only near the dwelling of man hover
those whose song is sweetest: in his garden they take
shelter and bring up their young; in the close copse or
mossy orchard they cower from the noonday heat; and
return again and again, in spite of the persecutions they
meet with at his hands, to heighten his enjoyments, to
cheer his social hours, and renew the sentiments of past
delight.   In the lonely mere, and over the dark moorland hover many birds, but they are such as only hoot
and scream; and where the wild waves play together fly
seabirds, whose only language is a dismal scream.

Nature pushes up towards the region of poetry in
sound as she does in colour.   As she weaves rainbows
from the fragments of a falling cloud, so she struggles
to weave music from every voice of animate and inanimate
things.   The wind howls in the November branches, but
sings amid the shrubby foliage of June; the rivulet
makes a whizzing sound while creeping through the
matted sedge, but laughs like a merry maiden when it
sparkles among the yellow pebbles, and tinkles like a bell
when it beats up a fallen rock.

It is because music stands above all the utilities of
sound,—because it appeals to the sentiments of men,
because it is soul claiming kindred with soul, that man
has loved it first among the spiritual possessions of the
world, and has sought in its voice an answer to his
longings for the good and fair.   Nowhere upon the face
of all the world is to be found a people in whose hearts
music has not a welcome.   The rude Indian stands upon

the shelly beach and listens in love to the singing of the
waves.   He suspends the hollow shell upon the delicate
fibre of the palm, and strikes it with his hand, that it
may give forth song.   He fashions the marsh reed or
the stem of grass into a flute, and enchants his listening
children with its voice.   And when the toils of the chase
are done, he gathers together his fellow-huntsmen, and
in the purple of the evening air they sing together their
songs of joy.

It was the consciousness of union between the soul of
man and the soul of song which begot those lovely con-
ceits of antiquity which represented nature as a musical
or rhythmic harmony.   Plato said, the soul of man was
itself a harmony, and had its nearest sympathies in music.
Bolder still was the sage of Samos, when he said that the
orbs of heaven were so harmonious in their motions that
it must be accompanied by ravishing songs,—that the
worlds warble in their ceaseless march, while the blue
deeps beat back the chorus and repeat the echo of their
psalms.

All fables, when understood, become facts.   Orpheus
is no fable; he is the poet skilled in harmony whom the
ages honour with the attributes of divinity in remembrance of the solace which men found in his songs.   The
Orphic hymns are lost, but fragments of his legendary
life remain to testify how closely men cling to the
remembrance of pleasure.   When Orpheus bewailed the
death of his wife Euridyce, the sweet sound of his lyre
caused a forest of elms to spring up, and the charm of
his harp was so great that the woods nodded, the brown
rocks broke their bonds and marched entranced towards

him. That the extravagance is only superficial, witness the repeated references of poets, who return again and again to these lovely legends because there is a truth beneath them which is universal:—

> " Therefore the poet
> Did feign that Orpheus drew trees, stones, and floods ;
> Since naught so stockish, hard, and full of rage,
> But music for the time doth change his nature."

The universal poet saw the breadth of the myth, and added:—

> " The man that hath no music in himself,
> Nor is not moved with concord of sweet sounds;
> The motions of his spirit are dull as night,
> Is fit for treasons, stratagems, and spoils;
> And his affections dark as Erebus."
>
> SHAKSPERE.

The spirit of the world was young when music was made the handmaid of religion ; and it still affords a glimpse of that antiquity to know that deeds of heroism and valour were sanctified in song, and that music completed the glory of the inauguration and the festival. Whether at the Olympic, Pythian, Nemean, and Isthmian games, or at the victories of Romulus, 750 years before Christ, when the army, horse and foot, followed the chariot of the conqueror, hymning their gods in songs of their country; or whether at the marriage feast or the funeral prayer, the charm of music still predominates,—interweaves itself with the fate and circumstances of man, and creeps into his heart like a sunbird seeking for a home. It is this power which rouses a rude peasantry from the lethargy of serfdom to repossess themselves of liberties long lost, under the impulse of their national melodies. The effect produced on the Swiss soldiers, when in the service of the French, by an ancient air of the *Rannes des Vaches*, was so powerful that it was forbidden to be played, so forcibly did it remind the men of the mountainous homes which they had left, and of the hearts that were beating and the eyes that were weeping for them.

National song, of all other, holds a powerful sway over the minds of those in whom it awakens thoughts of fatherland and freedom. What would be the poetry of any nation, or any age, if robbed of the spirit of its song? What would be left of Scottish character if the ballads of the Caledonian bards were swept away? if the harps of the minstrels perished with the fingers that first swept them? The song that cheered the shepherd boy while tending his sheep, comes back to him in the hour of oppression and danger; and even upon the battle-field, that melody calls up the moors and mountains of his native land; the wild woods and the streams come back, and the breezy freshness of the heather fans his cheek again, as he marches with a firm step and a nervous arm to win his liberty or die. It is said that he who writes the songs of a nation may at the same time predict its history, for patriotism has ever burned the brighter when music fanned the flame, and the human breast has ever throbbed with a holier devotion when the soul of song was stirring at the heart strings.

The same tender emotions which move the camel-driver to sing to his camel, as he shares with the patient brute his dates and barley-bread, and then ceases in his

song to hear the tinkling of the bells upon the desert
sand, animated the harper in the olden times when he
poured forth his wild songs to nerve the chieftain's arm
for battle. No music is there like the human voice :
harmony may flow from trembling strings ; but the
soul of song dwells sweetest on the human lips. It was
in musical sentences that Pythagoras uttered those
wonderful spondees by which he could suddenly pacify a
man that was in a violent transport of anger ; and in
the simple ballad sung to-day at the fireside, the heart
finds one of its sweetest consolations, and learns a sympathy which for ever links it in memory with home.
Virgil knew the value and the beauty of the voice when
he made Silenus sing of the Epicurean birthday, and in
a strain so thrilling that

> " Tripping satyrs crowded to the song ;
> And sylvan fauns, and savage beasts advanced,
> And nodding forests to the numbers danced."

And there are but few who could sit listless while the
lips of beauty were uttering the language of a tender ballad
—a ballad of the heart, woven of home joys and sorrows
—not the jingle of a heartless and abandoned fancy. Oh,
the magic of that tender touch !—the thrill of that
utterance of soul for soul—the glorious circle of associations kindled into being by the music of those household
words by which our mothers sang us to sleep,—by
which our sweethearts beguiled the evenings · of our
wooing, and by which, as age and trouble gather around
us, we hope to have for solace in the downward path !
The finishing touch—the completion of the household
circle—is this fire-side song ; enjoyed but once, it is

remembered for ever, and as a frequent pastime it is the purest and most refining antidote to the gilded allurements of gaiety and fashion. Picture the Christmas group sitting round the hearth of blazing logs, where the flames leap up, and up, and flash their ruddy radiance on the ruddier walls, playing in strange sparkles and gold drops on the old cornices, and leaving a strange Christmas light upon every happy face assembled there. The song is all that is needed to complete their joy, and that scene, completed by the fireside song, becomes a memory to each one there which none of the detergent vanities of the world will ever annihilate. There can be no limit to the moral beauty of this. Everything which refines the home, which makes it attractive, which endears it by spells and enchantments, and words of love, and songs of gladness, has an effect which abides through life, and gives force and reality to the domestic character, and which makes home a haven of refuge from the storms and whirlwinds of the world. Who, but the most abandoned and outcast, can for a moment picture such a scene without calling up from his own circle of associations a hundred memories of dear ones that have passed away,—of others that still linger —linger as if only to love—the joys of the world having all passed from them; and of others yet in the bloom and flush of life, stepping one by one into the circles of manhood and womanhood, to be cheered by-and-by with the prattle and the songs of their own babes, and to know how truly home is home when cheered by the breath of song.

The object of the ballad is to stir the feelings by a

gentle appeal, and to lift the heart into its highest region
of sympathy and moral beauty, by the blending into one
harmonious whole of the simple things around it. *The
Old Arm-chair ; Oh, Nannie ;* and the *Evening Bells,*
have kindled more pure aspirations and left dearer
memories behind than all the *morceaux* of the French
and Italian masters that ever were introduced into the
boudoir. The ballad is essentially the song of home;
its appeals are direct, and it plays upon the emotions by
a rhyming of the things that are near and dear to us.
Happy the child whose first sleep is softened by a
mother's song; happy the mother who sings her child
to sleep ! Happy the home where music supplants the
attractions of the tavern and the gambling-table ; happy
the bride who loves the wedding bells for their own
sake, and mingles with the first cares of the wife a song
to win her husband's kisses—for " domestic happiness
is of that quiet nature which the heart enjoys but the
tongue boasts not,—it is like that still music which the
ancients supposed is going on above—not the less sweet
for its making no noise in the ears of this world."

THE MYSTERIOUS BALANCE.

A TEACHING OF THE AQUARIUM.

IN the vast procession of beings which passes before the eyes of God as a panorama, and of which man catches but imperfect glimpses here and there, the many which drop out of the ranks into the jaws of death form the tesselated pavement on which the successive races tread, secure in their perpetuity. Life stands in fear of death, though death is but its servant—a faithful servant—appointed by the Author of life to gather life's tangled threads into an order of successive developments. The dying Christian may fear death, though assured of immortality; and the unthinking worm writhes in its expiring agonies, as if it would by a last effort struggle into strength once more. Deeply hid in the core of the organic universe is the secret of Death, " who keeps the keys of all the creeds;" yet man is permitted to read a part of the mystery in the experiences of his kind, and in the records of past ages. He doubts the fact of death, while openly admitting it; for his fear dictates a thought directly opposed to reason, to observation, and to the knowledge that has been revealed—

L

"He thinks he was not born to die,
       And THOU hast made him, THOU art just."

Yet when man looks upon Nature, he sees everywhere
the records of death's work among the representatives of
creative energy.   The stratified rocks are but the tomb-
stones in the great graveyard of the world ; they cover
the bones of a million generations, and the inscription on
them is, " The dust we tread upon was once alive." If the
infusion of life into countless forms, each in itself perfect,
needed nothing less than Almighty power, it needed
Almighty power too to complete the scheme in the
institution of dissolution ; and the grim king of terrors,
before whom the bee and the sparrow tremble, perhaps,
not less than man, became co-worker with God by a wise
and beneficent appointment : and so the orders of being
began, and have to this hour continued, as a series of
dissolving views, in which there is no hiatus, but only
change ; no shifting of the focus or the screen, no aber-
ration or intermission of the source of light, but an
unending variety in the pictures.   We know not how
other worlds may fare, but this we know, that *here*
death supplies from every extinguished picture the
colours with which the next are painted, and we live—
man and brute—on the *débris* of the past.

   I see all this and more in the aquarium ; it teaches me
lessons in physics, and, I trust, also teaches me that the
moral and spiritual truths of the universe may be illus-
trated, sometimes explained, by a patient study of the
commonest things.   The aquarium is a world in little ;
it sustains itself.   For the moment, I put aside the law
of gravity as a universal law, and the presence of the

atmosphere as a universal thing, and I call it a world, needing no aid for its continuance and the perfect adjustment of its balance of power from external things. I take a vessel of glass, a few pebbles, a few pieces of sandstone rock, and a sufficiency of water, and to that I commit my fishes and insects, and say, "There is your world; the order of nature is such, that you may henceforth live and die without human interference." I say nothing here of the details of management; I am looking for instruction in the laws of life and death.

The two requisites of animal life, food and air, must be generated in this world, or it ceases to instruct me; yet the water contains but little of each, and whence is its supply to come? God has ordained such a wealth of organic forms, that wherever the conditions of life are found, life takes possession of the spot, whether it be the bottom of the ocean, the dripping roof of a cave, the expanse of the viewless air, or the mimic lake I call an aquarium. Forthwith the dead stones become alive with greenness, the glass walls assume the semblance of a meadow, the milky hue of the water disappears as the earthy particles it held in solution subside, and the light that streams through it takes a tint of greenness. There is an order of vegetation appointed to occupy such sites, and almost every non-metallic, and some metallic substances too, become speedily coated with confervæ, when their surfaces are kept moist a sufficient length of time. Were it not so, the inhabitants of my world must perish; and to prove the fact I try an experiment. I place some fishes in a clean vessel of water, without pebbles

and without rock; the moment the first dim bronzy
speck appears, I rub it off the glass, and so thwart the
course of Nature. The fishes soon exhaust the water of
its oxygen, and though the water attempts to renew its
supplies by absorption from the atmosphere, the compen-
sation is too slow, the fishes come gasping to the surface, and in a short while perish.

Even then I learn something from their death, if I
leave the vessel in the hands of Nature. Death has no
sooner spread his black banner over my household gods
than life of another kind arises to confound him, and
the microscope reveals to me myriads of animals and
plants, and organisms that seemingly occupy an inter-
mediate place between the two great kingdoms, rioting
upon the wreck that death has made. My half-dozen
dead fishes have given birth to existences numerous as
the stars in heaven, or as the sand upon the sea-shore,
innumerable. While these devour the banquet death
has spread for them, while forests of confervoid threads
rise in silken tufts like microscopic savannahs, Nature is
passing portions of the ichthyic *débris* through her
laboratory, and the very source of life for which they
pined and perished—oxygen—is poured in in large
measure, and the corruption is quickly changed to sweetness. Of the once sportive fishes some portions have
become air, other portions have become water, but the
chief of their bulk lives already in the vegetation which
hides their grave, and the moving throng with which
that vegetation is peopled. God's purpose in the working of the laws in obedience to which these changes have
      'ce, is manifestly to keep ever true that balance

of life and death of which He holds the beam in His own hands.

But my aquarium which has not thus been interfered with, presents already a similar scene of life and bustle. When first supplied, the milky-looking water was abundantly full of gaseous matters, and every part of the rough rockwork was, for a time, studded with silvery globules. The fishes consumed all that in the process of breathing. As the water passed through their gills the oxygen was absorbed; that oxygen, by a process of refined chemistry, and perhaps by the help of iron also, gave their gills a bright red colour, gave their blood its red colour too, and by other processes not less refined, sustained the balance of life's functions within them, for without it they must perish. We believe that not the airiest particle of earth, atmosphere, or water, nor the most minute globule of condensed moisture, or the most infinitesimal point of meteoric dust, can ever be lost, at least during Time, from the fabric of the universe. My fishes tell me that the oxygen they absorb from the water, they again return to it, but *in another form*. They *in*spire oxygen and *ex*pire carbonic acid, just as a man does, and every other living creature that moveth upon the face of all the earth. Is it within the reach of human power, even when reason, imagination, and fancy combine together as a bold triad to look direct upon a fact, to appreciate that principle of terrestrial life by which animal and vegetable organisms reciprocally labour to maintain the balance of atmospheric purity? The carbonic acid given off by the animal is poison to it, if it accumulate while the supply of oxygen is cut short.

It was carbonic acid as much as absence of oxygen that killed our fishes just now, for though inhabitants of water they were not the less suffocated. Therefore I see *why*, in the tank that has been left alone, plants have cast anchor on the glass walls, the brown pebbles, and the gray blocks of sandstone rock. My fishes breathe, and breathe. If their numbers are properly proportioned to the area they occupy, they will never exhaust the water of oxygen, never render it fœtid with carbonic acid, so long as one necessity of vegetable life—light— is allowed to use its active influence to paint the plants green, even as oxygen gives a sanguine hue to the gills or lungs of the fishes. To those plants the carbonic acid which the fishes expire day and night, is as essential as oxygen is to the animal economy; and thus, without introducing a single scrap of any living plant, the balance is sustained, and death seems to be kept at a distance. If at first I threw in a tuft of callitriche or anacharis, or any other true aquatic vegetable, oxygen would be supplied abundantly; and in practice it might be well to begin so, because some little time elapses ere the seeds of the microscopic forest, the tops of whose trees present to the eye but a felt-like coating of superficial greenness, are developed into true plants; though with a fair amount of indirect daylight, and at certain seasons of the year, a few hours suffice to set the vegetative process, with all its proper consequences, in full action. Many of the readers of this paper will call to mind the aquarium that stands in my entrance hall. It contains twenty fishes large and small, and not a single scrap of vegetation except what has been developed *in situ* by spontaneous generation. It is five years since that was fitted and stocked, and committed to the management of Nature, with the sole exception of the external aid afforded by regular supplies of food for its inmates, which need not be taken account of, now that we are considering it as a world in which the balance of life and death is sustained by the operation of principles ordained by the Creator.

It is when we leave the principles, and attempt to classify the details of the scheme, that we become bewildered. The smooth revolution of the flywheel and the noiseless oscillation of the piston, convince the unprofessional observer of a great engine, that mechanical motions are possessed of poetry ; but if he would analyze the relations of the cog-wheels, the indications of the " governor," the " gauge," and the pressure-valve, he must descend to hard facts, and forget for a while the sublime suggestions of a system of mechanism that throbs like a living creature. Admit a full glare of summer sun to the aquarium, and forthwith the water loses its pellucid fluidity, and becomes deeply tinged throughout of a dull green, as if some pigment had been dissolved in it. Instead of ·plants attached to stones and glass only, and animals that float unseen, the whole of the water is occupied by visible masses of animal and vegetable life; and if the fishes suffer, it will be from undue heat, not from the addition to the element in which they live of this new mass of being. Shut out the sunshine, let the fresh air play over the surface of the water, let moderate daylight stream through it as before, and speedily the green ˙ fog clears away, the water again becomes transparent, and the balance is restored. Monas, euglena, uvella, cryptomonas, gonium, and other wondrous infusoria, may be detected as constituents of the cloudy mass while it lasts, called into being because the conditions of the tank were such as they required; as if life in embryo was everywhere locked up until the moment came for its liberation, and some particular circumstance was the talisman to set it free; or if we consider created forms to be marshalled in grand procession, may we not expect that every tribe will hurry to its appointed place the instant that a door is opened?

Microscopists have long been at war, but without bloodshed, as to the place to be assigned to certain organic forms which are hidden from our common eyesight. While the war goes on as to whether desmidiaceæ and diatomaceæ be animal or vegetable, or both, let facts suffice us here in the study of the aquarium. Does an animal exhale carbonic acid? Yes. Well, here are plants or animals, concerned in keeping up the balance, which exhale oxygen, and their name is legion. Volvox globator and the bacillariæ labour as hard to supply the fishes with the life-sustaining gas as do the silken threads of verdure that line the glass like a carpet. Is the possession of starch a distinctive feature of the vegetable? Perhaps so. Truly here are desmidiaceæ that contain starch, and if I make the possession of cilia the test for assigning certain forms to the animal kingdom, I find in the aquarium spores of algæ furnished with them. Motion I know to be no test, because algæ spores dance through the water gaily till they find a resting-place, and when the aquarium was first filled, it was by dancing they at last found where to pitch their tents, and cease their nomad wanderings. But they all work together to sustain the balance, and the law of "give and take" prevails amongst them—the stentor devours the oscillatoriæ, rotatoria, and monads, and the hydras swallow all; every darting speck is a tomb wherein some smaller speck of life is to be buried, and life thus prospers on the decay it is itself undergoing.

But all this while a fine deposit slowly settles among the pebbles, which form the lower stratum of this watery world. Between the stones a fine alluvial silt collects and thickens. The first frost, sufficiently severe to touch the tank, causes the whole green coating to peel off from the glass and rock, and while this subsides, to add to the thickness of the alluvium—how slightly, and yet how sufficiently for an example of Nature's working ! —a new growth commences, and *that* balance is restored. Do you not see that the chief teaching of geology—the piling of stratum upon stratum, the conversion of disrupted rock and decayed plant and animal into rock again—is here exemplified in the history of a domestic toy, which contains already one example of stratification in the silence of watery submergence ? A tank which has been fitted with loam, pebbles, and plants of the brook and river, will, if left undisturbed for three years, be in this state. Those plants will all have decayed, but there will be an abundant spontaneous vegetation. The accumulations of that short period will have settled into a close mass, almost as hard as stone ; and if fishes have died in the meantime, and have not been removed, their bones will be found overlaid with hardened mud, just

as we find them in the old red sandstone, or the chalk,
or the carboniferous rocks, and shall we not call them
our own fossils?   See again in this case in which death
has been very busy (for plants of large growth soon
perish in the absence of sunshine, and occasional
attendant accidents will carry off some of the finny pets),
how life has been equally active on the other side,
for such an aquarium will be a hundred times richer
in those spontaneous growths we have already spoken of,
and visible forms of infusoria and true zoophytes will
abound, and every class will be more fully represented,
down even to the twilight monad.

Though this paper must have an end, there is no end to
the teaching of the aquarium.   It is a watery microcosm
of living and dead wonders, and we need not marvel
that the balance of life and death may be observed in its
succession of changes, because all the physical forces
of the universe are locked up within a single bead of dew,
and all the functions of organic creation are comprised
in the economy of monas termo.   If God so ordains that
life shall be constantly soaring from the tomb, if the
story of the Phœnix ceases to be a fable, need man, the
victim of doubts and fears, ever fail in his trust of that
blessed promise, that " this mortal shall put on immortality, and this corruptible shall put on incorruption?"
Science may fix his mind on the appreciation of God's
wisdom and power as he reads the handwriting of the
Almighty in Nature, but through faith in another revelation must he hope to exclaim, triumphantly, "O death,
where is thy sting?   O grave, where is thy victory?"
Or, to pass from divine to human consolations, we may

take up the apostrophe of the great Raleigh, and say, "O eloquent, just, and mighty Death! what none have dared, thou hast done; what none have attempted, thou hast accomplished; thou hast gathered all the might, majesty, and meanness of mankind, and hast covered them with these two words, ' *hic jacet.*'" Nature's children have a dread of death, but Nature herself is in friendly compact with the master of silence. If the *types*, which are the ideas of God, have survived from the oldest rocks to this present hour, will not the spirit, which lives on ideas, and evolves them as the aquarium evolves its throng of animalcules, live for ever? It is not hard to believe with Tennyson :—

> " That nothing walks with aimless feet,
>   That not one life shall be destroyed,
>   Or cast as rubbish to the void,
>   When God hath made the pile complete."

"The pile" will be complete when God's purpose is fulfilled in man, to whom it is given to hope after eternal life, and with eyes of faith to pierce through the veil, and behold the wondrous things of eternity.

THE POETRY OF CHEMISTRY.

> " There's not one atom of yon earth
>   But once was living man ;
>   Nor the minutest drop of rain,
>   That hangeth in the thinnest cloud,
>   But flowed in human veins."
>
> SHELLEY.

So pass and change the elements of the world. So
separate and combine, so decay and revivify, so come
and go the creatures of the earth and air, and in due
time all the particles of the rounded world pass through
the life current of the human heart. Nature is a great
laboratory, a necromantic palace of mutation. Yet out
of all this passing and repassing, this flitting and fading
of her dead and living children, she still preserves the
old familiar face, and looks upon us with the same sweet
mother's smile which gladdened the hearts of the old
thinkers, and cheered the builders of the ancient temples.
Nature has but a few simple materials, and neither
crucible nor alembic in which to elaborate her new forms,
and yet with this poverty of means does she trick out all
the world in scenes of delicious beauty, and hedge round
the waking thoughts of men with wonder upon wonder.
" The whole code of her laws may be written on the
thumb-nail, or the signet of a ring. The whirling

bubble on the surface of a brook admits us to the secret of the mechanics of the sky. Every shell on the beach is a key to it. A little water made to rotate in a cup explains the formation of the simpler shells; the addition of matter from year to year, arrives at last at the most complex forms; and yet so poor is Nature with all her craft, that, from the beginning to the end of the universe, she has but one stuff—but one stuff with its two ends, to serve up all her dream-like variety. Compound it how she will, star, sand, fire, water, tree, man, it is still one stuff, and betrays the same properties."[*]

When men woke up from barbarism and night, and began to contemplate the beauty of the world, they saw that amid the multiplicity of colours and of forms, and in the endless metamorphoses of things around them, whether they looked upon the granite peaks piercing the blue heaven with their hoary pinnacles; the wild sea with its midnight moans and summer laughter; the blue heaven with its storms and starlight beauty; or the green earth with its clustering woods and waving grasses, blossoming all over from pole to pole with a garment of living verdure; still the same invisible forces were at work, weaving all things in a web of unity, and connecting the most incongruous things together. Hence, in their mystic worship, and in the poetic utterances of their untamed hearts, they pictured nature under the various forms of Buddha, Vishnu, Osiris, Proteus, and Pan; all of them symbols of the same thought, and representing the creative power which for ever and ever transmutes one form into another, and evokes from

[*] " Emerson's Essays," Second Series, p. 121.

corruption and death the creatures of a new creation.
The story of the Phœnix is the story of the world, and
as one form crumbles into ashes, another starts from its
dust, to continue the chain of beauty, and push on the
series of utilities.

> " Where is the dust that has not been alive?
>   The spade, the plough disturb our ancestors;
>   From human mould we reap our daily bread;
>   The globe around earth's hollow surface shakes,
>   And is the ceiling of her sleeping sons:
>   O'er devastation we blind revels keep;
>   Whole buried towns support the dancer's heel."
>
>   Young.

Of the sixty simple elements to which all the varieties
of dead and living matter are reducible, some fifteen or
twenty play the chief parts in the chemistry of the world.
All the phenomena which take place around us, whether
it be the upheaval of volcanic masses, or the floating of
a gossamer in the summer air; the sweeping hurricane
which tears up forests by the roots, or the blushing
promise of the spring's first flowers; the forked lightning, and the tramping thunder which shakes heaven
with deep pulsations, or the golden belts upon the body
of the bee, and the fairy song he chants among the
flowers; the trickling of molten metals into the fissures
of the earth, or the passage of an idea through the brain
of man; are dependent upon the separation and re-combination of various of these elementary principles; without the movements or metamorphoses of which, the
whole world would be one scene of darkness and desolation. Chemical laws operate upon the minute atoms of

which bodies are composed; and as all the atoms of matter have a spherical or globular form, the attractions and repulsions of atomic particles exhibit a close analogy to the attractions and repulsions of the worlds. It is possible, indeed, that there is but one attraction and one chemical law, and the phenomenon of an atom may be repeated in the dewdrop, in the bubble on the stream, and in the floating world. There is more poetry in the alembic and the test tube than the worldly dream about.

In one direction the earnest workers are probing the secrets of Nature, and unravelling one by one the mystic threads that run through all her fabrications; and in another, poet-minds are arranging and diffusing the facts which the former have made known, that all the world may become inheritors of the new possession, and dwell with increased joy on the contemplation of these new treasures of the Almighty's handiwork.*

If we trace back the history of our world into those remote eras of which the early rocks are records, we shall discover that the same chemical laws were operating then which control the changes of matter now. At one period the earth was a huge mass of fiery fluid, which, radiating or throwing off heat into space, gradually cooled, and became surrounded with a solid crust, entombing within itself a mere chaos of intensely heated materials, which now assert their existence in the shock

---

* "The Chemistry of the Seasons." By J. Griffiths, Author of "The Chemistry of the Four Elements," Chemical Lecturer to the Royal Family. London: John Churchill.

* "Chemistry, as exemplifying the Wisdom and Beneficence of God." By George Fownes. Ibid.

of the earthquake, and the awful outbreaks of volcanic
fires. In later ages, when the crust had cooled still
more, and the atmosphere let fall its showers, the still
heated surface, hissing and roaring with the contact of
the flood, was rent into enormous blocks, and dreadful
abysses; which still remain all over the world, and form
the wondrous monuments of an age of great convulsions.
Later still the seas gathered together, the rocky masses
were powdered into dust by the delicate fingers of the
dew and the shower, the green herbs sprang up, and the
monsters of the slimy deep appeared in obedience to the
Creator's fiat, and the whole earth became a home of
beauty in obedience to chemical law.   The ceaseless play
of the elements, and the mutations of the atoms, had
built up the whole into one gorgeous scene of luxurious-
ness; and man was awakened into being to render the
whole subservient to his wishes, and by tracing out the
harmonies of the natural world, to arrive at a more
exalted knowledge of his Maker.

The atom of charcoal which floated in the corrupt
atmosphere of the old volcanic ages, was absorbed into
the leaf of a fern when the valleys became green and
luxuriant; and there, in its proper place, it received the
sunlight and the dew, aiding to fling back to heaven a
reflection of heaven's gold; and at the same time to
build the tough fibre of the plant.   That same atom was
consigned to the tomb when the waters submerged the
jungled valleys.   It had lain there thousands of years,
and a month since was brought into the light again,
imbedded in a block of coal.   It shall be consumed to
warm our dwelling, cook our food, and make more

ruddy and cheerful the hearth whereon our children play; it shall combine with a portion of the invisible atmosphere, ascend upward as a curling wreath to revel in a mazy dance high up in the blue ether; shall reach earth again, and be entrapped in the embrace of a flower; shall live in velvet beauty on the cheek of the apricot; shall pass into the human body, giving enjoyment to the palate, and health to the blood; shall circulate in the delicate tissues of the brain; and aid, by entering into some new combination, in educing the thoughts which are now being uttered by the pen. It is but an atom of charcoal, it may dwell one moment in a stagnant ditch, and the next be flushing on the lip of beauty; it may now be a component of a limestone rock, and the next an ingredient in a field of potatoes; it may slumber for a thousand years without undergoing a single change, and the next hour pass through a thousand; and after all, it is only an atom of charcoal, and occupies only its own place wherever it may be.

It is from the unceasing interchange of the particles of matter that the living lustre of the world is born; it is the separation of one atom of water from one atom of starch which gives rise to the formation of sugar; and to this change, produced by the mutual influences of warmth and moisture, the germination of all seeds is due, and hence the continuance of vegetation. Neither the oaks of the forest, nor the grasses of the field, could ever have burst into their green beauty but for this simple change in the elements of their seeds.* The

* Seeds contain a large quantity of starch, a material best of all suited to resist the destroying influences to which seeds are sub-

M

maltster takes advantage of this, to produce that delicate
flavour in the barley which, when combined with the
intoxicating product of a second change in the sugar
itself, has proved the source of physical suffering and
social misery to millions.

If the imaginings of the early world were brilliant and
startling, the facts of modern chemists are embued with
a poetry more lofty still, while they have for their basis
the solid ground of truth, and stand separated by a wide
gulf from the phantasies of fiction. What Oriental
picture of aeriel temples, or rainbow daughters of the
sky, can for a moment be compared with the simple
chemistry of the atmosphere, or the rainbows themselves?
This soft, universal, azure medium in which the round
world swings, and which holds the clouds in its arms,
letting them fall drop by drop in fatness to the earth, or
that spanning archway of the angels, formed by millions
of separate particles of rain, each particle a prism, which
cuts up the rays of light into separate parts, and explains
their anatomy and their colours? What fable of old
can stand side by side with the fact that—

> " Each drop of water is a world, containing
>   Creatures more numerous than the men of earth ;
> The April shower upon the green tree raining,
>   To fresh creations in each leaf gives birth :
> Nature, her balance everywhere regaining,
>   New breathing things to form, leaves nothing dearth,—
> Spitzbergen's ice and Afric's sandy field
> To Nature's living mass their tribute yield ? "

---

ject; but which the young plant is unable to absorb into its tissues ;
hence the necessity, during germination, for its conversion into
sugar.

No! there is more wonder in truth than fable; more poetry in fact than fiction.

But there are revelations of this wonder-world of change more startling than these, and perhaps more truly poetic. The most obdurate and inflexible bodies seem destined by a law of their nature to work their way up through successive orders of being, till they reach the highest of them all; and when there, to fill a purpose essential to the very existence of man himself. Thus, without phosphorus, and sulphur, and potash, and lime, the human frame would be destitute of outline and power of locomotion, for with these materials its bones are formed; so also, without a supply of common salt, which is a compound of a brilliant metal and a poisonous gas, the alkaline character of the blood could not be maintained, and the frame would soon fall into corruption, and perish; and in like manner, without iron—the identical metal of which ploughshares and steam-engines are formed—life could not be sustained even for the shortest space of time; for, by the presence of the metal in the globules of the blood, that fluid maintains its brilliancy of colour, and is enabled to take up the vitalizing atoms of the air, and so continue the enjoyments of a happy existence. While still more wonderful, perhaps, are those discoveries by which Liebig has rendered himself immortal, and which reveal to us the chemical phenomena involved in the operations of the brain, and which indicate that the amount of phosphorus and nitrogenous principles, removed continually from the nervous system, are in direct proportion to the intensity and continuance of thought, and which

point to the immediate relation of the material to the
spiritual.

Passing from these things to matters less directly
associated with the phenomena of life, we find beauty
still predominant, and poetry of the most lofty character
the presiding idea. A dark surface absorbs more heat
than a light one; at the same time it radiates or parts
with heat more rapidly than a light surface. The
chemist exposes the backs of his hands to the noonday
sun; the one bare, and the other covered with a black
cloth. The uncovered hand will be at a temperature of
from 85 to 90 degrees, and the covered one at from 98
to 106 degrees. The black colour absorbs about 15
per cent. more heat than the white one, and yet the
covered hand is uninjured, while the other is scorched
and blistered; in this way, although apparently in opposition to the result required, has God provided for His
children who dwell under the fierce heat of the southern
sun. He has made them black, that they may live in
harmony with the golden sunshine above them, and not
as the objects of the white man's tyranny, when he for-
gets *his* God, and darkens the green wilderness with the
shadow of a devil.

There is poetry in such facts as these; and when the
human mind has achieved for itself a nobler inheritance
of wisdom than it now possesses, and true genius takes
the place of commercial craft, we shall find the poet and
the painter combining to do honour to the men by
whose labours these wonderful truths have been unfolded.
The picture of Faraday turning a ray of light from its
course by the power of a magnet, under the direction of

his own poet-mind, will be looked upon with profound reverence; and the names of Davy, Liebig, Berzelius, and Dumas, will adorn the poetical annals of generations now waiting to be born. The same scrutinizing power which detects ozone in the atmosphere, and in this way accounts for the peculiar odour of the electric spark; which traces out the analogy between that same atmosphere and nitric acid; which discovers the method of converting old rags into sugar, and sawdust into bread; which detects the service of the humble moss in cleaving and crumbling the rugged rocks on which it chances to grow, by means of the oxalic acid which its roots contain; which observes the effect of sunlight in elaborating the juices of the fruits, and makes the same sunlight a painter of pictures; which compounds a material which acts as an antidote to pain, and proves one of the greatest of auxiliaries in the service of humanity, under the name of chloroform; which not only finds

> "———— Tongues in trees,
> Books in the running brooks, sermons in stones;"

but travels up

> "—— Through the measureless fields,
> Where the silver moon and the comet wheels,"

and measures the magnitude of those lamps of God;—will deal with higher than physical things, and learn to attach its sympathies with a moral law; securing for itself a nobler salvation than from the choke-damp of a mine, and inheriting a purer religion than the worship of organic compounds.

Meantime, the elements wait on man, and combine to do him service; he has made matter subservient to his will, and in this conquest of the material by the immaterial, the world reads the idea of its advancing humanity. The lesson is one which humbles, because it points to a dependence on God, and suggests that there are regions into which the mind will yet have to enter to learn its spiritual duties, and connect them with its conquest of the world.

"In whatever light we consider these matters, the argument of benevolent design and contrivance, deduced from the obvious facts themselves, remains unaltered. The care and beneficence of the Creator is not less shown in the connexion He has established between physical and moral health. The labour which a man is obliged to exert to procure for himself the necessaries of life, is not less essential to the maintenance of a healthy tone of mind than of a sound and active condition of the bodily organism. No evil can be greater than the rust, alike of body and soul, which results from inactivity. The state of labour is the very condition of enjoyment; not, indeed, the excessive and slavish toil to which a very large portion of mankind have, by a most unfortunate combination of circumstances, been reduced; but that moderate and well-regulated labour of mind and body which conduces so much to the welfare of both, and which would be, under more favourable auspices, fully sufficient to impart comfort and abundance to all. If men only knew and felt how inseparably their own individual happiness is connected with the welfare and prosperity of their species; if those who have intellect and power,

and wealth at their disposal, could only be persuaded to
thrust aside the petty jealousies and cares, the idle
parade and prejudices of society, and join heart and
hand in the great work of human improvement, how
much might be effected! How much happier, and how
much better all might become, if a sound and universal
spirit of philanthropy were once awakened, capable of
embracing within its pale all orders and conditions of
men: considering them as they really are, the children of
one common Parent, bound together by the ties of
brotherhood, each having a special duty assigned to
him to perform, not independently of, but in conjunc-
tion with the rest, and exciting all to render each other
mutual assistance in surmounting the difficulties and
trials of this life of discipline and pupilage." *

* Fownes.

MEDITATIONS ON A BROOMSTICK.

" I am sent with broome before
To sweep the dust behind the doore."
—Midsummer Night's Dream.

SUNSHINE prosper thee, sweet lady-birch! Softest of
dews and holiest of showers fall upon thy tasselled sprays
and trembling foliage, and ruddiest of morning glances
break upon thy silver bark! And thou, bonny broom,
hiding thyself in the moorland hollows, how many belted
bees have visited thy ringlets since the spring began?
how many wanderers hath thy perfume solaced? over
how many aching heads hast thou shook thy rushy
branches, hushing the lone wayfarer into Elysian dreams
as he lay on the pliant moss beneath thee? It is in the
greenest of glens and the mossiest of woody nooks that
broomstaffs flourish,—on the healthiest of wild moorlands
that the bonny broom comes to birth. Blue and golden
flowers watch over them in infancy, and bearded oaks
bend above their lusty youth. A broomstick! Are
" proper people " shocked at the suggestion—to them—
of the vileness and scullery refuse which the broom is
used to sweep away? No matter—what is mere fuel to
them shall be philosophy to us; and with the reverent

stump of a superannuated besom before us, we will let
the caprice have its course, and see for once what suggestions may come from a broomstick.

Were you ever young?—of course you were, and
made your first triumph before family friends by trotting,
full speed, into the midst of little Jemima's muslin
friends astride a broomstick, and had at least a hundred
kisses from dear old Granny, who sat in the corner, and
vowed it was vulgar to trot broomsticks in doors, while
she secretly loved you all the more for it. There, too,
was the old Captain, in his skull-cap, and barnacles, and
purple nose, who gloried in a romp, and yet, for fear
of offending the young ladies, suffered innumerable pangs
when he said, "Charley, you're a naughty boy, sir!"
Well, that day has blended with the mists of memory,
and the broomstick is the only talisman to summon its
pictures to the present.

> "———From the age
> That children tread the worldly stage,
> Broomstaff, or poker, they bestride,
> And round the parlour love to ride."
>
> PRIOR.

The broomstick went the way of all toys—petted to-
day, burnt to-morrow; and to avenge the degradation
inflicted upon it then, its ghost came back to us at
school, inflicting stripes, and, in the compound of fools-
cap and pickled birch, torturing the affections as well as
the flesh, and making youth's season of song and sunshine one of wailings and tears. The pickled birch—
how barbarous in itself, and still more barbarous in its
frequent and untimed use, marking more the phases

of the teacher's temper than the dulness of the pupil's
mind. Stupid old doctrine! to imagine that what the
mind was incapable of grasping could be beaten into the
body—that to make an impression on the memory, blood
must trickle from the skin. Well, that time has past
also, and memory seems to hallow even those barbari-
ties; and we catch sight of the modern cane, so sparingly
used by men who have adopted love as an element
of education in the place of the old sottish spite. When
we see that, we sometimes imagine that things have
sadly degenerated since we went to school, for to us *now*
the pickled birch is a thing of poetry, if it be the poetry
of pain, while the cane is mere prose, and suggestive
of sugar-candy at the highest. But the birch has its
moral for after life,—

> "———As fond fathers,
> Having bound up the threatening twigs of birch.
> Onely to stocke it in their children's sight
> For terror, not to use; in time the rod,
> More mocked than feared."
>
> —*Measure for Measure.*

It is a serious question how far principle actuates us
to duty rather than fear of consequences. We are,
perhaps, little better than schoolboys, and feel the moral
birch of the world, and the stripes of conscience, in more
cases than we love its tasks and burdens : –

> "But though no more his brow severe, nor dread
> Of birchen sceptre awes my riper age,
> A sterner tyrant rises to my view,
> With deadlier weapon armed."
>
> JAGO, Edge Hill, b. iii.

But leaving private experience, which lacks largeness

and universality, let us take this crippled stump, worn as it is to a mere shadow in the service of that which is next to godliness. It was once a comely, upright, lusty broom, with a stout birchen body, and a green bushy head; and though ever standing with its one leg in the air, yet always ready to be useful, and run the risk of apoplexy for the service of a good cause. Its wretched stump, now reduced to the last extremity of vegetable suffering, was, in time gone by, a waving branch of lady-birch, and was clothed in silver bark, and tasselled over with delicate twigs and little fairy leaves. When spring came, it danced to and fro in the sunlight, and its shadow glided up and down the white ledges of the rocks, over which its pensile sprays peeped to see the water trickle down the ravine. Glorious was the lady-birch at any season; glorious, too, the hale green broom; the one gleaming in the morning sun, where the wood-pigeon built her nest, the other dressing the stony moor with yellow livery, and both living to make the world more beautiful. It is this birch* which supplies the best of wood for broomsticks, and whose young feathery branches often take the place of the green broom in the completion of the besom. In the Highlands they use it for tanning, for dyeing wool yellow; its bark supplies Highland candles and Norway bread; its wood, charcoal and printers' ink; its leaves, fodder for horses, kine, sheep, and goats; and its seed, food for that pretty

---

* BIRCH—Celt., *betu;* A. S. *birc;* Dutch, *berke;* German *berkan, birchenbaum;* Fr., *bouteau;* Ital. *betulla.* Pliny, I. 16, c. 18 speaks of the *mirabilis candor* of the birch. " It showeth wonderful white," says Holland.

songster of the wood, the aberdevine. The sap of the
birch makes the birch-wine of English housewifery, of
which those who know how to make it are not a little
proud :—

> " And though she boasts no charms divine,
> Yet she can make and serve birch-wine."
>
> WARTON.

It will flourish in English woods, and there is not a
wood worth rambling in which has not many of these
light, fairy creatures, pencilling the sky with their
trembling, spidery network of leaves and branches.   It
was this same birch from which the Gauls extracted
bitumen, and which the Russians now use to prepare the
celebrated Russian leather; which the carpenter finds
best of all wood for rafters, ploughs, spades, and carts;
which the Highland peasants use for harness, ropes, and
basket-work, and with which they symbolize, under the
name of *Betu* or *am beatha*, the clan of the Buchanans.
It is the same birch as that from which our poor imbecile
stump was cut, which forms the great forests of the
North; which climbs up rugged mountain-sides, to peep
over the precipices, and fling the light of vegetable grace
and beauty over the giant solitudes of snow.   It is the
same birch which fills us with forest lore when we see
its silvery stem towering up, straight as an arrow, to the
sky, and waving its plumes of pensile beauty in the
sunlight.

   The bonny broom,*

   * BROOM—A. S. *brom ;* Ger. *besen ;* D. *beren,* from D. *bremmen,*
because the seeds when ripe, burst from the pods with considerable
noise.   Ital. *scope garnate ;* Sp. *escobas ;* Rus. *metlii.*

" Yellow and bright as bullion unalloyed,
    Her blossoms "—

used by the good housewives of old to brush the crumbs
from the dressing-board, and the soiled sand from the
kitchen floor, is no less dear for its touches of memory,
and pictures of green imagery, than the lady-birch. It
grows on the moorland, where there is no shelter from
the blast of winter or the fierce heat of summer; where
drought, and swamp, and keenest frost have each unmiti-
gated vigour, and where the earth lies flat beneath the
blue sky, as if it had fallen prostrate, and had no friend
but the broom to cover it with garments. It is on the
dreary waste where the red deer loves to wander, and the
ptarmigan finds a home, that the bonny broom sprinkles
its round tufts of green, fresh as infancy amid the
fiercest frost—golden as day-break through the laughing
summer. There it creeps up and down the hills, and
amid the wild forest dells, far away from the haunts
of men, in company of creeping things, of gaps of sunshine, and of passing shadows.

" There lacked no floure to my dome,
    Ne not so much as floure of brome."
                                CHAUCER.

" In yonder greenwood blows the broom ;
    Shepherds, we'll trust our flocks to stray,—
Court Nature in her sweetest bloom,
    And steal from Care one summer day."*

It was the rushy branches of the broom which sup-

* Langhorne, "The Wilding and the Broom."

plied the old Greeks with ropes and cordage; * which
now provides the "simple sheep" with the best of food,
the cattle with the best of litter, the cottager with the
best of thatch—

(He made carpenters to make the houses and lodgynges of
great tymbre, and set the houses like stretes, and covered them
with rede and brome, so that it was lyke a lyttel towne.—
FROISSART.)—

and the wild bee with the most delicious honey. It is
the bonny broom which serves us as well whether we cut
its tufts for sweeping, for tanning leather, or for the
manufacture of coarse cloth; which is almost as useful
as hops in brewing; which furnishes a wood capable of
the most exquisite polish; which, in its ashes, gives
a pure alkali, and in its pods and blossoms, perfume
and medicine. Dr. Cullen and Mead both esteemed the
broom in cases of dropsy.

> "E'en humble broom and osiers have their use,
>   And shade for sheep and food for flocks produce."

It was the bonny broom which the Scottish clan of
the Forbes wore in their bonnets when they wished
to arouse the heroism of their chieftains, and which, in
their Gaelic dialect, they called *bealadh*, in token of its
beauty. It was this very broom from which the long
line of Plantagenets took their name, and which to the
last they wore on their helmets, crests, and family seal.
It was thus:—Fulke, Earl of Anjou, having committed
a crime, was enjoined by a holy father of the church,

* *Spartium*, from σπαρτον, cordage. *Genista spartium* has thick-
set rush-like twigs, very tough and fibrous.

to make a pilgrimage to the Holy Land by way of penance. He went, habited in lowly attire, with a sprig of broom in his hat to denote his humility. The expiation finished, he adopted the name of Plantagenet, from *Planta* and *Genista*,* the old name of the broom, and transmitted this to his princely descendants.† As an emblem of humility, too, it was worn by St. Louis, in 1234, on the occasion of his marriage with Margaret, eldest daughter of Raymond Berengarius, Count of Provence, and a new order of knights was instituted to commemorate the event. The motto of the order was " Exaltat humiles," and the collar of the order was made up of the flowers and seed-pods of the common broom, enamelled and intermixed with fleur-de-lys of gold. This *Ordre de la Geneste*, or Order of the Broom, continued till the death of Charles the Fifth.

> " Though the feeblest thing that nature forms,
>   A frail and perishing flower art thou;
> Yet thy race has survived a thousand storms
>   That have laid the monarch and warrior low.
> The storied urn may be crumbled to dust,
>   And Time may the marble bust deface;
> But thou wilt be faithful and firm to thy trust,—
>   The memorial-flower of a princely race.

Then hail to thee, fair Broomstick! herald of a thousand years, memorial of human trials, triumphs, and sufferings. Abide with us, oh! tough and well-tried

---

* GENISTA.—The Celt implies *small bush;* or from *genu, a knee,* from the bending of the twigs; or *geno, to produce,* on account of its abundance.

† Sandford's " Genealogical History."

friend; and now, too feeble for thy office of cleanliness, hint to us of the old Roman pageant, when the *noblesse* of Rome assembled, and the officers swept the hall with a green broom affixed to a sturdy broomstick. That was the honour paid by Roman patricians to intellect, energy, and virtue, which, however humble in their origin, had an equal chance with wealth and ancestral title in sharing the offices and honours of the state. The broom was as conscious of its dignity as the newly-elected councillors just lifted from the ranks of the people; and the moment its green and flowerless branches touched the floor of the assembly, it broke into golden blossoms, a mute symbol of the fertility of virtue.* Hail to thee! for all the legends of old Time thou bringest us, from the state processions of Rome down to the hanging of a broom at the door of a Russian maiden pining for a lover. The broomstick was the chosen Pegasus of the midnight hags, when, gliding like bats through the midnight, they laid plots and counterplots to involve poor human nature in the sufferings of superstition :—

> "Do not strange matrons mount on high,
> And switch their broomsticks through the sky,—
> Ride post o'er hills, and woods, and seas,
> From Thule to the Hesperides?" †

Verily they do; but they are only the embodied sins of men's consciences, which have taken shape and come

---

* This story is related by Marcellinus Ammianus. The custom of publicly sweeping the hall on occasion of those assemblies was maintained for a long period. The verbena and sagmina were carried by the Roman fetiales instead of the caduceus, as emblems of peace.

† Somerville, "Epistle to Allan Ramsay."

back again and again to stick pins in sinners' sides; stifle the babe that has been neglected by a harsh mother; fling cattle which want tending into bogs which ought to have been drained; spoil milk which has been left by sluttish dairy-maids; and jabber, scoff, and torture men in the reflected images of their own wickedness. Why always in the night, amid

> The dark sublime of extra-natural scenes?
> The vulgar magic's puerile rite demeans;
> Where hags their cauldrons, fraught with toads, prepare,
> Or glide on broomsticks through the midnight air?*

Why, but that all evil spirits are but human vices riding on the broomsticks of memory, and compounding in the cauldron of remorse the toads and snakes of retribution. The diseased mind peoples the night with hags and witches, and influences dire, as excuses—lame as they are—for its own wickedness and folly, which dare not face the daylight.

Some strange old customs suggest themselves in connexion with broomsticks. There is the salutation of the broom, which, like the throwing of old shoes for luck, has a smack of poetry in it, and recals Arbuthnot's remark on the brooming of servants, who, "if they came into the best apartment to set anything in order, were saluted with a broom." The hanging out of the broom at the mast-heads of ships offered for sale originated from that period of our history when the Dutch admiral, Van Tromp, with his fleet, appeared on our coasts in hostility against England; and to indicate that

* Amwell Scott—*On Painting.*

N

he would sweep the English navy from the seas, hoisted a broom at the mast-head of his ship. To repel this insolence the English admiral hoisted a horsewhip, equally indicative of his intention to chastise the Dutchman. The pennant, which the horsewhip symbolized, has ever since been the distinguishing mark of English ships of war.* The custom of hanging out the broom has another meaning in Russia; there it is the custom in the villages for parents who have marriageable and un-betrothed daughters to hoist a broom over the cottage doorway, that the swains may know where to seek for virgins.

Few associations of the broomstick are more inter-esting than those of the poor Flanders peasantry, who a few years ago came to this country in vast numbers, to penetrate into every nook and corner of every town in the land with the cry, "Buy a broom!" There are few of them left, and those few have modern airs and modern dress, which separate them entirely from the upright, short-coated, wooden-featured "Buy-a-brooms" of our infancy. We well remember the favourite ditty, sung in a plaintive voice at the parlour window, or on the doorstep,—

> A large one for a lady,
> A small one for a baby,
> Come buy, my pretty lady,
>   Come buy of me a broom,—

which touched many a heart, and secured for the singer many a basin of warm soup and lapful of kitchen-pieces,

* "Notes and Queries."

besides some halfpence for the immortal "brooms." In
the most squalid wretchedness, confined within the pre-
cincts of Whitechapel and Petticoat Lane, these modest
broom-merchants took up their abode, to sally forth every
morning into the genteel squares and by-streets of
London, having a bobbing courtesy ready the moment
a face was seen at a window, and a song at the first
appearance of a child. William Hone published an
engraving of them in his inimitable "Year Book," with
the following doggrel of his own composition attached
to the print :—

> "These poor ' Buy-a-broom ' girls exactly dress now
> As Hollar etched such girls two centuries ago;
> All formal and stiff, with legs only at ease,
> Yet, pray judge for yourself; and don't, if you please,
> Like Matthews's 'Chyle,' in his Monolo-play,
> Cry, ' *The Every-Day Book* is quite *right*, I dare say.'
> But ask for the print at old shops (they'll show it),
> And look at it ' with your own eyes,' and you'll *know* it."

We took Hone's advice, and found they *wouldn't*
"show it" at the print shops, and so waited for an
opportunity to see it at the British Museum, and then
were satisfied as to the identity hinted at by Hone.
Was ever dress so comical? The hair skewered into an
immense tight knob, and covered with a cap too small
for an infant, and tied under the chin; the body as
unbending as an oak tree, and apparently encased in
metal clothing set out in formal flutes, like a large bee-
hive or cone of carpentery; and the grey legs—oh,
for Bloomer trousers to hide such! our veritable broomstick is more flexible. But they were poor, and suffered

N 2

much; and though most comical illustrations of the
Flemish costume, there was always something sad about
them as they courtesied at the windows just before
dinner-time, and sniffed the odour of the kitchen with a
relish which told too plainly of their condition.

Of all the quaint literary allusions to the broom,
nothing can surpass the passage in Richter's story of
Lenette, in the fifth chapter of the "Thorn Pieces,"
where poor Lenette endures one of those many perver-
sions of thrift, for the exercise of which the crooked-
minded adventurer had such a peculiar gift. Those who
have read "Jean Paul" will see in this much more than is
apparent on the surface of the incident; it is, in fact, a
masterly illustration of crotchetty-mindedness :—" On
the morrow he sat in judgment on everything that was
going on behind him (continuing to write, however, at
the same time, but always worse and worse), and exam-
ined one thing after the other, in order to decide whether
or not it had the free pass of necessity. The writing martyr
endured much with tolerable fortitude; but when
Wendeline went into the bedroom, and swept the straw
under the green marriage *torus* with a long broom, this
last cross was too heavy for his shoulders. Besides, he
had read yesterday, in an old journal of natural history,
that the theologian, Johann Pechmann, could not endure
the sound of a broom, that the rustling of a broom
almost took away his breath, and that he had once fairly
taken to his heels and run away from a street-sweep who
chanced to push against him. Such reading had the
effect of making him more attentive to a similar case,
and at the same time more intolerant. Without rising

from his seat, he called out to the domestic sweep in his bed-chamber—'Lenette, pray don't scratch and scrape with that broom; it prevents me from thinking. There was once an old clergyman, named Pechmann, who would rather have been condemned to sweep the streets of Vienna himself, than to hear them swept; yes, who would even have preferred a flogging with the birch to its horrid whetting and grinding noise : and do you think I can have one sensible thought fit to appear before the compositor and printer, in the neighbourhood of this house-broom ? Only think a little of this, Lenette.'" *

Here our broomstick would have told its story, but that its fallen state is so suggestive of the fate of man, that we should lose the very pith and marrow of its teachings were we to lay down our pen without deducing this moral epilogue. The history of a broomstick is a fit emblem of the history of man; for its green vigour when flourishing in the woods, and its neglected and enfeebled state after a life of good services, are exact counterparts of the sunny freshness of early life and the imbecilities of age. The most useful labourers in the van of progress, those who sweep away the abuses of society, are not they who reap the largest rewards : poets, philosophers, and philanthropists fall friendless and penniless into old age, and, like worn out broom-sticks, are cast aside and forgotten; while the fawning and hypocritical too often feather their nests snugly, and retire from a world which they have defiled, into a retirement which laughs nobler souls to scorn.

* See also pp. 136, 142, of the English translation of the " Flower, Fruit, and Thorn Pieces."

Illustrations may be drawn from a thousand sources
to help out this meditation on a broomstick.   It would
not be too great a stretch of fancy to picture the Roman
Fetiales carrying a broomstick in place of the caduceus,
and thence to make a disquisition on the Verbena and
Saguina as kindred with the bonny broom.   "Kenealey
Brallagan on the Dienosophists" would furnish an
episode, and Wordsworth's quotations of the broom, in
his adulation of Brougham, would give excuse for a
chapter on the origin of Broom as an English surname.
We could then retreat upon Hogg's lines of the "Broom
sae Green" and Aird's "Buy a Broom," without fear
of wearying the reader.   But even a broomstick must
have an end; ours shall not end ingloriously, so this
paper shall conclude with a reproduction (*verb. et lit.*)
of a forgotten scrap of wit from the pen of that master
of satire, the immortal Dean Swift :—

A Meditation upon a Broomstick, and Somewhat Beside; of the
same Author's.

Utili dulci.

London : printed for *E. Curll*, at the *Dial and Bible*, against
St. *Dunstan's* Church, in *Fleet Street ;* and sold by *F. Harding*, at
the *Post Office*, in *St. Martin's Lane.*   1710.   Price 6d.

THIS single Stick, which you now behold Ingloriously lying in
that neglected Corner, I once knew in a Flourishing State in A
Forest, it was full of Sap, full of Leaves, and full of Boughs; but
now, in vain does the busie Art of Man pretend to Vye with Nature,
by tying that wither'd Bundle of Twigs to its sapless Trunk: 'tis
now at best but the Reverse of what it was, a Tree turn'd upside
down, the Branches on the Earth, and the Root in the Air; 'tis
now handled by every Dirty Wench, condemned to do her Drudgery,
and by a Capricious kind of Fate, destin'd to make other Things
Clean and be Nasty itself: At Length worn to the Stumps in the

Service of the Maids, 'tis either thrown out of Doors, or condemned to its last use of kindling Fires.   When I beheld this, I sighed, and said within myself,

Surely Man is a Broomstick;

Nature sent him into the World Strong and Lusty, in a Thriving Condition, wearing his own Hair on his Head, the proper Branches of this Reasoning Vegetable, till the Axe of Intemperance has lopt off his Green Boughs, and left him a withered Trunk: He then flies into Art, and puts on a *Peruque*, valuing himself upon an Unnatural Bundle of Hairs, all covered with Powder, that never grew on his Head; but now should this our *Broomstick* pretend to enter the scene, proud of those *Birchen* Spoils it never bore, and all covered with Dust, tho' the sweepings of the Finest Lady's Chamber, we should be apt to Ridicule and despise its Vanity, partial Judges that we are! of Our own Excellencies, and other men's faults.

But a *Broomstick*, perhaps you'll say, is an Emblem of a Tree standing on its Head; and pray what is Man, but a topsy-turvy Creature, his Animal Faculties perpetually a Cock-Horse and Rational; His Head where his Heels should be; grovelling on the Earth, and yet with all his Faults, he sets up to be an universal Reformer and Corrector of Abuses, a Remover of Grievances, rakes into every Slut's Corner of Nature, bringing hidden Corruptions to the Light, and raises a mighty Dust where there was none before, sharing deeply all the while, in the very same Pollutions he pretends to sweep away: His last Days are spent in Slavery to Women, and generally the least deserving; 'till worn to the Stumps, like his Brother *Besom*, he's either kickt out of doors, or made use of to Kindle Flames, for others to warm Themselves by.

THE SEASON OF BROWN LEAVES.

Race after race of leaves and men
  Bloom, wither, and are gone;
As winds and waters rise and fall,
  So life and death roll on.
And ever as the ocean heaves
  So life and death roll on;
Drop, drop into thy grave, old leaf,
  Drop, drop into thy grave."

ELLIOTT.

THE spring time came with green and gladness, and the summer followed with its rosy flowers and fruits; and now, after so brief a season of exuberance, the green things fade and die, and the joy of the year withers with the browning of the leaf. For a few moments, ere the branches are stripped of all their russet glories, let us reflect on these autumn changes as they hint of analogies in life and nature, and suggest ideas of hope and duty.

That view of the world which represents the outward and material forms, as perishable symbols of imperishable ideas, is that which should guide our first steps into this region of comparison and speculation. Nature is a series of progressions or unfoldings, and all her creatures are representative of ideas. The human form sinks into decay, and perishes; the individuals pass from existence one by one; they do not live as individual types, but collectively, as representatives of Man. So the year, with its manifold changes and unfoldings, its many forms, and colours, and voices, has its spiritual and moral analogies, which are infinitely more poetical and instructive than any of its details of animate or inanimate beauty. All through the universe the same few laws peep out under an unity of expression which makes them all parallel. Spring, summer, autumn, winter; infancy, youth, manhood, age. The seasonal unfoldings of the individual; the spring, summer, autumn, and winter changes of the man are seen again in the progress of the race; and the ages of gold, silver, bronze, and iron are but other modes of expressing the same fact. The tree of life has its budding and blossoming, its fruitage and decay; and one simple thread of related harmony runs through all its metamorphoses.

The leaves that brown now, and fill the forest paths with pliant matting, from which, as we tread the solitude, a moist odour arises, were in their day rife with life and luxuriance; and having accomplished their work, go back to the soil whence they sprang, to supply the nourishment of another generation. All things change together as the autumn air creeps over the fields. The sun sinks slanting to an early bed; and the day, like the human heart after the shadows of many years have gathered upon it, is less merry than of yore. The golden corn becomes a grey stubble, the green tree a naked brush of branches, and death comes up from the grave to breathe a freezing air upon the world, and to

usher in the days of silence. Yet these leaves, which
flutter into autumn graves; this grey stubble, which
stands where waved the green before, are the harbingers
of spring-life yet to come, and the types of an unceasing
series of renewals which eternity may develop, but
cannot exhaust. Man gathers the harvests, and survives
many generations of falling leaves; and the very wind
that beats the trees in their waning life, is to him as a
breath from that blooming summer beyond, in which the
growths of these years shall still strive for completion.
He looks complacently on this flowing of the ages, and
as these shadows of destruction weave around him, he
sees the rainbow of hope spanning the dark gulf between
the summer here and the summer there, and borrows
from the joy of this the glory of his future years. What
is this, then, but the law of progress, of development for
ever of those possibilities which are locked up within the
soul of man, and which the changes of the seasons teach
and the cycles of the ages help to perfect? Let it once
be known that the soul of man is capable of never-end-
ing youth, and this browning of the leaf is a lesson of
hope rather than fear, and the story of Æon is seen to
be repeated for ever and ever. When the spring of the
world was here, and the creatures were creeping up to
higher forms by the same law of development, the grey
mosses, sown on barren rocks by singing winds, crept up
and down the sea-beat solitudes, and there was no man
to watch their growth, no man to appreciate their beauty.
The grasses came and waved their silken tassels, and the
forests followed with their great brown arms and leafy
fingers; and when the turf rippled into waves of green

and gold, the master of the wild appeared, breaking the
silence of the desert, and singing the story of the ages.
The civilization which now puts out its buds and shoots
of moral beauty is but a part of the same series of unfoldings which in the primal age covered the granite
with greenness, and now begets the consciousness that
man, like the world on which he lives, is made to grow
—to grow.

In this partial life, in which shreds and patches of
existence get mistaken for the full completion of being,
the browning of the leaf is fraught with sadness, and the
death which follows seems a thing of gloom. Yet, in
nature, death is as beautiful as life, as needful, and for
that reason as good. The decaying leaves form odorous
mounds from which, in the spring, new generations of
things beautiful will burst, and without which no troops
of flowers would arise to sweeten the breath of another
summer. The dead bird, the dead insect, are each fitted
to form the nourishment for other forms of life, and fill
a place in the world which they could not occupy when
living. From out of all this death and destruction,
nature weaves the warp and woof of future fabrications,
and new races spring, Phœnix-like, from the ashes of
those which have expired. Why, then, fill the house with
mourning and the eyes with tears when Death shows his
presence in the home ? Is he not also one of God's ministering angels, sent to bless rather than to ban, and, like
other ministrants, filling a place in a series of changes
which shall never end ? Look at the tree, it stands
upright in the sun, and confronts heaven as if worthy of
the light which drops down from the blue ; while man

creeps into towns and hides his head from the daylight,
too conscious as he is that the tree shames him. The
tree has filled its place, has developed all its energies to
their full possibility; while in man the will has usurped
the instinct, and the faculties remain unfolded. Therefore the tree fears not death, while man weeps before the
falling of the leaf, and surrounds the death of his kindred
with emblems of contrition and sorrow. But in nature
man is no better than the tree, and the individual, of
whatever tribe, is of no value but as a fragment of the
type on which the race is built. Hence the tree has all
the elements of growth within and around it, and as it
has no will to draw it aside, it grows up to the limit
of these possibilities. When, as a member of its
race, its work is done, it falls, rots, and becomes the
food of successive plants and creatures; and there is
no weeping in the wood, no weeds of sorrow in the
solitude.

Thus, in reality, there is no death; and that which we
regard as the cessation of existence, and which the
browning of the leaf teaches us with shame and weeping,
is only one of many changes through which all the
types must pass, as they fulfil the universal law which
requires them to grow—to grow. And because man has
all the faculties of all the creatures combined, together
with a will which allows of no limit to its choice, a mind
which knows no limit to its power, death is still less a
truth to him, who can transmit the faculties of the
inward as well as the outward life, and perpetuate, even
in dying, the chain of circumstances through which he
has already passed. This civilizing, railroad building,

freedom-loving race of beautiful souls, are only the fruits
which hang on the branches of the tree of human
history, and which, in their turn, become the food of
generations which are to follow them. Each man lives
to enjoy that which past ages of suffering and trial have
procured for him, and suffers in his turn that the next
may derive happiness from his scars and trials. Thus
all the aims of all the ages are locked in this, and each
individual man carries within him the germs of an
infinite progression.

But this will, which wars with instinct, which draws
him from the wood where he had learnt to worship, and
thrusts him into the city where he may learn to swear,
is also a thing of nature, a part of the being which claims
its possession; and if now acting in opposition to his
aboriginal impulses, and impelling him to deeds which
his moments of high sanity—when instinct alone speaks
—proclaim false to his nature as a whole, acts thus only
that it may one day harmonize with his whole life, and
become the helpmate of his highest gifts and powers. In
the child, where instinct acts almost alone, the aims are
pure, and there is no food for contrition; in the man,
where the will is paramount, and the instinct but a
secondary trait, the soul is covered with blots, and
embittered with infinite compunctions. Therefore, for
the soul which dwells within this clay, the ages have all
passed as successive generations of leaves, the browning
and falling of which were necessary to the perfection of
the type running through and surviving them; and for
the purposes of this day and hour, the brown leaves
of the human life, the perishing purposes of the human

spirit, exist but as materials for that future juvenescence, when the will and the intellect shall act together.

The history of man, no less than the history of nature, teaches this lesson of evolution. Wrapped up in the oval bud of spring are the blossoms and fruits of the summer; and in the impulsive heart, beating in harmony with the instinctive nature of the primæval man, are enfolded the acts of his illimitable successors. The shepherd-life, with its simplicity and peace, is seen again in the radiant face of the infant, and the violet tenderness of the spring. The age of chivalry, with its costly pomp, its clang and clash of arms, its great deeds of daring and sacrifice, break out in the hours of individual passion when manhood has not yet set its seal on the brow, and when the outward semblance of heroism is mistaken for the supporting and sustaining ardour which springs from manly determinations. The first flush of summer has it, too, when the fruits are yet unripe, and storms dash in and out between the leaf-laden branches. But the autumn and the browning leaf must come, and it is already here around us. Who, then, is worthy to die—worthy as the leaves are, all of whose duties have been fulfilled? Who is worthy to convert body and soul into a soil for the growth of the next generation of men, whose bodies are to be formed out of the elements of ours—whose spirits are to be fed with the aims, and hopes, and knowledge we have nurtured, and which we must bequeath to them by an inevitable necessity?

Who among us has been living all these years in vain, watching the greening and the browning of the leaves, without taking heed that his autumn must come, and that winter must heap snow on his tomb, as upon the graves of fallen leaflets? Of whom may it be said, in the words of Ovid—"Actis ævum implet, non segnibus annis." The listless heart, the idle brain, the lips that have breathed curses, are to live for ever; and the curses, and the evil passions, and the cherished hate, are to live also, and to grow as all things grow, through generation after generation. My child there has my face, my passion, my hope, my moral turpitude. Shall I not blush, then, that long ago I did not root out my sins and failings, and supplant them with a nobler growth of hopes and aspirations, that such only might break out in him, and that for his sake the browning of the leaf might find me worthy of the blessed hand of death? For, truly, the destruction of things is only a necessary step in this endless growth on growth, and Death is himself the most potent of creators.

If there were no browning of the leaf, how lost to hope and heart would be the fate of man! If the bud, once unfolded, had an individual life for ever, how localized, cramped, dwarfed, were those energies which now climb higher and higher on this ladder of created souls, to reach Heaven at last by that upward growth which death entails as a beautiful necessity! If the primal earth, with its unformed soil, its dreary swamps, and creatures in the first stage of development still revolved in sunlight and darkness, how aimless, hopeless, and stagnant were the frame of Nature! Yet, the moment that succession supplants this stationary life, every pulse of the world, every change of the seasons,

becomes an item in the universal progress, and Nature
stands in the presence of the Deity as a being endowed
with hopes and aspirations which, throughout eternity,
shall be ever developing, and at every phase claiming
closer kindred with the Divine. What to man this death,
but a pledge of his eternal endurance, and a warning of
the duties of the "eternal Now?" As the ages have passed
through phases to higher and higher growths, so shall
the individual, so shall the social circle, so shall the
nation and the race. Every age and every man has
lived to represent a thought, and the universal man is
embodied in the growth of all the individuals through all
the ages of their lifetime. It is but the browning of
the leaf. When Nature has attained perfection in one
type, she will not tolerate less perfection in another, but
raises each creature, step by step, into new perfections;
and as forests fall that more stately forests may flourish
upon their decay, so the conditions of humanity pass
and change, that others more noble may be raised
above them, and so on for ever. Greece built her
temples upon the ashes of Persian and Egyptian magnificence; Rome caught up and diffused the fire which
had burned upon the altars in the fanes of Greece;
and Europe has risen with its civilization, its poetry, its
moral grandeur, upon the ruins of the nations of the
past. Where blood flowed, and thrones crumbled to
dust, the green grass waves: and the man of science
learns, from its flexible sprays, the dependence of man
and nature upon God, and the necessity of both to
grow—to grow. It is only the browning of the leaf,
Autumn decay, and Spring revival; the perishing of

one tribe for the prosperity of the next; the transmission of the same sap, blood, body, and soul, through endless tribes of creatures, of which man is one, growing and growing through these multiform developments to a perfection which shall never cease.

FLORAL ANTIQUITIES OF THE EAST.

"Twining the floweret in her rainbow wreath,
    She bore it, followed by the golden beam,
    To bygone ages and to distant climes."

SOMETHING of the beautiful yet remains to man, something of the fair and good, to cheer the hours of the present, and serve as emblems of the future and the past. We talk of the gone-time as if dreams and shadows only peopled it—as if the spirits of the great moved amid forms of darkness—dealing only with their dreams; while we look forward through a hope whose atmosphere is rosy, and with many beatings of the heart and pulse, believe in the reality of the future. Yet the present is but another leaf unfolded on the tree of time; the future will be but a leaf added, and added too, as leaves are out of doors, certainly, but imperceptibly. The present is the only reality, and love as we may those reveries in which the past comes back in shadow, we may at least receive it as a reality for the time, and go back to it over a path of flowers. The future is a cloud, the past is a cloud also; but in it there are gaps of sunshine, and between its wreathing folds we see glimpses of men and women—breathing forms of thought—here

struggling, there embracing; here pining under false
faith, and despotism, and savagery; there giving the soul
room to grow in an atmosphere of love, kneeling together
before shrines of light. There are burning sands and
rocky heights, and giant caverns where darkness crouches,
and blood trickles unseen. Temples, altars, and sicken-
ing cities where Death holds carnival; and over all are
wreaths of flowers, twining, creeping—in thick bowers
of fragrance, in lovely forms of green leafiness, in mossy
slopes, and shady coolness and delightful umbrage.
"Flowers foreshadow the future," but they guide us
through the past; lead the way into its dark recesses,
and point us to the birthplaces of the holiest influences.
Strangely, but truly, do flowers mingle in all the events
and passions of the world, refreshing the heart of man
with their greenness, and binding life and love together
by plaited wreaths of beauty. Strangely, but truly, do
these plaited wreaths unwind from columns which have
crumbled in their embrace; strangely do they fall off,
sere and withered, from the stony faces of the temples
and idols of the past; and more strangely still, a fresh
group spring up there to hide the ghastly ruins from the
sun, and to throw over the white bones and powdered
granite a warm hue of life, making the two ends of the
world meet as they do often on the cheek of beauty—
life, fresh and beautiful, above; Death, with his stony eye,
lurking underneath.

And yet those fallen altars, those crumbling monuments, those lands dyed with the blood of the brave,
and sprinkled with fragments as with flakes of snow,
still hide under their coverings of flowers the records of

many generations of men, with whose lives such flowers as those were twined, and of whose acts, and thoughts, and impulses, those very flowers can repeat the history.

It was one of the redeeming traits of the old mythologies, that floral ornaments, sacrifices of herbs, and allegorical combinations of fruits and flowers were regarded as aids to worship, or as symbols of the Divine idea, or even as mediators between humanity kneeling in the dust, and the Supreme Being, throned upon a million worlds. India, with its memorials of blood, and tyranny, and fanaticism, looks even less fearful when its rites are seen to be surrounded with these mute poetic forms. The mighty Bhyroe, the Assura or evil spirit, gains something in the midst of his enormities, when his granite idol is seen adorned with flowers,* the offerings of the kneeling children of Brahma. The sacrifice of fire to all the gods, the third of the five great Hindoo sacrifices, with its impressive solemnity, becomes still more solemn when the priest, after many prayers and holy services, places the vessel containing the sacred fire on the spot consecrated to it ; and then sprinkles around it the green blades of the cusa grass,† and sitting on the ground, pronounces the name of the earth inaudibly. Then, after reciting a sacred mantra, more blades of cusa are placed around the fire, the sacred butter is poured upon the flame, and he sits down with his face towards the east, and meditates on Brahma, the Lord of the Creation.‡

* Jablouski, "Egyptian Pantheon."
† Poa Cynosuroides.
‡ Colebrooke on the Religion of the Hindoos.—" Asiatic Researches," Vol. vii., No. 8.

The grass is the key to the symbol, and while hinting that man is still close to nature, upholds the mystery of a consecration of the powers of the world, as visible emblems of the Lord of all things.

Thus, through all the mythologies and symbol images of the old world, the green things continually peep out, adding to the wild beauty of these aboriginal forms, which, begot in the infancy of the world, are full of that freshness of feeling, that love of allegory and symbol, which characterizes infancy in the individual man. In these devotions there is a largeness of character which shames the contracted piety of our own day and generation, and much as we may dread the features of those ancient faiths, and shrink, horror-struck, from their details of barbarity and absurdity, we must at least confess that faith had there a home. The legend of Rawana the good Brahmin, exhibits, in a powerful light, the sincerity of that age of idols. It was the wont of Rawana, to offer daily one hundred flowers to the god Ixora; and once, to prove his zeal, the god secretly took from the sacrifice one of the flowers, and then complained that the gift was too small. Rawana counted the flowers, and finding only ninety-nine, offered one of his eyes to supply its place; when the god, convinced of his piety, restored the flower, and blessed him for his confiding faith.

Soma, the moon, is, in the Indian mythology, as in those of the northern nations of Europe, a male deity; he is "born of the sun," and is the king of herbs and flowers. "Rain is produced from the moon," says the Rigveda; * and a Hindoo commentator on this passage

* "Asiatic Researches," Vol. viii., p. 406.

says, "Rain enters the lunar orb, which consists of water." This connexion of the moon with the changes of the weather is recognized by Shakspere, who calls her the "Governess of the Floods,"[*] and is a meteorological tradition. The Hindoos represent Soma as the god of showers and green things; when he descends in his car, drawn by antelopes, bearing in his bosom a sleeping fawn, he typifies the irregular motion of the moon itself, and the dependence of vegetation upon it for the necessary fluctuations of the weather. Barbarous as were the old Hindoo rites, the laws of hospitality were sacred among them; and he who planted a tope or grove, or opened a well and surrounded it with trees for the shade and refreshment of the traveller, was held for ever after a descendant of the gods. Timul Naik, Raja of Tanjora, became a deity for having built a choultry or resting-place for pilgrims, near the pagoda of Mandura; and to the neglect of these acts of benevolence by the wealthy British residents of Hindostan, the difficulties of Christianity have been increased tenfold—the Christian being regarded as selfish and uncharitable.

Among the plants sacred to the religion of the Hindoos, the cusa or cusha grass holds an important place. It is the poa cynosuroides of Linnæus : its leaves are long, acutely jagged downwards, but smooth on the other parts, and so sharp and tapering as to furnish the Hindoos with a favourite metaphor, in which it represents acuteness of intellect. The fruit-stalk of this grass rises about two feet from the ground, and is terminated by a

* *Midsummer Night's Dream.*

panicle, or head composed of brilliant blood-red flowers.*
To its beauty it doubtless owes its sacred character, for
the Hindoos suppose every object to be animated by a
spirit or divinity, and those which are most excellent or
remarkable, to be inhabited by spirits of the highest
order, or by gods. The blood-red colour of the flowers
of the cusa is frequently assigned as the origin of its
use in sacrifices; though Sir William Jones, the highest
authority on such a subject, believes that its name of cusha
is derived from Cush, the father of the Hindoo race.; and
hence it is regarded in the rites of Brahma as a memorial of the patriarch-father of the people.† The Cushites,
or descendants of Cush, came into Egypt under the
name of Aurilæ and Shepherds, as also Ethiopians;
hence Egypt also inherited that name. The Cushites,
styled Æthiopes, were the original inhabitants of India,
and wherever any portion of the history of the Cushites
appears, the name of India will be found likewise.‡ The
reverence in which this grass was held originated the
Indian custom of biting a blade of grass in token of
submission, and in asking for quarter in the field of
battle—

> " Her spear, not e'en Mahisha dare despise :
> The grass is bitten by her enemies." §

The cusa was also used in the preparation of the novi-
ciate for the pronunciation of the most holy word in the
creed of India. "Brahma milked out, as it were, from

---

* " As. Res." iv.   " Martyn Millar's Dict."
† " Diodorus Siculus," i. 17.   " Bryant's Analysis," iii. 212.
‡ " Philostrati vita Apollon," iii. 125.
§ " Metam. of Sona," v. 878.   " St. John's Indian Archipelago," i.

the three Vedas, the letter A, the letter U, and the letter
M; which form by coalition the tri-lateral monosyllable"
Aum,[*] pronounced Om, which is "the symbol of God,
the Lord of created beings." Each of the three compound letters of this word has its mysterious signification.
The first denotes Brahma, the second Vishnu, and the
third Siva. This syllable is never pronounced by the
Hindoos, except inaudibly, or, as it were, inwardly, and
never without many vigils and solemn preparations. "If
he have sitten on cushions of cusa, with their points
towards the east, and be purified by rubbing that holy
grass in both his hands, and be further prepared by three
suppressions of the breath, he may then fitly pronounce
Om."[†] This term appears to have originated the
Egyptian Om, the sun, and Omphi, an oracle, or presage
of futurity. Plutarch [‡] says ομφις was the name of an
Egyptian deity. The true rendering, according to
Bryant,[§] is Omphi or Amphi, from Ham, who was
worshipped as the Sun or Osiris. The mountains where
these oracles were delivered were called Har-al-Ompi,
from which the Greeks obtained Olympus, or from its
oracular prerogatives, ορος Ολυμπου. Among the Arme-
nians the same was called On, Eon, or Aon; hence it
was that Ham, who was worshipped as the sun, got the
title of Amon, and Ammon, and was styled Baal-Hamon.
It is said of Solomon that he had a vineyard at Baal-
Hamon,[||] a name probably given to the place by his
Egyptian wife, the daughter of Pharaoh.

<hr/>

* "Menu.," chap. ii. 76.　　　† Ibid, ii. 76.
‡ "Isis and Osiris."　　　§ "Analysis," i. 235.
|| Canticles, viii.

Another grass, called Durva,* is also held as sacred, and, in the mysteries of the temple, regarded as the symbol of fecundity. Its flowers, when in their perfect state, are amongst the most lovely objects in the vegetable world. Viewed through a microscope, they appear like clusters of minute rubies and emeralds in constant motion, and with innumerable changes of light and colour. It is the sweetest and most nutritious pasture for cattle, and so readily propagated by its creeping roots, that lands sown with pieces of them become completely swarded in a single season. Its extraordinary powers of increase render it an emblem of the reproductive powers of nature. In the worship of the divine Chrishna, or Heri, as he is termed by the poet Jayadeva,† the plant represents—in connexion with forms which to Europeans appear grossly licentious, but which, to the devout Hindoo, are holy allegories—the producing powers of the universe, the endless source of Nature and of Being.

Another plant, which the idolatrous worshippers of Brahma venerate, is the vata, or sacred fig, of which there are several varieties.‡ These are all holy plants, the pippala, or ficus religiosa, being the most sacred of them all.§ This species has perhaps a higher claim than any other to be regarded as sacred, on account of its curious growth, and the manner in which it extends

* Agrostis linearis of Linnæus.
† "Gitagovinda."
‡ Ficus religiosa, Ficus Bengalensis, and Ficus Indica, are the principal.
§ "As. Res.," iv. 27.

itself over the soil.   Its branches spread very wide,
about eighteen or twenty feet from the stem, and then,
bending down, the extremities thicken, and continually
approach nearer to the earth; when they reach the
ground they put forth roots, and each branch becomes a
stem or trunk, growing to the size of the largest
European oaks or elms.   The branches having thus
become trees, again shoot out branches bending down,
and rooting as before, still extending themselves, often
till the whole plant covers a very large space of ground.
One of these grove-like trees, growing on an island in
the Nerbudda river, about ten miles from Barouch, in
the province of Guzerat, has three hundred and fifty
principal stems, each as large as timber trees; and these
occupy a space two thousand feet in circumference, and
the branches, whose hanging extremities have not yet
reached the ground, extend much farther.   This tree
was once much larger than it is at present, for many of
the stems have been carried off by the floods of the river,
which have washed away part of the soil of the island.
The natives affirm, that it is three thousand years old,
and very possibly it may be; since, when any of the
older central stems decay and leave a vacant space, this
is in time re-occupied by fresh stems, produced by the
branches growing and rooting, as in the outer side of
the grove.   A plant possessing such properties as these
may be justly termed immortal.   Sanctity is very probably ascribed to this tree, because of its aptness to
represent the emanation of living things from the parent,
or creator, Brahma, who, having received the principle
of life from the great supreme Brahme, produced, by a

succession of agents, all the worlds, and all creatures, both animate and inanimate.* The Brahmins, however, assign a reason for the sanctity of this plant more suited to the understanding of the vulgar; and affirm that Vishnu, the preserver, was born under its shade. Under this legend is couched an ingenious allegory, significative of the salutary shade afforded by its branches, impervious to the rays of the sun. On account of the reputed sanctity of the tree, pagodas or temples are commonly erected beneath, or contiguous to its shade; in some instances, one of these trees is planted within the area of the principal court of the pagoda.† The Yogis, or religious ascetics, practise their austerities near it for the same reason; and any injury done to a twig or leaf is considered as a crime scarcely less atrocious than murder. Both the other species of the ficus, though less remarkable in their growth than the ficus Indica, resemble it in the rooting of their extreme branches, and are held sacred, probably, for that very reason; though some ascribe the sanctity of the ficus religiosa to the brown colour of the female flowerets, which bears some allusion to the preserver Vishnu.

But the most sacred of plants in the Indian mythology is the lotos, equally revered by Hindoos, Egyptians, Chinese, and Javanese, and associated with the most remarkable events in their cosmogonies, traditions, and creeds. In the religious services, and in the Sanscrit hymns and legends, the lotos is a frequent subject of simile and comparison. Lacshmi, the goddess of plenty, the sacti or wife of the protector Vishnu, is sometimes known by the names of Pedma and Camala, in allusion to the holy and increasing lotos. The author of the "Metamorphoses of Sona," frequently uses it to help out his classical allegories; describing the charms of Nerbudda, he says,

> "See, graceful wave, the lotos stalk her arms;
> Strive not, vain bracelet, to improve her charms;
> Fair lotos flowers her taper fingers glow,
> Tinged bright by lacsha,* like each slender toe."

This, like many others in the above poem, is borrowed from the "Gitagovinda"—"Madhava binds on her arms, graceful as the stalks of the water-lily [lotos], adorned with hands glowing like the petals of its flowers, a bracelet of sapphires." In the description of Deva, the lover of Nerbudda, the image occurs in a more beautiful form, in allusion to the powdered appearance of the lotos flower—

> "Light, graceful from his waist the jammah flows,
> Thus on the lotos blue the gold dust shows."

And in another passage, where Nerbudda despatches her slave, Johilla, to observe if the Deva be coming "in due array," she commands her to observe if he be

> "Such as becomes Nerbudda's birth and fame."

Commanding her to note,

> "If, lion-like, his port be bold and brave;
> If the blue lotus blossom on his face;
> If his form wear the palm's aspiring grace."

---

* Another wood-nymph pressed the juice of lacsha, to dye her feet exquisitely red.—*Sacontola*, Act. iv., scene 1.

The history of the lotos, though of highest importance as a key to many of the symbols and ceremonies of antiquity, is surrounded by many difficulties; yet this difficulty arises not in the fabulous details to which this plant is related, but in the intense reality of its uses and associations. Hindostan is the birthplace of the lotus, as it is also of the chief features in classical tradition and history. The lotos of Indian differs from that of Grecian, and that of Grecian from that of Roman mythology; though the lotos of India is the truly sacred plant from which the others derive both name and literary importance, and sacred investments. In Egypt the plant known as the lotos is the same in kind as that revered in India, and is a species of water-lily, called, in botany, *nymphæa*. The lotos of the Greek and Roman writers is falsely so called, for, of the true nature of the lotus they were unacquainted. Herodotus, however, who is generally correct in questions of fact where he gives a statement on the authority of his own experience, most correctly describes the lotos of Egypt as a lily of the nymphæa species. Its botanic name is traceable to its place of growth, as it flourishes in bays and inlets of fresh water, and on the broad waters of great rivers, where a rich mud lies near the surface. The Greeks, borrowing their idea of the lotos from Homer, describe it as the produce of a shrub. The lotos of Homer, however, is distinct from that of ancient India and Egypt, and it is slightly probable that, when Homer sang, it was known in Greece only by name. It could not have been the Egyptian water-lily which formed the bed of Jupiter and Juno, according to Homer; nor

could the horses of Achilles have regaled themselves
upon its herbage. It could not not have been any
species of nymphæa which so enchanted the companions
of Ulysses when they landed on

> "The land of lotos and the flowery coast;"

For, in describing the resources of the inhabitants of
this region, the poet says—

> "The *trees* around them all their fruit produce,
> Lotos the name, divine, nectareous juice."[*]

Ovid makes the same mistake, or rather adopts an
error which had become very prevalent in his day; for,
in his elegant fable of Dryope, he derives the name
of the lotos from the nymph who escapes from the law-
less lust of Priapus :—

> "Not distant far a watery lotos grows;
> The spring was new, and all the verdant boughs,
> Adorned with blossoms, promised fruits that vie
> In glowing colours with the Tyrian dye.
> *   *   *   *   *
> Upon the tree I cast a frightful look,
> The trembling tree with sudden horror shook.
> Lotos, the nymph (if rural tales be true),
> As from Priapus' lawless lust she flew,
> Forsook her form; and fixing there, became
> A flowery plant, which still preserves her name."[†]

---

* Pope is inclined to believe that it is this kind of lotos which
the companions of Ulysses tasted, and which was the reason why
they were overcome with it; for, being a wine, it intoxicated them.
† Lotis, or Lotus, a beautiful nymph, daughter of Neptune.
Dryope, a virgin, Æchalia, beloved by Apollo, and afterwards
married to Andræmon, was said to have been changed into a lotos.

There Ovid describes the lotos as a tree with " verdant boughs ;" and Theophrastus, in his fourth book, makes reference to it in similar terms, describing it as a tree ; but, in his details, he is more correct, where he describes its fruit as resembling a bean, and makes reference to it as an immortal plant—an idea essentially Indian in character.   Strabo, in his seventeenth book, also refers to it, and states that Syrtes, on the Mediterranean, as well as Menynx, were said to be lotophagitis.   The compass of the gulf, which modern geographers represent as composed of two immense sand-banks, comprised, according to Strabo, about sixteen hundred furlongs, the breadth of the mouth being six hundred ; and it was extremely fertile in the growth of the lotos.   But Strabo, whose accuracy is seldom impeachable, represents the lotos as a tree, and says that Menynx was the country of the lotophagi, or those that feed on lotos trees, of which Homer makes mention ; and further informs us that monuments of Ulysses, as well as his altar, remain there ; and that the country abounds with lote-trees, the fruit of which is exceedingly sweet.   The account of Strabo is confirmed by Pliny,* who describes the lote-trees as growing in abundance on the two-sand banks of the Mediterranean, though Pliny was well acquainted with the distinction between this and the true Egyptian lotos. It is needless to repeat minute and copious narrative here ; suffice it that the "lote-trees" of these later authors, which are doubtless identical with the thorny shrub discovered in Africa by Mungo Park, is distinct from the true lotos of antiquity, and deserves none of

* Book xiii., chap. 7.

the honours which have been heaped upon it by authors
who were misled by its spurious name. The plant
described by Herodotus is not only the true lotos of
eastern antiquity, but, in its essential character as a
plant, has the highest claim to symbolical uses. It is
one of the plants indigenous to the mud of the Nile, and
grows plentifully also in the great streams of India. It
is a plant of great beauty, closely allied in botanical properties to the water lily of Britain; its roots creep along
the bottoms of lakes and rivers, and are fleshy, bulbous
masses, containing a mass of white pulp, as Pliny saith,
"delicious to eat." It is a stately and majestic creature
of the waters; its leaves are heart-shaped, targeted,
slightly waved, from four to twelve inches long, of a
greenish purple hue, and float in broad rich masses on
the surface of the water, so as to defend the flower
in the centre, whether in deep or shallow water; the
leaves always lies flat on the surface, the hollow petiole,
to which they are attached, increasing in length as the
waters deepen. The flowers are produced upon a stem
rising about two feet above the water; they are as large
as the palm of the hand, of a tulip-like form, with fifteen
pointed petals. When full-blown, the flower is often of
a beautiful rose colour, sometimes white or yellow, and
always delicately fragrant; it has forty or more stamens,
and one inversely bell-shaped pistil,* with sixteen or seven-
teen cells, containing seeds half an inch long, with a rind
black and smooth, and, when ripe, of a taste finer than
almonds. The description of Pliny is correct, with one
exception, and that is, he tells us, in his simple manner,

* Polyandria monogynia of Linnæus.

that the seeds resemble millet, whereas they are of the size of a bean. "This bread, made from the seeds of this lotos," says Pliny, "is worked with water or milk. There is not any bread in the world (says report) more wholesome and lighter than this, so long as it is hot; but once cold, it is hard of digestion, and becomes weighty."

The curious germination of the seeds of the lotos rendered it the emblem of that successive production of created beings, taught in the holy Sastras.* In the sublime theory of the Brahminical code, the universe exists only in idea—or, rather, nature is but a system of ideas originating in Brahme, the supreme being, but actually or immediately produced by Brahma, the efficient creator, from whom, while he exerts his powers of combining ideas, things proceed into being; but when he ceases to exert his powers, things created die away, and return back to their primary elements. These periods of existence and non-existence the disciples of the Vedas distinguished in the biblical manner, by the allegory of day and night, or the waking and sleeping of Brahma. "When that power awakes—for though slumber be not predicable of the sole eternal mind, infinitely wise, and infinitely benevolent, yet it is predicated of Brahma figuratively, as a general property of life—then has the world its full expansion; but when he slumbers with tranquil spirit, then the whole system fades away."†

It was this plant which the Egyptians bound around their altars, and which the virgin priestesses wore in wreaths upon their hair. They were gathered with

* *Vide* "Floral Symbols," page 220.   † "Menu," ch. i., v. 52.

P

great solemnity by the Egyptian priests, and the deities
were painted sitting in their leaves. The creation of
Brahma on the leaf of the lotos was, however, the legend
which formed the groundwork of all others of the same
class; Osiris, Puzza, and Priapus being but modifications
of the same personage, less sublime in character, because
removed a greater or less degree from the sources of the
original thought. In Hindoo worship, its fecundating
properties associate it with the worship of the Linga in
the shrine of Siva, one of those mysteries of the temple
which, to an European mind, appears but an orgie of dis-
gusting indecency, but which, to the devout son of
Mizriam, whose chastity of character is too often a
rebuke to his Christian master, is purely emblematic of
the creative power of the universe.

Priapus, who, with the Greek and Roman poets, was
the son of Bacchus and Venus, the god of debauchery, a
sort of guardian devil, invented to countenance the luxury
of Athens and the sensuality of Rome, was a god of
highest repute in the Chaldaic and Egyptian mythologies, profoundly venerated under the names of Orus and
Apis, the god of light, the son of the world. The
Priapus of the Greeks is a compound of Peor-Apis,
according to the Grecian mode of adopting Egyptian
names; he is sometimes called Poer singly, sometimes
Baal Peor, the same with whose rites the Israelites are
so often upbraided. Phurmitus supposes Priapus to
have been the same as Pan, the shepherd god; who was
equally degraded on one hand and as highly reverenced
on the other. The Romans, reducing the ideas of a refined mythology to their own sensual imbecility, degraded

the one to a filthy monster, and made of the other a
scarecrow.* Under the name of Az-el,† he was the
supposed son of Isis, who was herself but an emblem of
the ark—the mother of mankind—and from the Titans
he received all that Osiris suffered under the Typhon.

Both Orus and Osiris were styled Heliadæ, and often
represented the sun, which has led many writers to refer
what has been said of the personages to the luminary
itself. Orus was in fact the same as Osiris, but Osiris
in his second state; and therefore he is represented by
the Egyptians as a child swathed in bondage, a type of
the infancy of the world. At other times he shadows
forth the likeness of Saturn, the father of agriculture,
holding in his hand the implements of tillage, with a
ploughshare over his shoulder, and the blossoms of the
lotos on his head.

It is easy to trace, even in these confused and dis-
torted remnants of ancient creeds, an identity of idea
and a coincidence of purpose. Brahma waking from
sleep upon the bosom of the lotos, and Willing the
creation by a passing thought; Puzza resting his gigantic frame upon the Lien-uha, or sacred lotos leaf; Orus
brought back to immortal life when he lay dead in the
midst of the waters, are all emblems of the Supreme
Will, which called up the worlds from night, and by
a thought, changed the silence of chaos into the morning
song of creation.

All tradition and allegory go the same way; and
in the most perverted and sensualized of ancient symbols
we may still read the sublime thoughts; the overwhelm-

* Bryant, i. 141.   † Ibid, vol. i., p. 206.

ing truth, handed down by oral tradition and sculptured
emblems from one generation to another; pointing back
through the dark to the great fountain of all things, and
telling, in words and images not yet illegible, the simple
story of the birth of nature.   Beautiful indeed are these
revelations of the flowers; sweet old time that, when
green leaves and yellow blossoms were parts of the life
of man, and the fragrance of the wood-cups mingled with
the globules of his blood, filling his heart and hands
with a holy purpose, one with nature, with God, and
with himself.

   Amid the luxuriance of the land of the sun, man was
born into a world of flowers.   Nourished with the milk
of a mother whose life and love had flown together through
those channels of religious beauty, he goes forth in his
youth to the fields and the forests, and kneels before the
protecting lord of spirits, the adorable Ganesa, the
son of Siva, whose images are placed beside the high-
ways, in the jungles, and amid the pastures surrounded
with green beauty and with flowers.   The god himself
is represented by an upright stake of the plant Cacay,*
which of all green herbs is most sacred to Ganesa.
Round this rustic image of the god, the ground is
levelled and consecrated, and then the sincere worshipper
kneels and makes his offering of milk and honey.†
When his blood, warmed into the generosity of manhood
and love, beats and burns in his bosom, it is Cama,‡
the son of Maya, who, with a bow of flowers strung with

* Cassia fistula.
† Buchanan's " Journey into Mysore," i. 52.
‡ Cama is the Cupid in the mythology of the Paranas.

stinging bees, has shot an arrow, tipped with an amra blossom, at his heart.

> "Quick from his bee-strung bow an arrow flew,
> Its point an amra, fresh with morning dew."*

Neither a blind god nor a fat baby is this Cupid of the Oriental fiction. His mother, Maya, is imaginative power, since, according to some Hindoo philosophers, whatever exists, exists only in a system of perception, wholly dependant on the imagination; and hence all things are but illusions of the mind. "Except the first cause (Brahme), whatever may appear or may not appear in the mind, know that it is the mind's Maya, or delusion, as light and darkness."† The warm impulse of the brain being the parent of love, Cama himself, though sailing on the wings of the gay lory (or parrot), attended by his dancing nymphs, is a spiritual essence only; for Siva, writhing under the smart of his arrow, flung at him a flame of fire, and consumed his body, so sublimating that which is only beautiful when of the spirit.

Neither do flowers fail this son of Mizraim, when he subdues the raging flame into a genial and cheering warmth, and makes it burn as an oblation upon the altar of a home. His hand is bound to that of his bride by a wisp of the sacred cusa grass, by a priest whose vestments are wrought of the sara or jungle plant,‡ arranged in triple cords according to the precepts of the holy Sastras.§ If in his lifetime he perform good works, and

---

* "Metamorphosis of Sona," p. 6.   † Bhagavata purana.
‡ Saccharum spartaneum of Linnæus.
§ "Menu," ii ch. ii., v. 42, 43.

endear himself to his fellow-men, flowers are strewn in his path and honours heaped upon him—not as in the West, when death has sealed up the fountains of gratitude—but while *living*, that the heart, while it beats, may know it beats not in vain.*   And when, after a life sanctified in act and thought by the poetic breath and symbolic beauty of flowers, death at last imprints an icy kiss upon him, he goes up to the sweet gardens of Nandana to revel amongst the spiritual flowers or joys which blossom there.

But these things are of the past, and though fit for the age of mystery and Paganism, are painfully unfit for the age of Christianity and progress.   Beautiful as things of the past, noble memorials of an age of mystery and a race of giants, they would have died out long ago, had the Christian masters of the world been Christians in their life and character.   Debauchery, pillage, slavery, exaction, and bloodshed, have marked their steps; and the children of the sun have seen little yet of that spirit of love which forms the first feature of the Christian's preaching.†

* According to the Paranas, flower-strewing is an honour due to the benefactors of the people.

† The above was written ten years before the outbreak of the Indian mutiny, and might reasonably be altered, since Britain has shown herself the true friend of India, and her best of benefactors, during seasons of famine and pestilence.

FLORAL SYMBOLS.

SYMBOLISM plays a prominent part in the early history. of the human race, and manifests itself in an infinite diversity of forms. It had its first origin as a system among the imaginative people of Oriental climes. Under an intensely blue sky, glowing with unclouded sunshine or glittering with unnumbered stars, it is not surprising that the imagination, once kindled by the contemplation of beauty, should trace in nature a language expressive of the varying phases of the human mind. Religion and poetry thus found language and expression in the symbolic vocabulary of nature, and the most interesting features of Flower Lore are those that have originated in the use of flowers as symbols.

Of these floral symbols, some are of such a general character, and they would be adopted and appreciated so readily by any people, that it would soon become difficult to trace them back to their original forms. The brief existence of the flower would render it a fit representative of the life of man. Literature abounds with metaphors and symbols of this general character. Thus of Corinne, that warm-hearted daughter of Italy, whose affections were as warm and pure as the sunlight of her

native skies, Madame de Stael writes :—" This lovely
woman, whose features seemed designed to depict
felicity—this child of the sun, a prey to hidden grief—
was like a flower, still fresh and brilliant, but within
whose leaves may be seen the first dark impress of that
withering blight which soon shall lay it low. . . . The
long black lashes veiled her languid eyes, and threw a
shadow over the tintless cheek."   Beneath was written
this line from the " Pastor Fido " :—

> " Scarcely can we say this was a rose."

A similar passage occurs in a lament for Lady Jane
Grey :—

> " Thou didst die,
> Even as a flower beneath the summer ray,
> In incensed beauty ; and didst take thy way,
> Even like its fragrance, up into the sky."
>
> J. W. OAD.

In such a tone of subdued eloquence does the sister
of Sir Philip Sydney mourn over the memory of her
sainted and incomparable brother :—

> " Break now your garlands, oh, ye shepherd lasses,
>   Since the fair flower that them adorned is gone ;
> The flower that them adorned is gone to ashes ;
>   Never again let lass put garland on :
> Instead of garland, wear sad cypress now,
> And bitter elder, broken from the bough."

The language of deep feeling is always poetical, and
in every age of the world's history flowers have aided in
giving force to the utterance of the heart's passion,
whether of love, hate, sorrow, or joy.

> " If bliss be a frail and perishing flower,
>   Born only to decay ;
>   Oh! who—when it blooms but a single hour—
>   Would fling its sweets away ?"

Among the many chaste and poetical allegories which occur scattered up and down the Eastern literature, is the following :—" As this dark mould sends upwards, and out of its very heart, the rare Persian rose, so does hope grow out of evil: and the darker the evil the brighter the hope, as from a richer and fouler soil comes the more vigorous and larger flower." There is another of this class, which conveys in a most elegant form a symbolical embodiment of the refining influences of the pure and the beautiful. " A traveller, in passing through a country in Persia, chanced to take into his hand a piece of clay which lay by the way-side, and to his surprise he found it to exhale the most delightful fragrance. 'Thou art but a poor piece of clay,' said he, ' an unsightly, unattractive, poor piece of clay : yet how fragrant art thou! How refreshing ! I admire thee ; I love thee ; thou shalt be my companion ; I will carry thee in my bosom. But whence hast thou this fragrance ?' The clay replied, ' I have been dwelling with the rose !' " In another Persian legend, we are told that Sadi, the poet, when a slave, presented to his tyrant master a rose, accompanied with this pathetic appeal :—
" Do good to thy servant whilst thou hast the power, for the season of power is often as transient as the duration of this beautiful flower." This melted the heart of his lord, and the slave obtained his liberty.

The well-known " Language of Flowers " was first

introduced into this country by Lady Mary Wortley Montague; but in the modern system nothing is preserved of the fresh poetry and brilliancy of thought which characterized the floral symbolism of ancient Eastern nations. The rich imagery and startling truth of the Eastern metaphors and symbols have crumbled into ruin, like the temples dedicated to their gods. Sickly and weak as is the modern language of flowers, it has been rendered still more tame by its universal adoption in the intercourse of life; instead of being preserved as a part of religious worship, and of the highest forms of poetry. In Turkey, you may, through the assistance of these emblems, either quarrel, reproach, or send letters of passion, friendship, or civility, or even news, without ever inking your fingers; for there is no colour, no weed, no flower, no fruit, herb, nor feather, that has not a verse belonging to it. So, too, no Turkish lady would send a congratulatory message, or a ceremonious invitation, without sending with it some emblematical flowers carefully wrapped in an embroidered handkerchief, made fragrant by the odours of flowers, which convey also an emblematical meaning. But these are merely fragments of the ancient customs of the Eastern nations, where all was symbol, emblem, and allegory; and where the imagination usurped the power and controlled even the affairs of the State.

These emblematic verses are in the form of enigmas, and are founded on a sort of crambo, or *bout rime*. M. Hamma has collected about a hundred specimens, but they are exceedingly untranslatable. We quote three of the most manageable :—

Almonde.—Wer bana bir Ominde.
Pear.—Let me not despair.
Rose.—You smile, but still my anguish grows ;
Rose.—For thee my heart with love still glows.
Tea.—You are both sun and moon to me,
Tea.—Yours is the light by which I see.

But these are arbitrary and fancied similarities, founded on the mere rhyming and jingling of words ; and although occasionally conveying an idea, are upon the whole mere frivolities to fritter away the hours which might be better spent in the growth of ideas, in tracing out the symbolical expressions of nature, in establishing these as keys to the æsthetics of all beauty, and as the framework of the noblest poetry.

To catch a glimpse of floral symbolism, when yet in its pristine vigour and poetical sublimity, we must penetrate the dust of departed years, and make search among the literary and artistic remains of ancient India, Egypt, and Chaldea, where superstition clothed all things with a wild and terrible grandeur, and rendered natural objects emblematic of the highest spiritual truths.

Amid these relics of former magnificence, and within the walls of these crumbling temples, are yet to be seen the sculptured symbols which embodied the ideas of their daily faith. Dread and mystical as many of these are, even when viewed in the calm light of reason, there is yet a bewitching poetry and a sublimity of thought associated with them, as startling and wonderful as they are beautiful and true. The history of the universe has been written in living characters upon the obdurate granite in which those mystic caves are hewn. The dawn of creation is represented by a leaf divided into light and darkness; when

> " The heavens and the earth
> Rose out of chaos."

And the story of the ages has in like manner been written in symbols of leaves and flowers.

Of the flowers consecrated to religious deities by the symbol worshippers of India and Egypt, none occupy a more prominent position than the lotos. Its sacred leaf was the

> " Emblem and cradle of creative Night."

It was anciently revered in Egypt, as it is at this day at Hindostan, Thibet, and Nepaul, where they believe it was in the consecrated bosom of this plant that Brahma was born, and on which Osiris delights to float. Naturalists have differed in opinion whether the celebrated Lotos was a hero, a flower, or a tree. Some authors have affirmed that it was a rough, thorny shrub, the seeds of which were to make bread; but the testimony of Herodotus, that the lotos is a species of water-lily, which grows in abundance in the Nile during the inundations, is so very conclusive, that no other solution of the question can be accepted. Herodotus bears testimony to the high antiquity of the Egyptian veneration for the lotos, and M. Savary assures us that at the present day, the degenerate children of the Nile are animated by the same feelings of worship and veneration. It was called the " Lily of the Nile," from its growing in abundance on the banks, and in the marshes which form the delta of that river. It is a stately and majestic plant, of the Nymphæ tribe, and rises about two feet above the water, having a calyx like a large tulip, and diffusing an odour like that of the lily. The physical peculiarities in the growth of this plant rendered it an appropriate symbol in a worship of the most degrading and immoral character.

The plant grows in the water, and the blossoms are produced amongst its broad ovate leaves. In the centre of the flower is formed the seed-vessel, which is produced in the form of a bell or inverted cone, and punctuated on the top with little cavities or cells, in which the seeds grow. The seeds, when ripe, are prevented from escaping, in consequence of the orifices of the cells being too small, and so they germinate in the places where they ripen, and shoot forth into new plants, until they acquire such a degree of magnitude, as to burst the matrices open and release themselves; after which, like other aquatic plants, they take root where the current chances to deposit them. This apparently self-productive plant became the representative of the reproductive agencies of nature, and was worshipped as a symbol of the All-Creative-Power—the spirit which "moved upon the face of the waters," and which gave life and organization to matter. We find the same symbol occurring in every part of the Northern hemisphere where symbolic religion has prevailed. The sacred images of the Tartars, Japanese, and Indians are almost all represented as resting upon the lotos leaves. The Chinese divinity, Puzza, is seated on a lotos, and the Japanese god is represented sitting on a water-lily. The flatterers of Adrian, emperor of Rome, after the death of his favourite Antinous, endeavoured to persuade him that the young man was metamorphosed into a lotos flower; but the emperor created a temple to his memory, and wished it to be believed that he had been changed into a constellation. The plant is poetically described in the "Heetopades," as "The cooling flower, which is oppressed by the appearance of day, and afraid of the stars;"*—in allusion to the circumstances of its spreading its flowers only in the night. There is a beautiful passage in the "Sacontala" in reference to the palmistry of the Brahmin priests. "What!" exclaims a prophetic Brahmin, "the very palm of his hand bears the mark of empire, and, while he thus eagerly extends it, shows its lines of exquisite net-work, and grows like a lotos expanded at early dawn, when the ruddy splendour of its petals hides all other tints in obscurity."†

"This is the sublime, the hallowed symbol, that eternally occurs in Oriental mythology; and in truth, not without substantial reason, for it is itself a lovely prodigy; it contains a treasure of physical instruction, and affords to the enraptured botanist exhaustless matter of amusement and contemplation. No wonder, therefore, that the philosophizing sons of Mizraim adorned their majestic structures with the spreading tendrils of this vegetable, and made the ample expanding vase that crowns its lofty stem the capital of the most beautiful columns."‡

The onion was held in similar esteem as a religious

* "Heetopades," p. 282.   † "Sacontala," p. 89.
‡ "Maurice's Indian Antiquities," p. 527.

symbol in the mysterious solemnities and divinations of the mythologies of Egypt and Hindostan. Mr. Crauford has imagined that the delicate red veins and fibres of the onion rendered it an object of veneration, as symbolizing the blood, at the shedding of which the Hindoo shudders. But astronomy has stamped celebrity on the onion; for, on cutting through it, there appears, beneath the external coat, a succession of orbs, one within the other, in regular order, after the manner of the revolving spheres. We have the authority of Alexander,[*] that the onion was worshipped as a symbol of the planetary universe by the astronomers of Chaldea, before it was adopted by either Egypt or India. The Egyptian veneration for plants and animals arose from their symbolical representations of the benevolent operations of nature; while there were some which were held in abhorrence from possessing opposite symbolic meanings. Thus the onion, as a symbol of the spheres, was held sacred to Osiris—the soul of the material universe, the energy that generates and nourishes all things; and to his consort Isis—the nurse and mother of the world, the goddess of a thousand names—the Infinite Myrionyma.

Notwithstanding the extreme veneration for the onion as a noble astronomical symbol, yet when a more minute attention to its growth and cultivation had taught that it flourished with the greatest vigour when the moon was in the wane, the priests of Osiris began to relax in their worship, and by the priests of Diana, at Bubastio, it was held in abhorrence and detestation. These floral

[*] " Alexander ab Alexandro," lib. vi. cap. 26.

symbols of the ancient nations have elucidated some of
the most difficult questions concerning their history, and
have made it certain, that most of the Indian, and
Egyptian customs originated in Chaldea—that land of
serene and tranquil skies, where human society had its
origin, and where the observation of nature first grew
into a science, in the earliest ages of the world.

The rose has been a symbolic flower in every age of
the world. It has been the universal symbol of beauty
and love; the half-expanded bud representing the first
dawn of the sublime passion, and the full-blown flower
the matured sentiment which sheds a heavenly light upon
the domestic hearth, and hallows all who come within
its influence. The rose is the delight of the East, the
eternal theme of the poet, and the emblem of the highest
virtues. The Romans, whose profuse use of flowers
subjected them to the reproofs of their philosophers,
considered the rose as an emblem of festivity. The
Egyptians made it a symbol of silence, and crowned
Harpocrates with a garland of its blossoms.

The classical story of the death of the beautiful youth,
Hyacinth, has rendered that flower an emblem of grief.
It is very probable, however, that the hyacinth of the
ancients was the red lily, called the Martagon lily, or
Turk's cap. Virgil describes the flower as of a bright
red colour, and as being marked with the Greek
exclamation of grief, AI, AI, and which may be faintly
traced in the black marks of the Turk's cap. Milton
speaks of this as

     "That sanguine flower, inscribed with woe;"

and as there are no such marks upon the wood hyacinth,

that plant has been called *Hyacinthus non scriptus* (not inscribed). The Eastern poets have made the hyacinth subserve many poetical uses. By Hafiz it was adopted as the symbol of elegance and grace, and he delighted to compare his mistress's hair to its blossoms; hence the term, hyacinthine locks, which was originally an Oriental comparison. The asphodel was also an emblem of sorrow, and the Greeks used it at their funerals.

We cannot wonder that so fragrant a plant as the myrtle should become a symbolical teacher. It was most anciently the emblem of peace and quietude, and gave a living freshness to the annunciation of the angel mentioned by Zechariah, who said, as he stood among the myrtle-trees, "We have walked to and fro through the earth, and behold, all the earth sitteth still and is at rest." From being an emblem of peace, on account of its quiet beauty and perfume, it afterwards became an emblem of war, in consequence of the hardness of its wood rendering it very suitable for warlike instruments :—

"The war from stubborn myrtle shafts receives."

VIRGIL.

From the supple nature of its branches, together with the odour emitted by its leaves, it was largely used for entwining into wreaths, garlands, and crowns. These were worn at the Roman festivals, and the myrtle-boughs were steeped in the wine, to improve its flavour and fragrance ; and hence the myrtle became a recognized emblem of festivity. By the magistrates of Athens, it

Q

was worn as a symbol of office.   By the Greeks, it was
dedicated to Venus, either because it grows near the sea,
whence she is said to have arisen, or because the sweet
and unfading nature of its foliage made it a suitable
tribute to the goddess of beauty.   The Greeks planted
the myrtle abundantly in those groves which have been
so renowned in song, and where he who wandered was
greeted by such a succession of delightful odours, that
he might believe himself transported to some sweet land
of enchantment, where every breath was sacred to poetry.
The myrtle was sacred as a symbol of love and beauty,
and the first temple erected to Venus was surrounded
by a grove of myrtles.   When the ancient poets or
painters represent Venus rising from the ocean, they
tell us that the Hours or Seasons, who were the
offspring of Jupiter and Themis, present her with a
scarf of many colours, and a garland of myrtles.   There
is an old fable concerning Eratostratus, who burned the
famous temple of Diana at Ephesus, on the same night
as Alexander the Great was born.   He was a Naucra-
tian merchant, and during one of his voyages, there
arose a terrible storm.   Fortunately, he had in his
possession a small statue of Venus, whose protection he
immediately implored.   The goddess caused a prodigious
number of green myrtles to spring up in the ship, and
of these the sailors made garlands, and by wearing them
were saved.   They arrived in safety at Naucratis, the
great commercial city of Egypt, and from that period
the garlands of myrtle were called Naucratites.   By
Papirius Cursor, who erected the first sun-dial at Rome,
the myrtle was made a symbol of the Roman empire :

and to make the idea more capable of appreciation by the people, he planted two myrtles, one reputed plebeian, and the other patrician. The prosperity or decline of these trees was regarded by the Romans as ominous of party ascendancy in the government of the empire.

The floral symbols of Holy Writ are exceedingly beautiful, and are frequently used to convey a Divine command in a poetical form; and are usually remarkable for their botanical correctness. From the circumstance of Elijah having been sheltered from the persecutions of King Ahab by the juniper* of the mountains, that plant has become a symbol of succour, or an asylum. Britain might well adopt this as her national emblem, for truly, since the stirring events in the various European states, persons of all languages and creeds may say with the Psalmist—"Thou hast been a shelter for me, and a strong tower from the enemy." The almond was a symbol of haste and vigilance to the Hebrew poets—"What seest thou?" said the Lord to Jeremiah, and he answered, "I see a rod of an almond tree." Then said the Lord, "Thou hast well seen: for I will hasten my word and will perform it." The almond puts forth its delicate, blushing flowers so much in advance of other trees, that its adoption as a symbol of haste is very happy. With the Eastern poets it was a symbol of hope—

> "The hope, in dreams of a happier hour,
> That alights on misery's brow,
> Springs out of the silvery almond flower
> That blooms on a leafless bough." MOORE.

---

* This was the Broom, *Genista Monosperma*.

Q 2

But no floral symbol can equal in beauty or sacredness the passion-flower. It is so peculiar in construction, that when the Spanish conquerors of the New World first met with it in the woods, they gave it its name, and adopted it as an emblem of the sufferings of Christ. The thread-like stamens which surround the rays of the flower and some other portions, suggested to their enthusiastic imaginations the story of the Saviour's passion! and the sight of this wondrous symbol, in a wilderness in which they trod for the first time, seemed to them to betoken conquest, riches, and power—to be achieved under the sanction of religion. But they sought rather to insure a temporal dominion, than to act in obedience to that God who had planted flowers in those solitary wilds; and the very men who beheld in the passion-flower an emblem of mercy and of love, an emblem of faith in God and fellowship to man, carried malevolence and desolation wherever they trod, and made their standard a signal of blood, torture, and tyranny. Let the passion-flower be still an emblem, but let it keep us in the fulfilment of the benign precepts of the great Teacher, whose suffering is symbolized in the form of the flower—that by contemplating it, we may be raised in thankfulness to God, and learn to recognize the great truths taught by Him who

> "————— Trod
> The paths of sorrow, that we might find peace."

The clover has been revered from the most remote antiquity as a religious symbol. Its triple leaf renders it adaptable to a multiplicity of ideas. The Druids

held it in high repute, both as a charm against evil
spirits, and for its supposed medicinal virtues. They
were very confident in its powers, because its leaf represented the three departments of nature—the earth, the
sea, and the heaven. The legends of Ireland tell how
St. Patrick chose it as an emblem of the Trinity, when
engaged in converting the native Irish, and hence the
esteem in which it is held by the Irish people ;—for the
shamrock is only the common white, or Dutch clover
(Trifolium repens).[*] The ancients represented Hope by
a little child standing on tiptoe, and holding a trefoil in
his hand. Scarcely any religious symbol has been so
widely and reverently regarded as such, as the aloe.
Throughout the East it is held in profound veneration.
The Mahometans, especially those who reside in Egypt,
regard it as a religious symbol of the most exalted
character.   The Mussulman who has performed a
pilgrimage to the shrine at Mecca, ever after considers
himself entitled to the veneration of a saint, and hangs
the aloe over his door to signify his religious purity, and
to proclaim the great duty which he has performed.   It
is also highly esteemed as a charm against any malign
genius, and no evil spirit will pass a threshold where so
holy a symbol is suspended.   The Jews at Cairo have a
similar belief, and suspend the aloe at their doors, to
prevent the intrusion of these dreadful influences.   The
Mahometans, who plant their burial-places with shrubs
and flowers, place the aloe at the extremity of every
grave, on a spot facing the epitaph ; and they call it by
the Arabic name *saber*, signifying *patience*.[†]

---

[*] Or the wood *Oxalis*. [†] Burckhardt.

The Eastern poets usually make the aloe a symbol of bitterness, doubtless in allusion to its association with death, and to the bitter flavour of its juices. "As aloe is to the body, so is affliction to the soul—bitter, very bitter." It is usually adopted as an emblem of acute woe, of "Sorrow that locks up the struggling heart."

> "The woful teris that their letin fal,
> As bitter werin, out of teris kinde,
> For paine, as is lique aloes, or gal."
>
> CHAUCER.

The wormwood is also a symbol of bitterness. In the modern Language of Flowers it represents absence. Dr. Watts says, in his work on Logic, "Bitter is an equivocal word; there is bitter wormwood, there are bitter words, there are bitter enemies, and a bitter cold morning;" and the absence of those we love is also bitter, and may well be spoken by wormwood. The rosemary has a similar meaning, and has become a symbol of remembrance, from the old custom of using it at funerals, and perhaps from its supposed medical virtue of improving the memory. Shakspere uses it as a symbol of remembrance :—

> "There's rosemary for you—that's for remembrance :
> I pray you, love, remember,"

said the sad Ophelia: so Perdita, in *Winter's Tale :—*

> "[*To Polixines and Camillo.*] You're welcome, sir!
> Give me those flowers there, Dorcas.—Reverend sirs,
> For you there's rosemary, and rue; these keep
> Seeming, and savour, all the winter long:
> Grace and remembrance be to you both,
> And welcome to our shearing! .

Pol. Shepherdess
(A fair one are you), well you fit our age
With flowers of winter." [iv. 3.]

It is, perhaps, the greatest evidence of the transcendency of Shakspere's genius, that in the philosophy of little things there is a stern regard to truth of detail. Never does he mention an insect or a flower, but it is in harmony with the season, place, and moral of the event it serves to illustrate. In the same scene as we have just quoted, he makes Perdita give flowers to her visitors appropriate to, and symbolical of, their various ages :—

> "Here's flowers for you ;
> Hot lavender, mints, savory, marjoram ;
> The marigold, that goes to bed with the sun,
> And with him rises weeping : these are flowers
> Of middle summer, and, I think, they are given
> To men of middle age.——
> *   *   *   *   *   *
>   Now, my fairest friend,
> I would I had some flowers o' the spring, that might
> Become your time of day ; and yours, and yours ;
> That wear upon your virgin branches yet.
> *   *   *   *   *   *
>   Daffodils,
> That come before the swallow dares, and take
> The winds of March with beauty ; violets dim,
> But sweeter than the lids of Juno's eyes,
> Or Cytherea's breath ; pale primroses,
> That die unmarried, ere they can behold
> Bright Phœbus in his strength, a malady
> Most incident to maids ; both oxlips, and
> The crown imperial ; lilies of all kinds,
> The fleur-de-lis being one !"

But the most beautiful of Shakspere's floral symbols

occurs where poor Ophelia, in her madness, goes to make "fantastic garlands"—

"Of crow-flowers, nettles, daisies, and long purples,"

which are all emblematical flowers, and tell a silent tale of her broken heart. The first signifies *fair maid;* the second, *stung to the quick* the third, *her virgin bloom;* the fourth, *under the cold hand of death;* and the whole, being wild flowers, might denote *the bewildered state of her faculties.* No wreath could have been chosen more emblematical of the sorrows of this beautiful blossom, blighted by disappointed love, and withered by filial sorrow.*

* H. G. Adams.

FAIRY RINGS.

" In days of old, when Arthur filled the throne,
Whose acts and fame to foreign lands were blown,
The King of Elfs, and little Fairy Queen,
Gambolled on heaths, and danced on every green ;
And where the jolly troop had led the round,
The grass, unbidden, rose and marked the ground."

As the autumn green takes possession of the meadows, and the hope of another spring cheers the labour of the husbandman, a thousand curious things may be seen in hedgerows, on commons, in copses, and by the stony wayside. Not the least interesting of these strange sights and autumn wonders are those rings of rich green grass which appear on lawns and old pastures, familiarly known as "Fairy Rings"—subjects of inquiry to the curious, and of poetic interest to the imaginative. These rings are of all sizes, ranging from the circumference of a common cart-wheel to wide sweeps of fifteen or twenty feet diameter, and distinctly marked in outline by the rich greenness of the grass which forms the exterior circumference. There are not a few of those who love to ramble in green and shady places, and who know somewhat of the economy of the fields, who consider fairy rings mere pleasant fictions, whereas they are genuine realities, and may be seen by every observer who chooses to exercise patience and diligence. On the flats at Wanstead, towards the gate which opens on the road to the "Thatched House;" on the smooth lawn of Cheshunt Park, and especially in front of Cheshunt House; in the rich meadows between Highgate and Finchley; and on the "Rye," at Peckham; we have always succeeded in finding fairy rings; and in no meadowy district will a diligent search go long unrewarded.

In common with all appearances of a mysterious character, these rings have been long associated with the superstitions of the country, and time out of mind consecrated to the service of the fairies. They are, indeed, the impressions left by fairy feet upon the grass: where they have trodden in the giddy dance at midnight, rings of luxuriant verdure spring up; and so sacred are these circles of green, that the simple sheep abstain from them, and tread but softly where they grow. Shakspere makes beautiful use of this article of ancient faith, in that passage in the *Tempest* where Prospero invokes for the last time the supernatural powers to his aid:—

> "Ye elves of hills, brooks, standing lakes and groves;
> And ye that on the sands with printless foot
> Do chase the ebbing Neptune, and do fly him
> When he comes back; you demi-puppets, that
> By moonshine do the green-sour ringlets make,
> Whereof the ewe not bites; and you, whose pastime
> 'Tis to make midnight mushrooms."

Drayton, speaking of the fairies, says—

> "They in their courses make that round
> In meadows and in marshes found,
> Of them so called the fairy ground."

According to Olaus Magnus, this cause of the circles in the grass, called "Fairy Rings," was a general belief with the northern nations; and most of our poets who adopt it follow those traditions which the Norsemen left amongst us.

Some very curious legends attach themselves to these fairy rings, as, indeed, they do to every other branch of fairy lore. In Scott's *Minstrelsy of the Scottish Border*, a strange story is related of a poor man, who being employed in pulling heather upon Peatlaw, near Carterhaugh, had tired of his labour, and had lain himself down to sleep upon a fairy ring. When he awoke, he was amazed to find himself in the midst of a populous city, to which, as well as to the means of transportation, he was a stranger. His coat was left upon the Peatlaw, and his bonnet, which had fallen off in the course of his aërial journey, was afterwards found hanging on the steeple of the church at Lanark. The distress of the luckless adventurer was somewhat relieved by meeting a carrier whom he had formerly known, who carried him back to Glasgow by a slower conveyance than had taken him from thence. At Carterhaugh, at the confluence of the Ettrick and Yarrow, the peasants point out these rings as unmistakable evidences of fairy revels; and throughout Scotland, and more particularly in Selkirkshire, the belief in fairies and fairy influence is still pertinaciously held by the peasants. Moses Pitt, in a scarce tract, relates that his female servant—"Ann Jeffries . . . was one day sitting in an arbour in the garden, knitting, and there suddenly came over the hedge six persons of small stature, all clothed in green, which frightened her so much as to throw her into a sickness. They continued their appearance to her, never less than two at a time, nor ever more than eight. From harvest time to the Christmas following, these fairies came to her and fed her; and one day," says Moses Pitt—who was either a fool or a gross deceiver—"one day she gave me a piece of her (fairy) bread, which I did eat, and think it was the most delicious food that ever I did eat, either before or since." The same favoured Ann Jeffries was once presented with a silver cup by these fairies, and was often seen dancing around the trees, alleging that she was dancing with the fairies. Much as they favoured her, however, in her times of prosperity, the fairies fearfully deserted her in the hour of danger; for, being thrown into gaol as an impostor, instead of aiding in her escape, they forsook her—

> " To dance on ringlets to the whistling wind."[*]

It was one of the primary articles of Delta's faith, that

> " The leaden talisman of Truth
> Hath disenchanted of its rainbow hues
> The sky; and robbed the fields of half their flowers."

And in his poem of "Enchantment," he sets forth that poetry is being shamed out of existence by the march of modern science—an assertion which is untrue as regards the poetry of human experience and sentiment, though well borne out in the fate which has already fallen upon the legends and fancies of poetical superstitions. Truth and poetry may march together—truth widening the field, and opening up new resources for the growth of

[*] Hone's " Year Book.

poetry, and poetry shedding a sempiternal lustre on the acquisitions of truth. Newton dissects the rainbow, and, by showing its prismatic structure, disenchants it of its angel uses. Franklin analyzes the thunder, and, by pointing out its electrical origin, robs it of its avenging voice; and in the same manner, the man of science, kneeling on the green turf to speculate upon the fairy ring, finds that, like other natural appearances which have worn for a time poetical and superstitious attributes, this too must yield an answer to the touch of that "leaden talisman," and become a prose fact in the economy of nature. It seems at first sight a pity to sweep away a fancy so beautiful; but yet truth—though only the truth of a fairy ring—is superior to fiction; and while the cold inquiry of the student of physics clips the wings of the soul on the one hand, it enlarges its life on the other, and science, by increasing wonder, works in harmony with all truth in the extension of the field of poetry.

To disenchant the fairy rings has cost the philosophers considerable trouble. So sagacious an observer as Gilbert White never accurately fathomed the beautiful phenomenon; nor did Captain Brown, one of the ablest editors of the Selborne letters, who absurdly attributes them to electrical agency. The electrical theory of their production was a favourite one during the infancy of electrical science, when it was the fashion to attribute everything of a puzzling character to that subtle agency. Sir Walter Scott held the same opinion, and speaks of them as the "electrical rings, which vulgar credulity supposes to be traces of fairy revels." It is the more strange that this opinion should have been cherished, when the true cause had been hinted at again and again by the poets—whose words are as often prophetic, in regard to the discoveries of science, as they are of ethical and historical developments. Shakspere, in the passage already quoted, sounds the key-note where he speaks of the fairies as "making the midnight mushrooms;" and the author of "Round about our Coal Fire" speaks suggestively of the frequent appearance of these rings in spots "where mushrooms grow;" these luxurious rings of grass being caused solely by the growth of successive crops of certain species of fungi.

That law of agriculture which insists upon the rotation of crops has no more palpable illustration than these mysterious developments in the meadows. The recent discovery, that when one kind of plant has occupied a spot for a certain length of time the soil becomes unfit for that plant, but will readily nourish another kind, makes it evident that rotation of crops is no invention of man, but a provision of nature, and a prominent feature in her vegetable economy. Dr. Roget, in his Bridgewater treatise on "Animal and Vegetable Economy," gives the result of a series of experiments performed on plants, by immersing their roots in filtered water for several days; when, after the lapse of a certain time, the water became charged with certain excretions, or matters cast off from the plant; which excretions, in the case of the roots of the *Chandenilla muralis*, consisted of a bitter narcotic substance, similar to opium. M. Macaire found that neither the roots nor stems of the same plants, when completely detached and immersed, would produce this effect; and hence he concludes that it is an exudation from the roots, which takes place only when the plant is in a state of living and healthy growth. Now we can easily understand how it is that plants of one kind will not flourish in the same soil for any length of time. When rooted in the soil, the plant continues to excrete or throw off certain matters which are injurious to it, or which have served their purpose in its economy; and the soil getting charged with these exudations, becomes at last wholly unfit for the plant which has occupied it, though the principles which proved obnoxious to that one may be nutritious and desirable for plants of another kind. Hence, in clearing the American woods, it is found that if the ground is allowed to run out of tillage, the vegetable tribes which formerly occupied it do not spring up again, but trees of another order and different constitution take possession of the soil; and, in the same manner, the salicaria flourishes in the vicinity of the willow, and the broom-rape in that of the hemp.

Of plants which exercise this influence in a special manner, the fungi are among the most prominent; for wherever any of the tribe take root, they speedily render the soil unfit for their continued growth. The spot thus rendered pernicious to fungous growths is particularly suitable for grasses; and as the fungi disappear, grasses take their place in a rich and luxuriant growth. Here, then, is the secret of the fairy ring—the result of one of nature's systems of successive crops.

To pursue the inquiry a step further, and ascertain why grass, in preference to other plants, should flourish where mushrooms decay, we have only to analyze the latter plant, and a solution immediately presents itself.

The ashes of the various kinds of fungi found in fairy rings yield in analysis small quantities of silica, lime, magnesia, iron, sulphuric acid, carbonic acid, and soda. Potash and phosphoric acid occur also, but in very large proportions, the first amounting to fifty-five per cent. of the entire analysis, and the second to twenty-nine per cent., so as together to constitute the bulk of inorganic constituents. Now, phosphorus and potash are the finest of manures for grass; and hence, beside the fact of the soil becoming unfitted for the continuance of fungi, the latter may be partially driven from the field—choked out, in fact, by the rapid and luxurious growth of grass in the rich soil thus provided for it.

A question of considerable interest arises as to why these growths of herbage should take a circular form, and maintain, as they do, such an uniformity of arrangement and development. This question will be best answered by a consideration of the detailed structure of a fairy ring, and of the nature of the plants which compose it. A circle which has attained some six or eight feet diameter will be found to contain a considerable variety of the mushroom plants, and several distinct kinds of green herbage. In the centre will be found scattered several of the common edible fungi, and sometimes a few of the rarer species. The most frequent are the *Agaricus campestris*, or common mushroom; *Agaricus oreades; A. pratensis;* and *A. muscarius*, or fly agaric, and the champignon. The curious heart-shaped and stemless *Lycoperdon proteus* may also occasionally be found; but the most common plants are the champignons and *Agaricus pratensis*, both of which we have ourselves found in plenty on the rings at Cheshunt, the champignons being of an excellent quality. In the interior of the ring, forming the first portion of the ring from the centre, we find sweet-scented vernal grass *(Anthoxanthum odoratum)* ; next that, a broad ring of rank meadow grass ; and, beyond that, a circle composed of various meadow plants, as glaucous heath grass, common thyme, mouse-ear hawkweed, with occasional sprinklings of *Agaricus virosus* and *Lycoperdon proteus.* Of *A. oreades,* Withering says,—"I am satisfied that the bare and brown, or highly clothed and verdant circles in pasture fields, called fairy rings, are caused by the growth of this agaric. We have many of them in Edgbaston Park : the largest, which is eighteen feet in diameter, and about as many inches broad in the periphery, where the agarics grow, has existed for some years."

If we suppose, then, that some few specimens of mushroom spring up—as they do usually in the droppings of cattle—and, after attaining their full growth, scatter their spawn around them, we shall obtain immediately a miniature picture of a fairy ring. The fungi which first took possession of the soil have used up all its phosphorus and potash, and have charged the mould with excretions injurious to themselves. Hence, the crop of fungi which spring from their seeds, or spawn, will form a circle all round the spot which was occupied by their predecessors. The centre, deserted by the mushrooms, will be taken possession of by grasses, which, rooting in a soil prepared for them, find additional nutriment in the phosphoric acid and potash which the fungi return to the soil, when they pass into decay. Crop after crop

R

of fungi follow, each one receding from the centre, and
passing outwards on to new soil, followed up at the same
time by the rampant grasses. The central grass will
soon have used up the rich deposits formed by the first
crop of fungi, and, losing its rankness, will allow of the
growth of other meadow plants. Common daisy and
other plants will then spring up in the centre, and now
and then a few agarics will appear, and other tribes of
fungi, now enabled to vegetate in consequence of the
refreshment the soil has received from the grass—the
soil being charged with the spawn of various species,
waiting only the conditions necessary to their growth.
Thus the interior of the ring becomes a mixture of thin
grass, meadow and heath plants, and various fungi; and
while this has been taking place, the ring of rich and
rank grass has been following the outer ring of fungi,
luxuriating in the soil which each succeeding crop
deserts; and thus extending, by a steady though slow
process, the dimensions of the ring itself. In addition
also to the suitability of the soil for grass, when it has
become unfit for fungi, the latter retain the potash and
phosphorus of the soil in a collective form for the
nourishment of the grass, and take possession of new
soil beyond that they previously occupied. The fungi
and the grass are then pitched in battle one against the
other—the fight is unequal, and the grass conquers; and
thus, what it does not gain by the voluntary desertion
of the soil by the fungi, it accomplishes by overgrowing
and choking them—continually advancing from within
outwards, feeding, as it extends itself, upon the remains
of its fallen foe.

In the garden of Gilbert White, in the valley at
Selbourne, was one of these rings, which had occupied
the same spot for six successive years, and perhaps
longer; but for that period it had been annually
observed, hovering over the green sod on which the old
man's feet had often trod, like a fairy oblation to the
departed naturalist. Perhaps the circumstance of the
fungi being destroyed before they attain perfection, as
would naturally be the case on a lawn, may sufficiently
account for the ring above mentioned remaining of the
same diameter for several seasons. When they occur on
hill sides, the lower part of the circle is usually open,
and sometimes it happens that, owing to the new crop
of fungi which sometimes springs up in the centre, a
second ring of very rank grass appears within the larger
one, and forms in this way a very beautiful object. Such
rings as these we have often found on the grassy
embankment of the Birmingham Railway, near to the
London end of the Primrose Hill tunnel. In 1846, we
found a fine ring at Wanstead, in which the common
toadstool had taken up its abode, and flourished to the
entire exclusion of every other fungus. Only a few
weeks since, we found several flourishing rings on
Hampstead Heath, which were crowded with the finest
of champignons; a vast number of these we gathered,
and had the pleasure of making intimate acquaintance
with their excellence in the soup which appeared on the
table next day. In rich meadows, the interior of the
ring—at least, as far as our own observations go—is
usually bare and brown, without trace of fungi of any
kind, while the grass surrounding it is of a very rich and

luxuriant character. If the plants in the exterior be
pulled up, the spawn of the mushrooms will frequently
be found attached to their roots, and in the barren
interior of the circle, at the depth of two or three inches,
the soil will be found saturated with it.

Such is the disenchantment which the fairy ring must
undergo : not to the destruction of its beauty, nor to
the lessening of our interest in its growth, but to the
exaltation of our views of the vast economy of nature,
and of that wisdom which lies behind nature, whose
workings are seen to be as perfect and as beautiful in
the vast machinery of revolving stars, as in the successive growths of fairy rings. Of old, it was deemed
sacrilege to question the mysteries of nature; and to
pry into alleged supernatural powers brought shame and
suffering in return. Science, supplanting these unseen
powers with agencies more subtle and wonders more
enchanting, bids us ask and ask again, giving to each
trustful question answers full of wonder and full of joy.

THE RAINBOW.

> "I took it for a fairy vision
> Of some gay creature in the element,
> That in the colours of the rainbow live,
> And play i' the plighted clouds."
>
> MILTON'S *Comus*.

To lose a day out of one's calendar is like having to
endure the excision of a limb. There is somewhat of a
life gone, and no after activity will repair the loss. A
spider or crustacean may restore a lost limb; I have
seen a triton grow a new tail, after the loss of that elegant
appendage, but a day of vacuity is a bead dropped out of
the aggregate allotted us in the order of eternity, and an
eternity of opportunities cannot restore it. I am thinking thus, while in a very idle mood, on an afternoon of
alternating cloud and sunshine, endeavouring, if I can,
to quiet my conscience for the inactivity of my mind
and the idleness of my hands. It seems almost hard to
think, quite a trouble to observe; but still very unsatis-
fying to lie here on the grass, as immobile as a snail
enscouced in its winter retreat. Above me fly the fleecy
clouds, like a panorama of ships, mountains, and angels;
the sun breaks through their ranks, as if pledged to dis-

perse them, and is hidden again, as a bigger cloud than
the rest comes to the rescue, and by his huge rolling presence proclaims that Aquarius is in the ascendant.   I have
been scorched several times, yet was too indolent to roll
myself a little further on into the shade; now, I see, I
shall be wetted to the skin, for the first drops are splashing on the large leaves of the plane tree overhead, and
there is a lull of the western breezes, ominous of heavy
rain.   But I can still play my perverse part in resisting
the impulse to action, and be the more perverse, because
at this moment there is a general whirr of wings, a
greater bustle among the bees; the gardener has tied
his bunch of bast to the branch of a tree, and has run
for his jacket.   All that I shall do in this emergency
will be to creep into yonder root-house, and there repose
again, lulled by the music of the shower and the fresh
odours of the mignonette.   Now, it is coming down in
earnest, and I am safe.   Happy man, to be compelled
to quit the soft turf for the rough seat ·among ferns and
waving grasses; for, unless I had done so, I should
have missed a spectacle that one might honestly quit
almost any task to see, and that is, the RAINBOW.   The
sun has gone so far down, and my position is so far
elevated, that I see the entire bow as it dips down on
either hand, and suggests the idea that I have before me
a gigantic circle of colours, the lower half of which is
hidden by the earth; so that if I could travel with the
speed of lightning I might, on the far horizon, behold
it dipping into space, and completing its 360 degrees,
like the orbit of a planet.

It is not the first time I have seen a rainbow, yet it

appears such. A phenomenon of this kind is always new, and the very thoughts it may suggest seem new also, though they may have passed through the mind no end of times before, in the presence of the same illusion. It seems almost a profanity to call it an illusion; nor, perhaps, is it so, strictly: its colours are all real, and I can reproduce them by the light of a lamp in-doors, by the help of a prism, and see them repeated in the crystal drops of the chandelier. But art has nothing to match against the rainbow; the spectrum may give the prismatic colours, but we must wait for the shower and the sun to paint for us the grand aërial bow, touching the two extremes of the horizon, and apparently supporting the heavens on a solid arch, of an order for which we have no name. It gives me a better idea of the vastness of space than what the astronomers tell of the distances of planets and stars; the mind can grasp little without the help of the senses, and I *see* how vast a span nature works in, and how careless she is of inches, feet, yards, or miles, when she requires space for the exhibition of a picture, for a period of a few seconds, which shall overpass the achievements of a thousand years of human art.

The rustling of a leaf will sometimes start the mind into a train of thought; how much more the display in the heavens of a spectacle so unsurpassed in beauty? It is the apparent extent of the great arc that first rouses me from my lethargy, by the feeling of wonder; its beauty calls forth my admiration, and I reflect that this is a very cheap sight, and may be enjoyed by all who choose to look on it, whether they be learned in the lore

of the Muses and the problems of philosophy, or ignorant
of the very names and objects of either.   My rainbow is
vanishing away—in another minute it will be gone; and
I may sink back into my favourite seat, darkened with
the festoons of the elegant glycine, and revolve in my
mind whatever thoughts arise out of this glorious vision
of aërial colouring.

I begin to wonder who was the first man to analyze
the rainbow, and arrive at a clear idea of the causes which
combine in its production.   The falling shower and the
direct light of the sun or moon must, from the first unfolding of this wondrous revelation, have been seen to
be its primary elements.   The allegory of the winds,
in the twenty-third book of the Iliad, indicates more
than a superficial knowledge of this grand phenomenon.
Virgil, in the Æneid, almost antedates the philosophy of
Descartes and Newton,* and Martial † was not far from
a scientific definition.   Aristotle believed himself to be
the first who had seen a lunar rainbow, the loveliest of
all aërial spectacles, except on those rare occasions when
the aurora borealis displays its darting flashes, ruby and
emerald and amethyst, in this climate.   But Pliny knew
almost as much as we do about it—certainly as to its
primal causes—as he expresses it " *Quod ergo iris sit
refractio aspectus est ad solem, manifestum est,*" and

---

* ——————" Ceu nubibus arcus
Mille trahit varios adverso sole colores."

Lib. v. l. 88.

† " Cæsurus alte sio rapit Iris aquas."

Lib. xii. ep. 29, 6.

Plutarch cites it as an index of the knowledge prevalent in his time.

Whatever may have been the thoughts of Adam, when the sunshine first resolved into prismatic colours, in an arch expanding over the region of the happy garden, those of Noah might well be more profound, for the rainbow became a part of his life, and through him a pledge of Divine mercy to the end of the world. "I do set my bow in the clouds"—marvellous utterance of a Father considerate of His children's fears. Those words possess me, as I look out over the gray sky where the rainbow glowed a few minutes since, and they seem to me to have all the force of an authority for research into the mind of God, the mind of man, and the ways of nature. The cause of the awful devastation of the globe is for ever rendered beautiful; the descending shower, which for forty days continued to submerge the offenders against Divine justice, seems to be woven into a robe of divers colours, and made pre-eminently beautiful, that they may henceforth cease to inspire dread. The fleecy clouds that held me in listless reverie half-an-hour since, and that are now dimming into ashy hues, seem to be impressed with similar evanescence and unsubstantiality, that man may look upon them henceforth as his friends that once were the destroyers of his race. And how deep a hold has that post-diluvian rainbow taken of the mind of man. It must be records of that fact we find cropping out in the old mythologies, as in the carrying of the rainbow-coloured fans in the procession of Apis; and the combination of the rainbow and the dove in hieroglyphics and mythological rites. Bryant

cites the names of the two attendants on Cleopatra,
Eiras, and Charmion, the Rainbow and the Dove, as
indicating the priestly office, and bringing down to a
later epoch in Egyptian history a remembrance of the
circumstances under which the earth was again peopled.
The rainbow was certainly the most renowned of Arkite
emblems, and I know not why Hesiod should designate
it "The Great Oath," except through the prevailing
power of a tradition, divine in its origin.   As such,
Homer knows it well,* and, in accordance with established
usage in the ancient world, he calls it, in a hymn to Selene,
the sign and intimation (of Divine promise) to mortals.†
The appeal to it by the Deity as something superior to
the secondary gods is characteristic of Hesiod, who describes Iris as the servant of Jove, who fetches from
afar, in a golden cup, the waters of many names; making
her the representative of covenant and of purification.
Osiris entering the ark, Deucalion reproving the lawless-
ness of the men of violence by whom he was surrounded,
Nannacus sacrificing in the temple, are but versions
of a history, of which the heavens bear the best secular
memorial, after the special and Divine record given for
"our edification."   But did Noah understand the purport

---

* " Ἶρισσιν ἐοικότες ἅς τε κρονίων
   Ἐν νεφεῖ στήριξε, τέρας μερόπων ἀνθρώπων."
                                        IL., Λ. 27.

   " Ἠΰτε πορφυρέην Ἶριν θνητοῖσι τανύσσῃ
   Ζεὺς ἐξ οὐρανόθεν, τέρας ἔμμεναι."
                                        IL., P 547.

† " Τέκμωρ δε βρότοις και σῆμα τετυκται."
                                        v. 13.

of the rainbow, as a key to the mysteries of man's relations to the Divine essence? We know not, but it is a key for all that; and herein we see how the discoveries of science lend help to theology, and indicate truths that lie at the foundation of all harmonies, both of matter and of spirit.

Consider what a wonderful work a rainbow is. The passage of light through a refracting medium causes·the light to separate into its component parts. We see those component parts as it were in the colours of the arc. Ordinary daylight is a compound of all colours, say, to use a homely phrase, all the colours of the rainbow. The use of a prism is to anatomize a ray of light, and cause it to exhibit the violet, green, amber, orange, and red rays of which it is composed. Just as the prism dissects all rays of light, so does each drop of water of which the rainbow is composed; but those are *falling* drops; if they were suspended and immoveable, we might more easily understand the history of the phenomenon. All the colours we behold in the rainbow are around and about us in the daylight, so diffused and blended, that we can know nothing of their separate powers, until by some act of refraction each is made manifest. But each colour has its own peculiarity, so persistent that they may all be obtained from a pencil of light not thicker than a cobweb, as easily as from a broad band of uninterrupted sunlight. In a dark room, admitting light only by a small hole pierced in a shutter, the prism may be so positioned as that the place of the red, the orange, or the violet ray shall be determined beforehand; for each ray comes out at its own angle, and the places

of the rays are dependent on a fixed law of their variable
refrangibility. Suppose the angle of the violet ray to be
40° 17', then the angle of the red will be 42° 2', and
the difference between them will be the breadth of the bow,
or 1° 45'. So, if we suppose the bow to be divided in
breadth into 360 equal parts, the red will occupy 45
parts, and the violet 80; the orange 27, and the indigo
40; the yellow 48, and the blue 60; and mid-way between
them will be the green, consisting of 60 parts. So far
as I know, it has never been observed that these proportions are exactly adapted to the capacity of the human
eye for the distinguishing of colours. These are, in
fact, just the proportions in which a flower-bed should be
planted, or a coloured frieze arranged, to tell with best
effect as a pictorial harmony. The violet and indigo are
the least attractive to the eye, and they have a breadth of
80 and 40, respectively; the yellow and orange are the
most attractive, and they have a breadth of 48 and 27;
orange, moreover, is the most garish of colours, and, if
injudiciously used in artificial colouring, gives a vulgar
tone to the picture. Here observe, it is subordinate to
the group of colder tints, and has the least space of all.
Green, on which the eye always rests with complacency,
has a breadth of 60, enough to satisfy and harmonize the
colours of opposite classes on each side of it; and that
it may not obliterate by unhappy juxtaposition the blue
which joins it on the violet side, the blue has an equal
breadth, and cannot be dismissed by the most casual
observer. Mark, lastly, that the warm rays on the red
side of the green have an aggregate breadth of 120, and
the cold rays a breadth of 180—a system of compensations

which we know to be harmonious, because divine; but
the harmony is proved by philosophy and experience, and
the rainbow may be cited as the absolutely perfect example of the disposition of colours, for the gratification
of human vision.

But the prisms by which this spectrum is formed are
not fixed, but moveable—rapidly moveable; no one of
them for an instant keeps its place. How, then, is the
immoveable, apparently solid, and eternal arch sustained
in its prismatic completeness? The question is easily
answered. Just as in the glass prism the white light
refranges, and each of its component parts becomes
visible as a separate colour; so, for all practical purposes, the apparent fixity and permanence of the rainbow
is secured by the means of myriads of falling prisms. If
they did not fall, some other effect than that we witness
would be the result. The rays of light from the sun
are parallel, and for purposes of inquiry we may say
there is but one ray, and out of that proceeds the
variety of colours. So, instead of a million disjointed
water drops, let us suppose there is but one, and on
the surface of that one we desire the whole spectrum to
be displayed. Now, in falling, the *under side* of that
drop will first touch the ray; as it proceeds, the centre
will come to the ray; and lastly, the ray will fall on the
upper side of the drop, and at last above it altogether.
At each of these several positions the angle of incidence
will be such as to bring out the colours belonging to
each; and it is therefore evident, that if the colours
were of the same degree of refrangibility, there could be
no rainbow at all, and conversely, if their relative refran-

gibility were otherwise than as they are, the spectrum
would be differently proportioned. Severe mathematical
laws, therefore, are requisite in this (as in other cases),
to the production of a pictorial harmony unsurpassed
among the wonders and mysteries of nature.

But philosophy tells me I am only on the threshold
yet of all that the rainbow might teach of things mysterious in earth and heaven. The Scandinavians had a
glimmer of deeper truths than are apparent in their
wild mythology, when they made the rainbow the pathway for the gods, and assigned it to the guardianship of
Heimdaller. It is a connecting link between the human
and divine, much more definitely than the poets describe
it ; and an analysis of its constitution reveals harmonies
far higher in import than those of its perfect form and
exquisite blending of colours. It consists of seven
colours. SEVEN, the sacred number. In the recon-
struction of society after the Flood, it became the
heavenly symbol of the creation of the earth in seven
efforts of Divine power in seven periods of time. The
resting of the ark in the seventh month, and the sending
forth of the dove *thrice*, at intervals of *seven days*, has a
meaning in connection with the sign given afterwards as
an " everlasting covenant between God and every living
creature !" The clean beasts were taken into the ark
in sevens; and the whole round of feasts and fasts
prescribed in the Mosaic law were based on the number
seven, as indicative of the final fulfilment of the Divine
will regarding man according to a numerical law, more
than shadowed in the seven golden candlesticks of
the Apocalypse. But these mysterious sevens are of

secondary import. I cannot discover the presence of
the number even analogically in the nature of things. I
cannot resolve my body into seven parts; nor will the
elements group themselves in sevens, and I cannot force
by fancy a conclusion not based in fact. But so is the
division of the rainbow into seven parts apparent and
not real; it has but THREE. If the seven were
secondary, the three are primary; there are but three
primal colours. The orange of the rainbow is the result
of the blending of the red and yellow; the green the
result of the blending of the yellow and blue: the blue,
the indigo, and the violet, are deepening shades of one
primary colour—the red, the yellow, and the blue, are
three distinct elements which by association make up
the mysterious seven. Science tells me more than this.
She says each of these distinct rays has distinct properties. There is most light in the yellow ray, most heat
in the red, most chemical power in the blue. Light has
three properties, then, made specially known to me in the
spectrum; and I can find no more than these three
recorded in the books.

Now I understand how that, by a lens of ice, gun-
powder may be fired, and yet the ice through which the
heating rays passed, remains unmelted. I can understand, also, that the rainbow is a reality to the eyesight
only, a spectrum in truth, and that no two persons ever
saw the same rainbow, or ever will, though they may
proclaim their illusions to be identical; and for purposes
of intelligible speech, the rainbow seen at the same time
may be the same to all beholders. So, too, lenses trans-
mitting light on objects do get heated, though but

slightly, and a thermometer placed at the red end of the spectrum shows a higher temperature than one placed at the blue end, which blue end the photographer requires for his operations, in converting a shadow into a picture—as fixed as if painted in enduring pigments. If the heating power of the blue ray be counted *one*, that of the green will be *two*, and that of the red more than *three and a half*, and that of the colourless part just beyond the red about *four and a half*. The ripe peach, glowing with a vermilion blush, shows a response to the red rays by which it elaborated its sweet juices; the ripe apple, burning with red on the side next the sun, tells me of oxygen, *the sourer*, incorporated into an acid, by that very pencil of red light which forms the boundary at one side of the rainbow. The fading of my red window-curtains tells me of the energy of the blue rays in de-oxydising; for the pigment the manufacturer used was an oxide, and the blue rays mixed with the ordinary daylight, constantly operate in setting free the oxygen, and restoring the oxide to its metallic form. Three colours, three powers, and these variously proportioned in every climate of the world, so as to produce flowers of intensest hues, and fruits of delicious flavours, in the tropics, and in this country only during summer; pale-coloured flowers and less sugary fruits, in colder climates and at colder seasons in this country. The frame of nature seems now to be suspended on the rainbow—wonderful fabric, to be upheld by so fragile a thread! What is the story of Damocles to this enigma of the motherly Sphynx?

The grey of the evening thickens, the sun is nearly

down, but I see the rainbow still; not in the heavens, but in the hues of the deep green leaf, grey bark, tawny gravel, and thin mist rolling eastward. The world seems to be made of rainbows, and every one arches up to heaven, and invites me to try my trembling footsteps thither. That old apple tree yonder has been living on rainbows eighty years. If I cut it down and burn it to charcoal, I shall only learn that it abstracted charcoal from air and water by the agency of the sunbeams. And as the eye involuntarily resolves things into parts, so the mystical number of the rainbow is evidently written out. I can see but *three* parts therein. I believe in Goethe's theory of vegetable morphology, and that the tree is, therefore, an expanded leaf. It is all leaf, root, bark, branch, and ripened fruit stem. Its *oneness* is in harmony with its parent rainbow. But the oneness divides into three without force. The root is the leaf absorbing; the stem and branches are the leaf elaborating; the leaf itself is the leaf breathing; the blossoms are but leaves coloured; and the fruit only leaves gorged with acid and saccharine juices: it is a threefold being, and in harmony with the rest of the world, in which it has but a humble place. I look out into the vast space which evening has darkened, and on which the stars begin to glimmer, and can mentally pierce it only horizontally and vertically, and then the mind insists on a circumference. So space, in the midst of which the rainbow plants itself as if it would endure to the end of the world, has but three properties, and I can find no more. It is the same with tangible objects: they have length, breadth, and thickness—the last is their circumference;

s

and I revert in memory to Oken, who, with all his wild dreaming in the " Physiophilosophy," has shown that the number Three is the key to the universe. Take the whole range of nature—animal, vegetable, mineral; it is three-fold in form and properties: there is a numerical har-mony throughout, which the hardest anti-mystic cannot gainsay. All forms, animate and inanimate, appear to be modelled on one uniform plan. In the sphere I can find but three elements—the centre, the circumference, and the solid contents. In the qualities of matter, they must be either solid, liquid, or gaseous, and the old notion of the four elements shrinks to three; for fire is an effect, not an element, and earth, air, and water com-prise the category of created things. Dividing again, I can only count up three forms of matter—the metallic, the non-metallic, and the aeriform. In the organic world, animal and vegetable offer the most distinct duality, but science has not yet settled the question of the place that certain microscopic organisms should occupy; and as I assume nothing, I find three orders of animated beings. Dividing these, to the exclusion of the doubtful class, there are among vegetables—Acotyledons, Monocoty-ledons, and Dycotyledons. So among animals, there are —Inarticulate, Articulate, and Vertebrate; and I know of none but conform to the simple threefold arrangement.

What of myself?—the rays of light, and the colours locked up in every ray, reflect my being; the sunshine that browns the hand and bronzes the face brings with it a glow of health unknown to the man who leads a noc-turnal life, who is immured in a coal mine, or who dwells in permanent shadow. The prick of a pin informs me

of the reality of my corporeal frame. I know that two
is the multiple of one, and therefore contains one within
it : thereby I am informed of the reality of my mental
nature. I experience emotions that the mental nature
cannot analyse : conscience warns me, love animates me,
devotion calms me. I have a third possession—it is the
Spirit. The threefold man is a part of a threefold
system ; and in every trembling of the heart to God, he
bears testimony to the power of the rainbow to unlock
the secrets of earth and heaven.

I can now take comfort from the words of a renowned
thinker, and agree with him that "the day is not
wholly profane in which we have given heed to some
natural object." But I have lost all my faith in Emer-
sonian transcendentalism in the acceptance of a faith
which carries me far beyond the temporary shifts of a
perverted Platonism which has sought to graft old saws
on the root stocks of modern manners. One of Emerson's brightest and most attractive passages is that
wherein he pictures Nature as a duality ; to me Nature
appears as a triplicity, and in this view I find a solid
basis of fact to supplant the eccentricities of fancy. The
rainbow tells me of the presence of three powers in the
ordering of the universe ; and as its noble arch carries
my eye to heaven, so my thoughts go with it, and the
stars that have now succeeded to the spectral vision join
in the mighty psalm—"There are THREE that bear
record in heaven, and these three are one." Trinity in
unity is the thought forced upon us in every analysis of
material things. The rainbow inspires us with wonder,
not by its beauty only, but by its accord with a truth of

which man is the highest earthly representative. In the communion of the Omnipotent with man, it is appropriately the sign of covenant, and the visible reminder of the fundamental truth of human history, that "in the image of God" was man created, the possessor of body, soul, and spirit.

Considered historically and ethically, the rainbow holds the highest place among natural phenomena. It is the visible union of earth and heaven; it spans them both in an embrace so vast as to appear sufficient to make one for ever. It is the assurance to man that he shall run his allotted race in the enjoyment of seedtime and harvest, and summer and winter, without fear of the consuming flood which was once appointed for the destruction of his apostate predecessors. In this view it gives at least a hint of the triplicity of divine providences; for, in the re-peopling of the earth, *three* progenitors went forth of the ark; and the best summaries of ethnological research confirm the record that the existing families of men owe their origin to three distinct stocks, the types of which are still traceable. I can still apostrophise the rainbow, though it long since faded from its glorious place in the heavens. I will accept the poetic doctrine for the sake of the real poetry there is in it, that the rainbow bears the blue heaven on its sweeping arch, and that it is the pathway on which ministering angels descend to man with messages of mercy.

> "Still seem as to my childhood's gaze,
>   A midway station given;
> For happy spirits to alight,
>   Betwixt the earth and heaven."

The remembrance of its beauty fills me with adoration to Him who sitteth with a rainbow round about His throne; I tremble before the deep truths it has unfolded to me, and I offer my soul to God as an unworthy creature. It has suggested to me the affluence of that exhaustless energy which needs but to will and it is done; that same energy which to things of simplest use adds the touch of perfect and enduring beauty. It has shown me, too, how infinite variety may result from varied phases of the same facts, how a universe may partake of one idea in its elements, construction, order, and completeness. It tells me, too, of the tenderness of divine love, the sympathy, compassion, and gentle consideration of my God for the most ungrateful of his creatures; for the very rain drops that splash out of the rainbow on the green herb sing the praises of the Lord, and have for the burden of their song this monition for us— "Wide as the rainbow stretch all arms of faith, and seek happiness as the reward, not of proving, but believing."

The evening breeze has died away; the moon throws a yellow gleam athwart the grass. The dews thicken, and as I glance across the moisture-spangled herbage, I see a sufficient play of iridescence to be assured that every dew-drop bears a rainbow: and I remember that Shakspere saw the rainbow in a tear, and placed on record, in anticipation of philosophy, the fact, that there is the same completeness and the same properties in the spectrum formed by the minutest shining globule as in

the cloud-formed bow of iris.*   We are often reminded
that Lord Bacon uncovered his head to the rain.   I will
out-do the reverent lover of Nature by offering homage
to the rainbow.   I rejoice in the prismatic glitter of its
million disjointed water drops, for the rain is a present
harmony emblematic of the eternal harmony in which
all created things are as component colours.   How
much more homage, and of another sort, shall we pay
to Him who, having created all things in wisdom, now
sitteth on the throne judging His creatures in righteous-
ness, while holding the universe in the hollow of His
hand?

* Captain Scoresby was the first to use a telescope to view the
prismatic hues of dew on a grass-plot, and the method is one of
the prettiest ever devised in the study of natural philosophy.

FIDO FIDES.

FIDO and I have been companions so many years that we have learnt each other's language, and have succeeded in establishing between us a telegraphic system, as a re-source upon occasions when language is of no avail. We are just now enjoying the warmth of the fire, and the light of the lamp, quite ready for fun, if either should give the hint; yet sedate and quiet, and mutually thoughtful. Fido has serious objections to the noise the birds make. He dares not attempt to put a stop to it. He bears with it for my sake; but I know, by his looks, that he wishes the birds were fast asleep, as they were an hour ago, when all was quiet, and we were taking tea together in the lower room. There is a drop of bitterness in the cup of life given to every creature, and the drop in Fido's cup is to see my attention divided when the birds wake up at lamp light, and make a polyglot fuss and clatter. Old Poll is exercising her lungs in selling bonnet boxes, and calling me an "Old Silly." The canaries are sing-ing lustily one against the other, having enjoyed an hour's nap in the dark, during tea-time. "Trot," the sulphur-crested cockatoo, has taken his usual license of springing on my shoulder, and tapping his great black horny beak

on the tip of my nose—a performance which we call
"knocking at the door;" and "Rosy," the rose-billed
parakeet, is having a noisy quarrel with Patty, the red-
headed parakeet, about getting on the top link of the
chain, which is suspended in the bird-room for their
scansorial exercises. Rosy has touched the topmost link,
and her long tail is in Patty's way of reaching it, so they
are scolding each other most vociferously, and the excitement is shared by the rest of the family, and a terrible
screaming and trumpeting is the result. It so happens
that Trot is permitted to do things forbidden to the rest.
He is allowed to pull my hair, nibble my ear, and thrust
his mandibles into my waistcoat pocket, in a search for
nuts; now that a small confusion has arisen, he joins
the chorus, and is shouting at the top of his voice, and
displaying his daffodil crest, like the war gear of a white
Indian. Why I note these things is that they make
Fido sad. Fido is jealous. Fido desires to monopolise
my affections, and though he is on the best of terms,
apparently, with the birds, I believe that in secret he
would like to make savoury meat of them. But if some
intruder were to enter the house in the night, and
attempt to carry off one feathered pet from the family,
would Fido rejoice to see one rival taken? Not he.
Woe to the marauder while Fido has the use of his
limbs and fangs. But this noise must be stopped, and
it is but short work under my system of discipline. One
smart clap of the hands will suffice to demand attention.
There—all is quiet, and into their several cages they go
with wonderful celerity. Even Trot is disposed of, for
I am tired of his impudent fidgetting. Now it amuses

me to see the culprits looking through their prison bars
with envious looks at Fido. Poll says, in a serious voice,
"Naughty Dog." Betty says, " Hang that Fido ;" and
my pretty, amiable, forgiving "Dyardac" (self-christened)
whistles the chromatic scale in a low, sweet tone, as if
engaged in a music lesson. Now Fido knows that certain speeches refer to him, and with a flip of his ears,
he springs up with his fore-legs on my knee, and fixing
his bright eyes full on mine, sets his tail wagging at a
rate of rapidity which threatens to wag it off. Now
Fido speaks. You, my reader, would call it " a whine;"
but the words are, " You don't mean to hang Fido, do
you?" Being in a mischievous mood, I pucker my
mouth, frown slightly, and mutter "Well, we shouldn't
miss him much, he's a noisy dog." Fido plunges forward with a force that nearly throws me from my seat ;
he is at my neck—not to harm me, but to put his warm
face against mine, and say, in a louder tone than before,
" You'd never forgive yourself." "No Fido, no; good
dog."

Little events of this kind are fully as suggestive to me
of the diversity of talents with which animals are gifted
as the most curious anecdotes that abound in the books.
If I am in the garden, and I tell Fido to fetch my cap,
the cap is brought me as a matter of course. If I were in
a strange place, and threw down my purse, telling him to
mind it, I should know it to be as safe as in my own
pocket, though Fido is neither powerful, nor savage, nor
best fitted for encounters, of all the dogs I know. The
real source of enjoyment in companionships of this kind
is the establishment of a mutual sympathy and under-

standing; and I never kept an animal yet, not even a slow worm, but in course of time something of a mutual understanding was established, and thenceforward our communion bore more or less resemblance to a conversation. To talk *with* parrots and dogs is neither impossible nor difficult, but you must first learn to talk *to* them; after which the other is a work of time. The curious narratives that are related, as of the man who took a thorn from a lion's foot, and another who was on such terms with an oyster that it followed him about like a dog, have one common basis, the establishment of a conversational intimacy, if not in sounds, then by the language of the eyes. I am satisfied that Fido knows all my thoughts, and I am also satisfied that I know most of his; that is, so far as the thoughts of either party relate to things in which we are mutually interested. Now that our caresses are over, and the birds are getting drowsy again, Fido sees that I want half an hour's quiet, and he prepares himself to take a nap.

I like sitting here with these pretty creatures for an hour or two at night. The greetings I get on entering the room compensate for all the vexations and anxieties of the day; and I sit sometimes for hours, asking them mysterious questions about the origin of things, and the properties of life. I cannot say that their answers are such as can be written down literally as delivered, but they satisfy me, and if there is any one less perspicuous than the rest, Fido is interpreter, and explains the thing aright.

A friend who drops in at this moment with a message of good news asks me why I sit here, with a large fire and huge moderator lamp, keeping the poor things awake. I tell him it is for the mutual good of all parties that we should hold converse frequently. It so happens that the birds have now settled themselves for the night, the lamp light no longer disturbs them; they are now only so many feathery balls, each having buried its head beneath its wing. Fido having offered my friend a faint recognition, makes three turns like a horse in a mill, and then screws himself up on the rug, and like the rest goes to sleep and dreaming.

This friend of mine has, I know, come at this hour expecting a little amusement, in seeing me pass my birds through their tricks and performances, but it so happens he has come too late. Looking round the room, he sees that old Poll has waked up at his entrance, and he is about to address a word to her, when she says "good-bye," and at once tucks her head beneath her wing, and joins the rest in the region of slumber.

Friend.—What a curious bird that is, one might think she knew the meanings of our words.

Myself.—She does know their meaning, and rarely wastes a word or utters one inappropriately.

Friend.—Ah! you think so much about your pets, that you are prepared to go to any extreme.

Myself.—Not so, you have been here often enough to have observed that Poll invariably makes her speeches suit events or express her wants.

Friend.—I've seen some strange coincidences certainly, I shan't soon forget how she looked at the leg of mutton, and asked, "Is that for Poll?" But coincidences are to be rated at their proper value and nothing more, you don't mean to say that all talking birds speak with similar purpose and appropriateness.

Myself.—No : that is simply because they differ in
degrees of intelligence, Poll does not understand the
words she utters as we understand them, but by constant
practice and observation she has learnt to associate certain speeches with certain events, and that act of association it is that charms and surprises us. But it ought
not to surprise us, for no vertebrate animal could exist
unless capable of thinking.

Friend.—"Thinking!" well, you may almost say "thinking," for instinct manifests itself in marvellous ways occasionally, and comes very near to the borders of thought.

Myself.—When I say "thinking," I mean thinking :
they think as we do ; their range of thought is limited,
but is equal to the range of their existence, and it is a
settled conviction of mine (not hastily adopted), that
animals possess a power of ratiocination of precisely the
same kind as that possessed by man.

Friend.—What you mean is, that instinct often resembles intelligence, and might be mistaken for intelligence,
did we not know that man is the sole possessor of reason.

Myself.—No : that is not what I mean. I say that
that parrot and that dog both reason upon events and
circumstances in the same way as I do, and to an extent
commensurate with their wants and their place in the order of creation. Man is not the sole possessor of reason.

Friend.—Then you admit Fido to an equality with
yourself.

Myself.—Yes : in the possession of the faculty of reasoning I do. But mark : his reasoning powers are bounded by a circle of less radius than mine, that is the only difference.

Friend.—Then I suppose you concede to him the possession of immortality, because it seems to me that if the mind endures, and the brutes possess mind, there is no escape from the conclusion that they, like man, are destined to live for ever. That practically is your feeling on this matter.

Myself.—I have no objection to the immortality of any and every animal, whether an elephant or an earth worm, *that* is not my business; but I have yet to learn what immortality has to do with the subject.

Friend.—You assert that these people (as you call them) share, in common with man, the faculty of thought. Now, according to our faith, it is in the possession of thought that man is distinguished from the creatures around him; and it is his mental faculty which is pre-eminently destined to live for ever. If, therefore, we accept immortality for man, let us be fair, and do the same for these brutes.

Myself.—Let us be fair by all means, and if it is to be so, I have not the least objection to meet Fido in heaven. If there is a paradise for birds and dogs, and all the rest of the creatures, my disapproval will not affect the fact. But this is a point I do not raise. I know nothing about it; all I contend for is, that the mind of the animal is of the same kind as the mind of man, and that it differs from the mind of man only in capacity. The other points are of your introducing.

Friend.—It's getting late. We'll talk this matter over again. For the present, let me warn you: the conse-

quences of your opinion, I very much fear it, will be
fatal to your faith.

We did talk over the matter; and the following is a
summary of the conclusion we arrived at :—

The customary mode of ascribing the actions of animals
to the operation of a faculty called instinct, is not only
unsatisfactory but false. The word is used as a loophole
from a supposed difficulty; namely, that animals think.
Admitting that we know little or nothing of either
instinct or intelligence in their essence, we do know that
in their manifestation they are widely different. Let us
take the best known, and most wonderful, perhaps, of
all the recorded examples of instinct—the work of the
honey-bee. If we propose to call this intelligence, we
become responsible to prove that the bee is acquainted
with the laws of geometry, as applied to the economising
of the bulk and strength of materials. But the work of
the bee differs from the work of an intelligent creature
in its constant uniformity : when uniformity is departed
from, there may be some reason to conclude that intelligence is the moving power, and in the bee we occasionally witness exhibitions of intelligence, but in its whole
life it is pre-eminently a creature of instinct. What,
then, is instinct? It is a blind impulse, operating by
means it does not understand, to attain ends of which it
is probably ignorant. This definition may be unsatisfactory, but it will suffice to indicate the recognised
distinctions between instinct and intelligence ; the latter
has an object in view, and it reasons upon data, in order
to ascertain the best means to attain to the fulfiment of
its desires. Among the best known examples of instinct,

we may class the operations of the beaver, the flight of
wild fowl, the work of the ant, the wasp, and the madre-
pore. Some of these may appear to be partly the result
of intelligence and it is quite true, that the two powers
are often combined when one is insufficient for the
required purpose. Thus the bee may obey a blind
instinct, while constructing a cell in accordance with
mathematical law ; but it may be guided by intelligence,
when some obstruction has to be met, by a deviation
from the ordinary method of its work. A kitten will
watch at a mouse-hole before it has seen a mouse, and
a squirrel will deal with the first nut with as much skill
and apparent knowledge of the kernel it contains as
with any subsequent nut, in the opening of which it may
have the supposed advantage of experience. Who taught
the weasel the situation of the jugular vein, or the
butterfly the nature of the plant on which its caterpillars
will feed ? Take this last case as our best example, and
we can then pass on. A butterfly deposits its first egg
on the leaf which is best adapted for the support of the
caterpillar which will ultimately emerge from that egg.
The butterfly never tasted the leaf itself, never saw the
egg before, has never seen a caterpillar. It may be
that the odour of the leaf attracts it : it may be—to give
rein to conjecture—that the leaf possesses the property
of causing it to deposit its eggs thereon, when by chance
it alights there. All that concerns us now is to observe,
that these so-called instinctive actions are uniform in
character, and independent of acquired experience. It is
worthy of note, also, that where there is least intelligence,
instinct is most powerful, and *vice versâ*, as intellect

advances, instinct declines; so that in man we can but faintly trace its last glimmerings.

But it must be again asserted that instinct is not the only guiding faculty of the brute. It has been proved, for instance, that crows can count three. At any country fair you may see learned ponies, learned pigs, and learned dogs. Were those animals not possessed of mental faculties of precisely the same kind as the mental faculties of man, it would be impossible to teach them the difference between A and B, much less to spell words and count numbers. Some of the anecdotes told of elephants, in Sir Emerson Tennant's "Natural History of Ceylon," are sufficiently conclusive as to the perfection of the reasoning powers of that noble beast, to bring a blush of shame to the face of any who would take refuge in the word instinct, or endeavour to substitute for intelligence that less distinctive word "sagacity." But here is Fido; let him answer for himself. When he enjoyed fewer comforts than he does now, a bone was regarded as a treasure. If a nice bone came in his way when hunger had been satisfied, he found a place to hide it, and when hunger returned he found the bone acceptable. Now, instinct would not accomplish this piece of thrifty strategy. It implies anticipation of a future want, a knowledge of what will supply that want, judgment in the selection of a place of concealment, memory of its whereabouts, and a power of combining all these several ideas; so as to render them practically useful in regard to one object—bone. Now, if it be conceded that in one act, as in this case, of hiding a bone, an animal establishes a claim to be placed on the same footing with

man, as to the possession of intellect, the supposed
" consequences" of the concession cannot be aggravated
by the concession of mind to the whole animal kingdom.
Dr. Cromwell, indeed, in his recent work on the "Future
Life," puts it as a case for consideration, whether vegetables think. Let us here deal with certainties; let us
admit that animals are endowed with reasoning faculties,
and, for the sake of truth, brave all possible " consequences."

When this admission has been frankly made, the gra-
dations of intelligence in the animal kingdom are seen to
follow pretty nearly the order of organic development.
It may be very hard to discover any traces of intelligence
in a rotifer or starfish; but among the vertebrata, the
degree of intelligence is evidently related to the degree
of perfection of the nervous system. As we ascend the
scale of animated nature, we see intellect acquiring more
and more strength, and instinct declining, to make way
for it. The conformations of the nervous system are in
every case parallel to the degree of intelligence, and the
brain is, in bulk and quality, the measure of the mind.
Thus an observer, skilled in the dissection of the nervous
centres, familiar with the various dispositions of the
interlacing fibres (first fully demonstrated by Dr. Ma-
cartney), and experienced in the observation of the
. psychical peculiarities of various orders of the vertebrata
—an observer so fitted for the task could predicate, from
an investigation of the brain of an animal, its place in
the intellectual scale of being, as accurately as the physical place of an animal can be determined by an investigation of a few bones or a tooth. Mere size of brain,

T

irrespective of quality and structure, may be taken as a safe criterion of relative intellect for general purposes. Thus the pike has a brain only 1·1305 of the bulk of the body; the tortoise, lower still in the ranks of intelligence, has a brain only 1·2240 the bulk of the body; but in this instance the carapace increases the apparent disproportion beyond the reality. The sheep has a brain 1·351 that of the body. The only points of real interest in the recent discussions on the gorilla, were those relating to its osteological and cephalic homologies; and the last of these would have been valueless, if the size, form, and structure of the brain were not regarded by all the parties to the discussion as directly related to the degree of intelligence possessed by the creature. Intelligence dawns upon us as we ascend the scale of animated creation, and its growth is so strictly parallel with the advancing characters of the nervous system, as to establish indubitably the most perfect correspondence between them. If we cannot define what mind is, we can at least say, these are the instruments with which it works; and the better the instruments, the more extended its range, and the more complete its operations.

Man stands at the head of creation, because in him the excellencies of all nature are combined. In the expert Indian marksman there is the eye of the eagle; Deerfoot, who runs six miles in fifty-three minutes, has the fleetness of the horse. The Kalmucks have the scent of the hound, and can tell if a fox is in his earth or not. The Bedouins of the desert can hear the approach of a caravan, and determine the nature of it, while it is yet leagues away. We, who have not culti-

vated any particular bodily faculty, are too hasty in
ascribing superiorities of sense and muscular power to
hawks, and hounds, and horses; but, in truth, man can
match any of them, surpass them in perception and
strength, and assert his lordship on those grounds alone.
But it is the perfection of his nervous system which
enables him to compete with the horse, the fox, the
eagle, and the camel; for the system of communications
between his senses and his mind is elaborated to a
perfection excelling theirs, and his nutritive system is
equal to the demands of all possible circumstances of
ordinary or extraordinary effort both of the limbs and of
the will. Art appeals to us directly by means of the
senses, and the most attractive delights of literature
require the exercise of memory on the facts of sensation.
For what else does imagination work with, but stored
reminiscences of what has been previously felt, and seen,
and heard? But add to this perfection of his senses
the immense capacity of his brain, its refined construction and numerous convolutions: give him a hand in
which the sense of touch is wonderfully developed: give
him his upright attitude—and creation *must* own him as
entitled to dominion. But the superiority, so far, is
wholly physical. The brain of Homer or Shakspere is
not chemically different to the brain of a Hottentot;
and the brain of the Hottentot contains no chemical
principles not to be found in the brain of the Orang
Outang. It is not necessary to the determination of
distinctions, to insist that thought is a direct result of
the operation of the nervous system; but we should not
be deterred from accepting such a conclusion, if facts

directly point that way, through any fear of consequences. For my own part, I must incline to the belief that the correspondence between the development of the nervous system and the degree of intelligence is a correspondence of cause and effect; and, as my friend Fido thinks as I do, makes similar calculations, and is inferior in mental power only because he has a less perfect organization, I must acknowledge that in mental faculties we are not distinguished initially, though we may be so relatively. The difference between myself and Fido is in degree, not in kind; and if man is immortal because of his possession of a mental faculty, then Fido must enjoy immortality too, and, as my friend said, I must expect to meet him in heaven.

God has given man a power of thought which separates him by a vast distance from the animal; a quickness of perception, and a fertility of invention, that entitle him, even *as an animal*, to the lordship of the earth. But we must not mistake this for aught else than what the brutes, which own his sway, share in common with him. If the creatures that obey him were destitute of mind of the same nature as his own, he would find little in their history to interest him, and in their companionship still less to profit him. What would be the value of a charger, if, when his rider fell helpless on his neck, he should halt to graze and drink, instead of hastening to the camp with his bleeding burden? What the value of a sheep dog, if incapable of reasoning upon the facts of locality and property? What the value of a camel that could not count its driver's steps, and enjoy the cadence of an Arabian song

during its midnight marches? The brute and the man
are alike in these two points, that they possess body and
mind; and, if the first has no future life, no more has
the second. Twofold man is simply the best animal;
the finest example of organic structure. Physiology
cuts from beneath his feet the great hope of a future
life, and classes him at once with the beasts that perish.

But at this point physiology leaves us. It has not
told the whole story of the life of man, or the life of
brute. It can instruct us how we obtain impressions
from the senses, and perhaps indicate in what way the
brain of a philosopher differs from the brain of a fool.
What can it tell us of innate ideas? and who, after the
study of Kant, will deny that we possess them? Even
the laws of reason do not explain all the life that is
within us. Intellectual operations may depend on
sequence; but the moral feelings are above sequence,
and, in regard to logic, irresponsible. If every impulse
of man could be tested by the laws of mental philosophy,
psychological problems might be settled on the basis of
mathematics. The moral life of man cannot be put into
the same crucible as that intended for the analysis of his
thoughts. No exercise of the senses, no observation
of fact, no process of reasoning, is needed to give occasion to the experience of a moral faculty, or compel
attention to the voice of conscience. I find no conscience in the brute, no moral life in the creatures that
are happy in companionship with man. There are no
evidences of the idea of devotion, and with them even
love can only claim to be regarded as a maternal instinct
sufficient for the perpetuation of the species. There is no

advance, historically or individually. Fido is a clever
dog; but I am satisfied that the dog that kept Abel's
sheep was quite as clever. Much of the advancement of
man in civilization is the result of his superiority of
intellect; but it is the moral faculty which has sustained
him in the constant desire to overpass old boundaries,
and attain to something better and higher. We talk of
"progress," and we do injustice to ourselves in not at
once attributing all progress to the power of that principle within us, which is impulsive in its nature, and
independent in its action, both of sequence and sense.
This is the true line of demarcation between man and
animals. By mind he is related to the brute, even as by
the flesh he is related to the dust. But above that, superior
to it, and independent of it, is the moral life—the pole-
star of his spiritual firmament, shining on the borders of
both worlds; by *that* he is related to God.

Thus the study of the life of the brute is essential to
a fair apprehension of the life of man; and, in some
measure, it becomes an aid to faith. Man consists of
three elements—a body to feel, a mind to think, a spirit
to love, fear, and worship. The aims of the spirit are
above the earth, and beyond the life; it vindicates the
moral justice that presides in this world, and explains
the moral perfection that reigns in heaven. As the
brute is threefold—body, soul, and instinct, so is man
threefold—body, soul, and spirit; and the harmony of
creation with the God who ordained it is established by
the aid of a concession which appeared to be fraught
with disastrous consequences.

As to the future life of animals, we know nothing.

Job speaks of the "spirit of a beast that goeth downward." In the correspondences of things, from which we derive our idea of harmony, instinct is the spirit of the brute; but, for all we know, instinct may be as much the product of matter as mind, for its successional developments are in a downward course, just as those of intelligence are in an upward course. We can only reason upon what we know, and we know this—that within us is a life added to that of thought, and that when intellectual parallels are at an end, man acquires a distinct place in the universe, by virtue of his impulses to moral good. The doctrines of Kant have never clashed with the conclusions of physiology. We may fearlessly connect thought with organization; and then Kant would ask about ideas *à priori*, about the spiritual resources of man, about his power of conceiving things that lie beyond the region of experience—such as infinity, God, the supreme Good. The answer must be, that man is a threefold creature; that these, his highest efforts, are the province of his imperishable spirit; and that thence his faith, though reason may assist it, is above reason in its nature, as it is also in its destiny. Intelligence drags him down to earth, conscience lifts him towards heaven, as a creature desirous of attaining "to the all good and the all fair." His aspirations are upward; such, too, is his path. It is his spirit that leads him; and only by so much as he trusts to *that* will his aims be purified, his faith perfected, and he himself fitted for an inheritance of eternal joy.

MEMORIES OF MISCHIEF.

"Oh, the happy days of youth
Are fast gaun by."

GILFILLAN.

HE must be either a very bad or very wretched man who does not look back with fond pleasure to the days of his boyhood—"the days when hope and life were young"—and bring back from that garden of green memories some fruits so refreshing, that now and then a tear shall fall on them like a joy-token, which the heart is willing to drop as the price of its new gladness. Boyhood! Ah, how racy is the very word—how suggestive of impulsive generosity—of hearty abandonment—of wild, hilarious joy—so brimful and excessive, that it scruples at no mischief, so its mood be served, and will dare anything to gratify its individuality. How unlike girlhood, too—how contrasted with the quiet refinement which marks the woman, even in the bud. Noise, confusion, nonsense, and unbounded laughter, with an innate love of mischief, which no philosophy can account for, form the elementary traits of boy-life: but the girl steals away to her beads, her doll, and her skipping-rope—dreading to be thought a "romp," and looking suspiciously on manifestations of boisterousness in any of her fellows.

Boys are boys, and not little men. They are all alike, except as to the colour of the hair and knickerbockers. They all inherit the same pride, the same "devil-may-care" ambition, the same spirit of mischief, and the same freemasonry of mutual confidence in all affairs relating to the government of the boy-world. Where is the boy who is willing to be outdone by a playmate? Where is the boy who will acknowledge to being beaten in a fight with one of another school? Wherever such an one is to be found, guard him well, for fear he should grow up silly. It is positively astonishing what hair-breadth ventures boys will engage in, merely to gratify some pride of rivalry, or satisfy the eternal longing of a boy "to do something." In fact, there is nothing within the range of possibility which a boy will not do, let the consequence be what it may, provided there is no unmistakeable criminality; and then you learn what an honest nature lurks beneath that Puck's grinning countenance, resting on its own self-trust, and to be neither bought nor sold.

With what pleasure did we prepare our little sailing-boats, and our pack-thread fishing-tackle, dreaming all the while of Robinson Crusoe and the desolate island, and entertaining, much to our parents' sorrow, serious thoughts of "going to sea"—a threat that every boy indulges in when he has read that most seductive of books, and gained sufficient knowledge of navigation to send his sailing-boat safely across a river. There was one out-door sport of ours for which we can never forgive ourself—it was so thoroughly mischievous—and that was, throwing a bench-ball at the church clock, a feat which we then considered as of the first order, so much strength of arm and skill in aiming did it require. Whenever we now make a sojourn to our native suburban district of Stepney (it was a green village, with meadows and windmills, when we were young), we look up sorrowfully at the clock of the old church, and regret that we could ever have committed such a sacrilege as to join in a party to pelt it.

But the crowning joys of all were "buttercupping" and "blackberrying." As soon as the spring warmth brought forth the golden dandelions, and gave a new greenness to the grass in Stepney churchyard, away we went, inspired by the sunshine and rich greenness everywhere, in parties of six or eight, to gather buttercups and daisies in Bow Common fields. Alas! that spot is now a busy town, covered with houses, factories, and railway stations. It was then divided by hedgerows and gravel paths, and stile after stile led the way from "Cut-throat Lane" to "Old Ford" and "Twigg Folly." There we rolled and gambolled in the meadows, and sometimes lay on our backs and shaded our eyes with our hands, while we watched the lark in his ascending flight far into the blue, and almost melted into the embracing spring air under the influence of his joyous carol. There our arms were filled with the long stems of the buttercups; or we sat on the grass eating "cock-sorrel" to satiety, and got home at dusk, so tired with happiness, that sleep was a real relief. Orchard-robbing we never indulged in but once, for the good reason that "*our* village" had few orchards. I remember old "Captain King," as he was called, who kept a house and garden at the corner of "Ben Jonson's Fields." He was a retired sea captain, and spent his whole time in the culture of his garden. As we passed his garden-wall every day in little parties to and from school, we were always attracted by a large pear-tree which loomed above the wall, and which in autumn was always loaded with large baking-pears. On the occasion of our expedition we had formed a conspiracy to attack this pear-tree; and although the pears were yet far from ripe, and hence as hard as bullets, the enterprize was considered one of the finest we had ever engaged in; for, to tell the truth, our pride had been wounded by the boastings of a country lad who came into our class, and whose whole conversation consisted of recitals of former orchard-robbings. We planned to play at "Nickey Night, strike a light," in the adjoining field, at dusk; and while one party kept up the noise of the game to lull suspicion, a small detachment was to scale the wall and secure the booty. The evening came, and at last the hour. Myself and a dark, determined boy, were chosen to scale the wall— three others, who had promised to aid us, having lost their courage and bolted. Choosing a spot where the bricks were loose, we at last gained the top of the wall, and looked down in the moonlight on the old gentleman's garden. We paused a moment, and then down we both dropped. We stole along the garden, treading on strawberry-beds, and breaking the flower-laden branches of the rose-bushes. There were grapes in one place, nectarines in another; the walls all round were hung with unripe fruit, and presented stronger temptations than the chosen pear-tree. We were treading in the

thick of a strawberry-bed, in order to get at some green
peaches, when there was a noise at the garden door, and
we saw the servant busy scouring a tub.   By this time
several of my playmates had mounted the wall, and were
occupying themselves in bawling out directions and
exhortations to us, thereby increasing our danger of
detection.   The noise of our companions attracted her
attention, and she understood in a moment the meaning
of their exhortations.   She ran towards us: we dropped
our fruit and ran also, but knew not whither.   The dark
boy made for a buttress of the wall, and began to ascend;
I shot straight across a bed of celery, tripped over a
frame, and fell sprawling, and the next moment the
broom was belabouring my shoulders.   My companion
escaped, and regained his fellows; but I was dragged
like a poacher to the county justice—into the presence
of the grey-headed captain, who sat, in his velvet cap
and slippers, smoking in the parlour.   The old man
looked at me through his spectacles, read me a lecture
on the wickedness of theft, and then ordered my liberation.   It was a loud "pit pat" my heart made against
my waistcoat when, shy, pale, and trembling from head
to foot, I sought my companions, and found they had
taken the alarm and decamped, leaving me to my fate
with the injured captain.

But the supreme joy was blackberrying.   Long before
August had tipped the trees with red—before, indeed,
there was a single gauze frill unfolded on the bramble—
we began to arrange our blackberry-parties.   Topo-
graphical debates took place every day, much to the
detriment of school studies.   Very soon the whole school

was absorbed in warm discussion on the relative merits of Hornsey, Finchley, Wanstead, Epping, and Woodford, as suitable places of resort for blackberry gathering. At last September came, and the first jaunt took place. We took our dinners with us in our wallets, though many went without dinners, as they did without parental permission; and sometimes a whole class " played the wag," and started direct for the forest instead of going to school. Many canings and boxings of ears followed these expeditions. Many a red mark on hands or face betrayed how this or that boy had become a martyr to his love for blackberries—though his pride never suffered him to acknowledge it. Lips bore their black stains for days afterwards: scars and thorn-marks were to be seen; and a general dulness in learning told plainly enough of the store of blackberries which had been brought under cover to the school, and which, in the hours of work, were eaten with indescribable relish.

One striking trait of boys is their extraordinary appetite. Did you ever know a boy who had had enough to eat? Fill him tight as a blown bladder at the dinner-table, and he will go to school with his pockets filled with grey peas, or sweetmeats, or cocoa-nut. I can vividly remember how, when " flush" with money, I ate no end of luxuries: but when the money had dwindled down to a last penny, a single rosy apple was regarded as a feast. There is scarcely anything that boys will not eat; their test of the worth of a thing is, " can it be eaten?" We always made it a point to get home soon at dinner-time on washing-day, in order to fill the ash-pit of the copper fire with potatoes and onions for roasting, the cooking of which occupied our whole thought during the afternoon, and kept us in an excited state until school broke up, and we returned home to feast upon our luxuries. Then there were the roast apples, which, like joints, were suspended by a string from the stalk, and swung from the brass crane to hiss and spurt before the heat. That they were taken up half done, and the mouth burnt by eating them too hot, were conditions as essential to such a treat as the apples themselves. Spanish liquorice-water, and orange-peel-water, were each luxuries in their way very early in life; though we soon came to regard them as treats more adapted for girls—certainly not for such as called each other "fellows." The putting of milk into bottles, and churning it into butter, was an amusement which we never tired of, though many a scolding for stealing the milk, and many a threat to "take away that nasty bottle," made us wary how we were detected in that class of experiments. We were very young indeed when we made toffee "on the sly," in a table-spoon; but we never entirely got rid of one dream, which was that of having nothing but toasted currant-buns for breakfast —a fancy which haunts us even now occasionally, and which, strange to say, we have never realized.

Pocket-money was always an important matter. The boy who could afford to buy a whole cocoa-nut—and a Jew always stood near the school to tantalize us with a bag-full, while he held several open ones in his hands, and offered "'arf a nut for twopence; a 'ole un for fourpence,"—a boy who could do that was accounted very rich, and was looked at many times in the course of a morning's conning; the younger lads especially eyeing him, as if to ascertain whether he exhibited any unusual traits in his features. The amount of money which a boy had, very much determined his rank in the world. The more money he had, the older he was regarded, and hence the better entitled to smoke pieces of cane, or even to chew tobacco if he thought proper. If either of these operations made him sick, not a word was said about it; but if a poor boy, or one who seldom spent money, ventured on so bold a step, he became a target for ridicule, and was so jeered by his comrades, that life, for at least another year, must be a burthen to him.

> My boyish days, my boyish days,
>   Were happy days for me;
> Then tripped my life all joyously,
>   In childish mirth and glee.
> I had no cares nor sorrows then
>   To home within my breast,
> Nor ghostly dreams nor fantasies
>   To mar my peaceful rest.
>
> I gambolled down the mountain's side,
>   And revelled in the glen;
> And skipped, on merry feet, away
>   From haunts of churlish men.
> Oh! yes, in truth, my heart was light,
>   My life was glad and free;
> My boyish days, my boyish days,
>   Were happy days for me.

Then there is the strange hope which possesses boyhood—the strange hope in the future. They talk about what they intend to be; and how they like this trade or

that trade, or this or that profession. Life is all mystery
to them, yet they are not wholly dead to a sense of
what its reality may be; and as their years grow towards
youth, and give hints of coming adolescence, this thought
of the future grows into an excitement which, for a time,
eats up the whole of life, and bears them along into all
manner of strange dreams, and schemes, and wayward
imaginings—the reality all the while lying beyond them,
but revealing itself in shreds and patches, till they grow
into the full consciousness of its serious import, and feel
the first pressure of responsibility.

So life passes, phase after phase, and manhood comes
by a slow growth, and continues to ripen until we have
so grown out of the boy-skin that we can look down upon
it, almost doubting that it was ever ours; until a flood
of these boyish memories encircles us, and we are once
more assured of our beginning in the world, and rejoice
that we were boys indeed.

For ourselves, we would be boys ever; not in orchard-
robbing, milk-churning, or pelting at the church clock;
but in freshness of feeling—in freedom from conven-
tional rules and the coldness of polished hypocrisy—in
hearty fellowship with all we meet, and in the strong
hope in the future; the forward-looking, earnest-striving,
hopeful ambition to tear aside the cobwebs of prejudice
and falsity, and enter with pride and hilarity into the
life that lies before us. Off with your kid gloves, man,
and pluck the blackberries.

SUMMER PICTURES.

" The mountains high, and how they stand!
The valleys, and the great mainland!
The trees, the herbs, the towers strong,
The castles, and the rivers long.
  ●   ●   ●   ●   ●
On hills then show the ewe and lamb,
And every young one with his dam;
Then lovers walk, and tell their tale,
Both of their bliss and of their bale;
Then everything doth pleasure find,
In that that comforts all their kind."

EARL SURREY.

EACH season has its own pictures, and each picture its own peculiar feature. In nature nothing is repeated, though the whole economy of nature is endless repetition. You may have travelled all over the round world, and witnessed scenes innumerable, and the productions of nature under every variety of aspect, but you never saw the *same* picture twice. The summer-scenes of England are peculiarly beautiful, and there is no spot in the world which can equal the domestic rusticity and rich verdant beauty of English out-door pictures—although I am an Englishman, and say so. Italy, the garden of the world, is parched up as brown as an old hat, at the season of

Midsummer. The plains of Judea, and the valleys of
Jordan, though extolled by travellers, are, nevertheless,
during the most charming portion of the year, nothing
more than wide carpets of a dull melancholy green; for
the shapeless olive-bushes, which grow so numerously in
those districts, wear, when in their most luxuriant condition, nothing but a mass of dull, dingy leaves, destitute
altogether of either grace or verdant beauty. We shall
therefore turn with some gratulation to glance on a few
pictures from our own fields, drawn, it is true, with a
very weak pen, but still copied from nature, and if not
truly in the letter, at least in the spirit by which they
were prompted—genuine transcripts of the real thousand
brambles, and rose-blooms, and frutful fields, for which
our beloved country is so justly celebrated.

Well, there are so many, I scarcely know with which
to begin. Do you see yonder gipsy-tent, sending up a
blue wreath of smoke among the elm trees—a soft curling stream of the purest azure, flinging a most beautiful
shadow upon the leafy branches, and diffusing an odour
more potent than that of violets—to give an idea of the
comfort of the country? There is an old knotted oak to
the right, which looks as venerable as St. Pierre; just
below it is a wooden bridge, which cracked its ribs long
ago, and now threatens to go in the back, and let some
poor fellow souse into the water, some fine morning
before breakfast. The water-weeds and forget-me-nots
are fond of these maimed and broken-winded tim-
bers, and grow in rich festoons of green and blue
about them, as if they were adorning the portico
of Flora's temple. The elongated mass of green algæ

which clings to the last plank by the willow-tree, and
hangs down into the slow current, as if it had nothing
to do but dream of water sprites and fairy grots, will
wake up some morning and find that it had been
clinging to a forlorn hope, and must get out of the rubbish and masses of rotten timber the best way it can, or
perish amid the ruins of its lost home.

Well! swing round a bit over the common, and get
upon the hillock of gravel; and now look all around
upon the rich masses of waving fern, and the glittering
light which plays amid the cool green of the oak leaves;
see the winding river, like a clear silver line, cutting its
way through green oases of willows and tall reeds; look
further on over the heath-covered hill, sheltering the sweet
village in the valley at its feet; look at the strange play
of the sunshine, as the huge clouds go sailing along like
mighty spirits in the vast abyss. Here is the broad
highway, dotted here and there with moving figures and
stately clumps of pines, and the sun shines upon the
white sandy road, as if it would blind the very hedges
which stand along the pathway to hide the fields from
wayfarers. Down yonder lies a broad reedy marsh, and
the clouds hang above it to see their faces reflected in
the waters which look so blue and cool, and which go
lurking here and there beneath rank sedges and osiers
and tall rushes, where a heedless footstep might lead to
our entanglement in a muddy sepulchre. See the ten
red kine, and the five long-tailed plough-horses, leading
an amphibious life there in the shady corners, and envy
them their freedom and companionship in the dense
shade and delightfully cool mire.

It is glorious now, as Thomas Miller hath it, to wander "through green lanes which lead nowhere," into dreary old woods, where little hillocks of red leaves spin round and round in a giddy dance with the "wild west wind," and where crisped leaves overhang the pathway, and where you get into the thick underwood, and are so shut in from the sky and the country round, that you despair of ever finding the path again, and would fain pass the rest of your days in such a dark green covert— to drink from the crystal spring, eat the water-cresses that check its course, recline in happy abandonment on the mosses and tormentil blossoms, and talk to the thrushes that come there to drink.

Up from the broad corn-fields green hills arise, whose boundary fills the sky, and the white patches here and there upon the upland horizon show the villages which nestle there; and as these landmarks fade from the sight, and become again visible, you can tell when a thick cloud is passing over, even at that distance, and if you watch, you will see the sombre shadow gliding noiselessly along towards you. It passes over the meadows, changes the line of the river, and at last glides over your own head, and you feel a few drops of rain while the gloom lasts, and, gazing on it as it recedes towards the opposite horizon, you see the shower growing steadily, until its watery vastness fills the landscape round. Then, as it gathers strength, the sun's rays fall upon the dropping cloud, and the majestic arch of many colours spans the scene from one horizon to the other.

Lovely, indeed, are the little sheets of water, which seem only made for the frogs and toads and yellow flags and bulrushes to play in, and which nature must have dug for the wood-birds to go to and drink, when the July sun had sucked up all the forest runnels. Amid the reedy brakes, you sometimes start the black water-hen, and she shrieks with alarm for her downy family of helpless little ones; and at the same moment down goes the water-rat with a deep plash, to rise again at some goodly distance, and immediately commence swimming round and round some broken branch which dips into the pond, and nibble a leaf here and there, as if trying to persuade himself that nothing has happened, and that there is no need to fear intruding bipeds.

Sometimes you come suddenly upon a quiet village embowered in ancient trees, on the border of a thick wood; and there are two or three huge sign-posts, and sundry stacks of hay, with homesteads and barns pitched about in the oddest of ways, but all roofed over with thick velvet mosses or tufts of whitlow-grass and stone-crop. The cottage roofs and chimneys are covered with snapdragons and orange-coloured lichens, which harmonize most beautifully with the hues of the cracked and twisted trees. There are timid wreaths of smoke curling up among the tall branches of the elms, and you catch the homely smell of ash-wood fires; you gaze upon the scene, and read, in the white-washed wall and the low cottage, with its acre of potatoes and well-stocked kitchen-garden, the unwritten history of English worth, and the peaceful content of an English home, nestled amid the land of ancient trees. You think of old customs—of May-day, of sheep-shearing, and of harvest-home; you remember that such scenes were to be found

long ago, in the days of good king David, upon the
sunny slopes of Palestine; and although you have not
the pencil of a Morland, a Wilson, or a Collins, such a
picture is painted for ever on the living canvas of your
heart.   As you turn off into the narrow by-path, to see
whereabout the village church is hiding itself, you come
upon a picture which every artist has tried his hand at.
A quiet pond, overgrown with duckweeds and bulrushes,
with a group of cattle of white, russet, and grey, loitering about in the most picturesque positions, the cows
looking particularly motherly and stupid, and all of them
flickering their tails about to drive away the swarms of
insects which annoy them.   There are two or three old
pollard-willows, and an oak tree, with neither head nor
limbs, stands staggering at the brink in a half horizontal
position, as if he contemplated suicide by drowning his
body; he is covered all over with scars, and wounds,
and blotches, which tell most significantly of the many
affrays he has had with the midnight-winds, and the
north-east blasts of January.   If you come here next
summer you shall find him leaning over the water in the
same melancholy pondering mood, shaking a few green
leaves in the wind, just to divert the attention of
passers-by from the deed he is evidently contemplating;
and it will be many summers before he will resign
himself to his fate.   There will be one mourner in that
solitary ass, standing not far off, as immoveable as a
petrifaction.

The fields around wear the promise of plenty; the
rye has a yellow and a hearty look, the horned barley
makes a rustling sound, as the soft wind sweeps gently

through its long plumy ears. The pendulous oats quiver
and tremble in the dancing sunlight, and the wheat gets
whiter and fatter day by day. The mole-hills on the
common are purple with the clumps of wild thyme, and
a drowsy, overpowering fragrance comes from the blossoming bean-field, "reminding us of Proserpine and her
fallen flowers." The hedges are covered with the foam-
like cymes of the wayside elder, and woven in a network
of the wild convolvulus and the white bryony, which
throw their glossy trails in all directions.

But we leave the land of flowers, and, led on by the
witchery of the clear sunshine and the deep blue sky,
studded with masses of cloud as bright as molten silver,
tumble over the brink of a little hollow, scooped like
that of Cowper, by Kilwick's echoing wood. There is a
small mud-walled cottage, partially white-washed, standing upon a little plot of chalky ground, partly fenced,
and planted with cabbages and potatoes ; and just at the
foot of a tall perpendicular cliff, on a small round grassy
hill, lies an ill-favoured mongrel, fast asleep. The upper
edge of the cliff is fringed with coppice wood, and a
straggling hazel hangs carelessly over the brink, the
shadows of which, as it sways to and fro in the wind,
dance like grim spectres on the white chalky ramparts,
and hold a sort of demon dance with the light steamy
smoke which curls gracefully upward from the little
hovel below. Beyond the young coppice rises a rich
plantation of Scotch firs, and their tall grey stems swing
mournfully and change places with each other, alternately forming long and regular vistas, at the end of
which you catch enchanting glimpses of the blue sky,

and then lose them again behind a forest of silvery stems, whose dark-green leafy summits shed on the brown slopes and grassy avenues below a calm and softened twilight. It would be impossible to gaze on such a scene as this without thinking of Longfellow's lovely stanzas :—

> "Before me rose an avenue
> Of tall and sombrous pines,
> Abroad their fan-like branches grew,
> And, where the sunshine darted through,
> Spread a vapour soft and blue,
> In long and sloping lines.
>
> "And falling on my weary brain,
> Like a fast-falling shower,
> The dreams of youth come back again,—
> Low lispings of the summer rain
> Dropping on the ripened grain,
> As once upon the flower."

When you get up there, underneath the rich festoons of foliage, and feel your eyes aching with the strange intersections of the stems crossing each other, and thinned here and there by time or accident, and observe the cones and broken twigs which sprinkle the green sward, you think of Wordsworth's "sheddings of the pining umbrage," and of those firs which live in their green beauty for ever in his graphic verse, and perhaps you detect yourself involuntarily quoting the lines :—

> ————— "Above my head,
> At every impulse of the moving breeze,
> The fir-grove murmurs with a sea-like sound."

Bundles of poetical associations come tumbling upon

you,—Thomas Hood and the Midsummer Fairies, mingling with the weird tone of the "Bridge of Sighs;"
Spenser and his Catalogue of Trees, wherein he indivi-
dualizes each by a happy choice of epithets :—

> " And forth they pass, with pleasure forward led,
>   Joying to hear the birds' sweet harmony,
>   Which, therein shrouded from the tempest's dread,
>   Seemed in their song to scorn the cruel sky;
>   Much can they praise the trees so straight and high,—
>   The sailing pine, the cedar proud and tall."

And as you get into a day-dream, and gaze upon the blue
snatches of sky through artless breaks in the foliage, and
upon the "half-excluded light which sleeps in patches
upon the shadowy verdure below," your thoughts turn
to Robin Hood and John Keats; to Scott and his
"forest fair;" to Coleridge and the "leafy month of
June;" to Robert Bloomfield and quaint old Herrick.
And from the solemn quietude and beauty of these pictures, the fancy draws innumerable beautiful figures,
such as the poets have ever delighted to revel in; and
they come up successively upon "that inward eye which
is the bliss of solitude," like stars peeping through the
cool twilight, or young hopes, hallowed in their birth by
those boyish tears, not unfrequently shed over fancied
disappointments. And then bitter memorials of old sins,
and feelings of remorse for broken ties and rash follies,
overwhelm the soul like a November fog; and we feel,
that if we had the power, we could gladly blot out all the
history of our past. But there are those who love us
now, and the world is not all desolate; and if the heart
is in unison with the external world of beauty, we shall

find that the influences of nature have a balm for the recesses of the deepest sorrow, and that a spirit of gloom and discontent is an iniquity against the universal spirit of love, which fills the earth with gladness.

Push on, for the voices multiply both near and far, and the hour of sunset approaches. We must cross the sheep-lea and the broad lawn meadows before we can rest our limbs, and in reverie recal these pictures. What is that sharp rasping sound? It is the mower, whetting his scythe in yonder meadows, where the work of haymaking has commenced. What a rich waving sea of emerald and golden billows is the unmown hay-field! How calm it lies in the beauty of the sunlight, with its spikes of chaffy blossoms and sprinkling of buttercups and cowslips! And beyond, the homely farmstead rises half-hidden amid tall elms, and leaning upon the sky like the shadowy painting of a dream. There are groups of sturdy men, with iron sinews and sunburt faces, all occupied in the busy work of the field. The mower sweeps down grass and flowers altogether, laying prostrate the pride of the summer, and turning swath upon swath with his sinewy arm, mingling the star-like daisy, the honey-scented clover, the buttercups, yellow trefoils, and long grass altogether; and before the sun has sunk into the west, their beauty will have perished for ever. He heeds not their beauty, but, like a destroying angel, hews down all before him— perhaps without a thought that he is thus the emblem of death. He leaves them piled ridge upon ridge, until the field is at last filled with round hillocks, beneath which the flowers lie, withered and dead, as in sepulchres,

whence they throw rich perfumes upon the air, to tell
how sweet was the sunny current of their lives, and suggest the fancy that their spirits still hover above the
spots which their beauty had sanctified.

Now, down the steep hill-side into the old wood, and
feel the mystery which always hangs about these ancient
trees, and the thick underwood which gathers at their feet.

> " How sweet the shade of this magnificent wood!
> The gnarled oaks, upon whose hoary,
> Tempest-stricken brows, Old Time
> Has chronicled a thousand years."

Millions of flowers grow in these dark untrodden
solitudes; thousands of birds have made their homes
amid these leafy coverts; innumerable strange beasts
and reptiles crawl and prowl among the moist leaves,
which lie rotting in fragrant masses where the underwood forms an impassable jungle, or burrow under the
hollow trees, or bask beside the hidden water-courses, or
on the great mossy branches of the trees which have
been hurled down by winter storms, and have been since
overgrown by rank weeds and flowers, which strive from
year to year to hide their hoary ruin and decrepitude.
The twilight gloom seems to enter one's very heart, as
we gaze upon the dim shadowy grandeur of these green
and mysterious woods, which have grown old and patriarchal in the light and darkness, the sunshine and the
glooms, of long, long centuries. But there is no time
to think of the Druids and the ancient Britons, and we
must find our way through deep dells where the foliage
darkens, and where gnarled and withered stems stretch
upward beseechingly, like troubled souls in purgatory,

and get once more into the broadlands and the field
paths. The moment we leave the skirts of the wood, we
encounter a picture of surpassing loveliness; there is a
broad footpath leading over a wide common, and a sweet
little river wends its way silently along under the shadows
of stately trees, circling like a silver line around the foot
of the furze-covered hill, till it vanishes like an evening
cloud in the distance. There are lambs and sheep scattered among the bushes, and the musical jingling of
their bells comes floating on the soft air like the music
of a dream. There are glorious hillocks of purple heather
and wild thyme, haunted all day long by humming bees;
and down in yonder green valley lie the cattle chewing
the cud, and almost buried among the grass and flowers;
while out afar lies the little village, with its cracked and
tattered windmill, and its white cottages and clumps of
tall trees, looming upon the blue horizon like an island
floating in the sky.

Who would not leave the crowded city, with its
eternal dust and din, and black walls and sooty atmosphere, for such lovely scenes as these? Who would
not leave the stiff forests of chimney-pots for the green
waving forests of beech and oak, and to lie idly by the
banks of singing streams?—to see the hawk poised
motionless in the air, the timid hare bound through the
green fern, and to hear the ring-dove cooing? A walled
city is a prison for the human heart; and to shut ourselves up from beholding the beauty with which the
hand of God has clothed the earth, is like choosing the
apples of Sodom, while luscious fruits hang tempting on
the bough.

THE LOVE OF FLOWERS.

"Our human souls
Cling to the grass and water brooks."

ATHANASE.

THE sentiments of the human heart are instinctive; they are born with us, and in saddest moments shed a light about us like spring sunshine, when clouds begin to break. Our best sympathies are unteachable, not to be imparted. They lie slumbering within us till awakened by kindred sympathies, and then we know their worth. Some of our sympathies are special, and some we share in common with all the world. The love of flowers is one of the universal sentiments. In childhood, we roam through lanes and fields, and amid the leafy garniture of woods, to hold communion with them, fancying we hear them talk, till our eyes fill with strange tears of pleasantness. As we grow into manhood, and mingle in the busy world, the heart still cherishes its love for flowers; and when the spring sunshine falls upon our path, sweet memories come over the spirit, and the heart seems to gush with flowery voices of its own. Even in age, when time has ploughed deep furrows in our brow, and the snows of life's winter lie upon our heads, this passion dies not. The eye, which was dim and lustreless, kindles with new light; and the step, which was feeble and tottering, becomes firm and steadfast, when nature sheds her sweet influences around us; and of those influences, how many are mixed up with flowers!

Flowers are friends that change not. In youth, they greet us with their sunny smiles; in age they speak to us of boyhood, and lead us back to the scenes made dear by recollections of home; year after year, as we hasten onward to complete the cycle of our being, they still abide with us, and offer solace. And when sickness and sorrow have broken down the spirit, and we lie down to rest, with the red earth for a pillow, the flowers come in joyful troops to guard our resting-place from rash footsteps and unhallowed intrusions. And then the "green grass, and clover, and sweet herbs"—made fragrant by the soft dews and early glances of the sun—sanctify the air which sweeps above our graves; and all day long the grasses wave in the wind, and the flowers sing sweet dirges over the green mounds which mark our resting-place; and at night, the sentinel stars come forth to keep watch over us, and the flowers become sorrowful in the still silence, for, as the poets say, they are stars too, though set in a firmament of greenness.

Come with me, thou toiler in the dusty city; shake off the cloud from thy brow; forget for awhile the pence and shillings for which thou hast sold thy soul; and I will lead thee under green forest trees, over soft mossy hillocks, and beside cool running brooks, where the water-flags play with each other, and look at their own merry faces in the glassy stream. Come to the thick brake, and lie down upon the grass till thou hast forgotten all the cares of life. Doth not thy heart now throb with emotions of thankfulness to God, for making the earth so fair, so redolent of beauty, in its garniture of flowers? and for having scattered these silent teachers up and down the world—things of beauty and joys for ever? The soul must be fed; we must have inspiration from stars, and sunbeams, and flowers,—and not be always chewing corn. We must hear the voice of God in the elements, in the winds and the waves, the rattling of the thunder, and the howling of the storm. We must see His face in every flower, and feel His breath in the odour of forest leaves and banks of wild thyme. Now, dost thou not long to be a child once more, and to live out thy days in one frenzy of joy? Wouldst thou shrink from cold hearts, and disappointments, and regrets, and live for the love of flowers only?—to gather round thee glowing visions of floral loveliness; to fill the air with angel shapes and rainbow hues; to breathe an atmosphere of perfume like that which floats over the green pastures of Paradise; to feel the sense overwhelmed with droppings of rich music, as though angel lutes were tuning their anthems to the Omnipotent; and, amid the grand symphonies of nature, to feel the soul hallowed and becalmed, as the sea in summer time, when the winds have gone to sleep upon its bosom?

Nature is the property of all. Flowers are the ministers of her commonwealth. They bloom for old and young, rich and poor; and, to every true heart, are messengers from heaven! The great duty of flowers is to teach us to be always children, to be ever fresh, and budding into new beauty; for the poetry of our lives is all that can ennoble us. It is in the morning of existence that

> " Hope looks out
> Into the dazzling sheen, and fondly talks
> Of summer; and Love comes, and all the air
> Rings with wild harmonies."

Because time has led us a little further towards the tomb, we need not become so engrossed with sordid pursuits as to shun the world of beauty, the creation of poetry, which exists around us in the semblance of perpetual youth. Oh! "let the blood of the violet trickle in our veins." Let us mingle with the sweet children of the woods, and hold communings with nature in her own peaceful solitudes. We will lie in green meads where daisies grow, and bask us in the sunshine; lie by the streamlet's brim, and plait rushes, and talk to our own images in the reflecting waters; hide in flowery nooks and dingles, and murmur snatches of wild old songs, until we laugh ourselves into a very incarnation of gladness; we'll build our fairy palaces with a geometry of sunbeams, and climb upwards on our dreamy destiny till the universe becomes our temple.

It was the love of flowers which gave to the pages of the old poets that freshness which is the true image of life. The wisdom of Solomon was so much the greater that he loved flowers; and it is the same sentiment which sweetens the pages of Spenser, Chaucer, Clare, Carrington, Gilbert White, and Chatterton, and makes them lustrous, like unclouded sunshine in the month of June. If we had not this love of flowers in our hearts, we should not feel the freshness and brilliancy of their descriptions of nature, sweeping over the spirit like a fragment of old music, or breathings from a blossom-scented valley. Now we can go to the silvery streams in company with old Izaak Walton, where the whirling currents play with the reeds and water-flags, and the green willows bow down to kiss the flowing stream; then we remember the milkmaid, and the draught of cow's-milk; the shelter under the honeysuckle hedge; the fish fried in cowslips; the little sleeping-room, smelling sweetly of lavender; and the flowers, which old Izaak thought too beautiful to be seen at any other times than holidays. We love the old man, who in the innocence of his heart could sing—

> "I in these flowery meads would be,
> These crystal streams should solace me;
> To whose harmonious, babbling noise,
> I, with my angle, would rejoice."

Pleasant it is to wander forth, as did Solomon of old, "into the fields, or to lodge in the villages, to see the fruits of the valley, and to go into the gardens and gather lilies;" and to inhale the perfumes of the banks and fields. The royal garden of an eastern prince is called the "Garden of God," a name which is usually supposed to refer to the Garden of Eden, and a promise adapted to the love of nature and of virtue. To the faithful follower of the Prophet, the Koran promised greetings of "good tidings, gardens through which rivers flow; and ye shall remain therein for ever."

The flowers of the wild have ever a greater hold upon the affections than the nurtured beauties of the garden or conservatory. Wild flowers form a chief part of the love of country, they are our associates in early life, and recal, in after years, the scenes and recollections of our youth; they are the true philanthropists of nature, and their generous and smiling faces give us kindly greetings and sweet memories of the first impulses of love and friendship. The poor mechanic may leave his dull bench when Sunday comes, and breathe the fresh air on the green hills, and gather cowslips and daffodils to cheer him, and to teach him that, although begrimed by toil, yet he has within him a soul capable of feeling, and a spirit which can woo the inspiration of nature, and grow green again in the love of flowers.

> "Aud such are daffodils
> With the green world they live in : and clear rills
> That for themselves a cooling covert make
> 'Gainst the hot season : the mid-forest brake,
> Rich with a sprinkling of fair musk-rose blooms."
>
> KEATS.

Of all things sent from heaven to minister to man's happiness, flowers are the most gentle, confiding, and un-resisting; he may crush them beneath his footstep, and their only murmurs are made in the sweet scent which they immediately emit; they may be plucked and scattered to the four winds of heaven, but a fresh troop bloom in gladness and delight; they may be gathered by the soft white hand of beauty, to gladden the eye which has never known a tear, and by the hard and iron hand of toiling industry, to beautify the window where the meek wife sits pon-dering, and the children play at kings and queens.

It was the awakening of the sentiment of love for
flowers which brought back the prisoner of Fenestrella to
the acknowledgment of a God; maddened by solitude, and
exhausted by profligacy and the unceasing anxieties of a
troubled soul, he denied his Maker, and cast himself into
the black and desolate regions of infidelity; but while
expiating, within the walls of a prison, for the rash im-
petuosities of his youth, a little flower springs up between
the chinks of the stones, and becomes to him a messenger
of love and mercy, while his soul is on the very threshold of
moral despair.   It is pleasant to read how the botanist,
Douglas, was cheered in his wanderings in America,
when he met with a blooming primrose high up on the
bald summit of a rocky mountain, where the clouds
rolled in darkness, and mingled their dense whiteness
with the giant masses of eternal snow.   The explorers of
the rocky mountains of the West were, in a like manner,
comforted, and reminded of the flowery valleys and fertile
plains which they had left far behind them, when, amid
the desolate and barren hills, where not even a blade of
grass was to be seen for miles, they saw a little bee,
humming along as if in quest of flowers, and in a
region many thousand feet above the level of the sea.

Schimmelpenninck* tells an anecdote of the philosopher of Geneva, which illustrates, in a pleasing manner,
the close bond of union between mind of the highest
order and the simple beauties of nature.   During the
earliest and happiest years of the life of Rosseau, he was
one day walking with a beloved friend.   It was summer

* " Theory of Beauty and Deformity."

x 2

time: the evening was calm, quiet, and serene. The sun
was setting in glory, spreading his sheeted fires over the
unrippled surface of the lake, staining the water with
Tyrian dyes. The friends sat on a mossy bank, enjoying the calm scene, and conversing upon the varied
phases of human life, in the unaffected sincerity of true
friendship. At their feet was a bright tuft of the lovely
Germander speedwell, covered with a profusion of brilliant blue blossoms. Rosseau's friend pointed to the
little flower, the *Veronica chamædrys*, as wearing the
same expression of cheerfulness and innocency as the
scene before them. Thirty years passed away! Care-
worn, persecuted, disappointed, acquainted with poverty
and grief, known to fame, but a stranger to peace, Rosseau again visited Geneva. On such a calm and lovely
evening as, thirty years before, he had conversed with the
friend of his bosom, and had received a teaching from
the simple beauty of a flower, he again was seated on the
selfsame spot. The scene was the same. The sun was
setting; the birds sung cheefully; the western sky
glowed like fire; the waters of the lake were skimmed by
glittering boats. But the house wherein the first feeling of love and friendship, and the first fruits of his
genius had budded, was now levelled with the ground.
His dearest friend was sleeping in the grave. The generation of villagers who had partaken of the bounty of
the same beneficent hand was passed away, and none remained to point out the green sod where that benefactor
lay. He walked on pensively; the same bank, tufted
with the same knot of bright-eyed speedwell, caught his

eye. The memories of past years of trouble and sorrow came upon him, he heaved a sigh, and turned away, weeping bitterly.

" The plant that bloomed along the shore,
    Where there in happier hours he strayed,
Still flourished gaily as before,
    In all its azure charms arrayed ;
There still it shone, in modest pride,
While all *his* flowers of joy had died.

It seemed to say, ' Hadst thou, like me,
    Contented bloom'd within the bed
That Nature's hand had form'd for thee,
    When first her dews were on thee shed.
Then had thy blossoms never known
The blasts that o'er their buds have blown '"

It is because flowers are emblems of innocence, so like the merry face of childhood, that they have a large place in our best affections. They remind us of our days or boyhood and buoyancy; when Nature, our fond mother, sat upon the hills, clapping her hands with joy, and giving us all the earth, with its landscapes and rocks, and hills and forests, for our school and play-ground; when quiet nooks enclosed us with their greenness, and we found companions in the wild bee, and the morning breezes, and in everything which wore the impress of beauty, whether animate or inanimate; when all things were clothed with beauty, and were worshipped with a veneration beyond utterance; when a bower of leaves was a palace of enchantment; when we picked up lessons of love by river sides, and hawthorn paths, in quiet glens and in green fields, and inhaled, from every passing breeze, health, intelligence, and joy; when the world became a picture of peace, without one flaw or frown, as a bright vision by a sick man's bed. Then, too, the holy memories which they embalm in their folded buds and undewed chalices—memories fraught with sorrow, but not less welcome to our hearts. Tender recollections, perchance, of parents now sleeping in flowery graves, no longer controlling our actions with a judicious watchfulness and care; no longer checking us as we are about to pluck the fatal weeds of folly, and to inhale the breath of the sinful blossoms which pleasure scatters in our path —beautiful and fragrant, but fraught with the bane of self-reproach.

> " Oh, lovely flowers! the earth's rich diadem,
> Emblems are ye of heaven, and heavenly joy,
> And starry brilliance in a world of gloom ;
> Peace, innocence, and guileless infancy
> Claim sisterhood with you, and holy is the tie."
>
> MRS. HEMANS.

Flowers blend by association of ideas the experiences with the pleasures of life; they refresh the worn mind with waters from the untainted fountain of pure feeling, which flows from the emerald meadows of childhood, and lead us from the world's thorny and flowerless desert to oases, blossoming acacias, and waters sweet to the taste. How often, when disease has wasted the frame, and anxiety and suffering have well-nigh done their work, the sufferer awaits calmly the approaching dissolution, and stands pausing on the brink of another world in majestic hope and confidence—the joys, sorrows, and fears of life's fevered dream banished from the memory— and the scenes and associations of childhood come flooding upon the memory in all their flowery freshness and beauty! Flowers are antetypes of the angelic, tokens of the perfect, the peaceful, and the just. Well might Keats,

> " Who grew,
> Like a pale flower by some sad maiden cherished,
> And fed with true-love tears instead of dew—"

say, on the couch of death, that he "felt the daisies already growing over him."

Mrs. Hemans believed that "the fine passion for flowers is the only one which long sickness leaves untouched with its chilling influence. Often, during this weary illness of mine, have I looked upon new books with indifference, when, if a friend has sent me a few flowers, my heart has leaped up to their dreamy hues and odours, with a sudden sense of renovated childhood, which seems to me one of the mysteries of our being."

The physical history of our world teaches us that flowers were created for spiritual, rather than material purposes. They were sent by God to give us constant revelations of the beautiful, and to keep us in the perpetual presence of innocence and virtue. There were no flowers among the wondrous vegetation of the world during the myriad ages preceding the creation of man. As there was no moral nature to be comforted, so in the workings of creative energy flowers had no place in the wild profusion of palms and cycads, and conifers and ferns. When the fulness of time had come, and man was to take his place in a world prepared for him, the world broke forth in full flowery beauty, and "the Lord God planted a garden eastward in Eden." The history of man has for prologue and epilogue the beauty and the glory of flowers. They beautify the path of Time, and are emblems of eternity. If we rejoice now in the changes of the seasons, and find in life so many flowery consolations, how much more perfect will be our joy when this mortal shall put on immortality, and faith, and hope, and love shall adorn the brow of the spirit as a threefold chaplet of imperishable beauty, in that happy Eden, which has oftentimes been spoken of as the land of flowers! Let us use the world, and all its gifts, as means to an end, and that end a happy one. We must recognize all things about us as Relative, though the absolute is our final goal; and every touch of adorning grace upon the tapestry of nature will hint to us that the moral is wedded to the physical, only that the first may ultimately triumph. These perishable flowers sweeten the garden of the body, but imperishable ones are blooming in the garden of the soul. To behold the lilies of the field is good for us while we continue in our sensuous probation; but when that is at an end, we shall behold the face of the Good Preceptor—" We shall be like Him, and see Him as He is."

W. H. Collingridge, 117 to 119, Aldersgate Street, London, E.C.

BIBLIOLIFE

Old Books Deserve a New Life
www.bibliolife.com

Did you know that you can get most of our titles in our trademark **EasyScript**™ print format? **EasyScript**™ provides readers with a larger than average typeface, for a reading experience that's easier on the eyes.

Did you know that we have an ever-growing collection of books in many languages?

Order online:
www.bibliolife.com/store

Or to exclusively browse our **EasyScript**™ collection:
www.bibliogrande.com

At BiblioLife, we aim to make knowledge more accessible by making thousands of titles available to you – quickly and affordably.

Contact us:
BiblioLife
PO Box 21206
Charleston, SC 29413

Lightning Source UK Ltd.
Milton Keynes UK
27 April 2010

153355UK00001B/13/A